"Natalie pulls us along happily into her wide world of wine—you are right there with her at the table or in an underground cellar. The conversations are lively and the wine flows. And when a winemaker pours a glass for her, you might look around wondering, 'Where's mine?' She made me itchy to get on a plane and hit the wine route myself."

—**Kermit Lynch, award-winning wine merchant and author of** *Adventures on the Wine Route* *continued . . .*

"The writing is light, breezy, and engaging. MacLean's trips to vineyards and wineries illustrate her theme well. Most readers will appreciate the refreshing angle she brings to an industry that can be too steeped in its own traditions."

—**Bloomberg**

"Like a breath of fresh air through a vineyard, award-winning wine writer Natalie MacLean's new book *Red, White, and Drunk All Over* breezed onto store shelves recently. Whether you've been no nearer a vine than watching the movie *Sideways* or are an experienced oenophile, MacLean's book will educate, entertain, and, best of all, make you laugh out loud."

—*Food & Drink*

"Never pedantic, but always erudite and eminently readable, MacLean's book is a terrific beginning for the inchoate wine connoisseur. Here, one will find advice and information on everything from cellaring to proper stemware, how to order wine in a restaurant, differentiations of grape varieties and regions, the myths of winespeak, and much more. . . . After reading this book, the wine neophyte is likely to be as enthusiastic about her love for the grape as is MacLean."

—**Rex Pickett, author of *Sideways***

"MacLean's enthusiasm for wine is contagious. For the winner of the prestigious M.F.K. Fisher Distinguished Writing Award, each glass represents a personal history, 'a secret cellar in our minds where we collect our empty bottles filled with memories.' . . . For casual wine lovers, MacLean deciphers the perplexing dilemmas of appropriate wine aging without pedantry. . . . Solid research, a breezy style, and commonsense advice prove invaluable for the novice, while her good humor will delight the connoisseur."

—*Publishers Weekly*

"Unlike so many wine 'guides,' this one is an adventure story. Natalie MacLean takes us along as she navigates the sometimes treacherous wine landscape, from vineyard to wine store to restaurant to her own kitchen, putting it all in perspective and even putting a wine snob or two in their place. We finish the journey far more confident—and with a craving for great wine."

—**Edward Deitch, wine critic for NBC and MSNBC.com**

UNQUENCHABLE

A TIPSY QUEST
FOR THE WORLD'S BEST
BARGAIN WINES

Natalie MacLean

A PERIGEE BOOK

A PERIGEE BOOK
Published by the Penguin Group
Penguin Group (USA) Inc.
375 Hudson Street, New York, New York 10014, USA
Penguin Group (Canada), 90 Eglinton Avenue East, Suite 700, Toronto, Ontario M4P 2Y3, Canada
(a division of Pearson Penguin Canada Inc.)
Penguin Books Ltd., 80 Strand, London WC2R 0RL, England
Penguin Group Ireland, 25 St. Stephen's Green, Dublin 2, Ireland (a division of Penguin Books Ltd.)
Penguin Group (Australia), 250 Camberwell Road, Camberwell, Victoria 3124, Australia
(a division of Pearson Australia Group Pty. Ltd.)
Penguin Books India Pvt. Ltd., 11 Community Centre, Panchsheel Park, New Delhi—110 017, India
Penguin Group (NZ), 67 Apollo Drive, Rosedale, Auckland 0632, New Zealand
(a division of Pearson New Zealand Ltd.)
Penguin Books (South Africa) (Pty.) Ltd., 24 Sturdee Avenue, Rosebank, Johannesburg 2196,
South Africa
Penguin Books Ltd., Registered Offices: 80 Strand, London WC2R 0RL, England

While the author has made every effort to provide accurate telephone numbers and Internet addresses at the time of publication, neither the publisher nor the author assumes any responsibility for errors or for changes that occur after publication. Further, the publisher does not have any control over and does not assume any responsibility for author or third-party websites or their content.

Copyright © 2011 by Natalie MacLean
Text design by Tiffany Estreicher

First edition: November 2011

Library of Congress Cataloging-in-Publication Data

MacLean, Natalie.
    Unquenchable : a tipsy quest for the world's best bargain wines / Natalie Maclean.
        p.   cm.
    "A Perigee Book."
    Includes index.
    ISBN 978-0-399-53707-3 (hardback)
    1. Wine and wine making.   I. Title.
    TP548.M1953   2011
    641.2'1—dc23   2011024632

PRINTED IN THE UNITED STATES OF AMERICA

10   9   8   7   6   5   4   3   2   1

For my mother, Ann;
my husband, Andrew; and my son, Rian:
I raise my glass to you all.

CONTENTS

A Nose for a Bargain: Opening Thoughts   xi

Beyond the Adventures   xvii

1. SUNDAY: The Wine Wizards of Oz   1

2. MONDAY: The Unbearable Lightness of German Riesling   41

3. TUESDAY: Helicopters, Hawks, and Hellacious Ladybugs   83

4. WEDNESDAY: The Cape Crusaders of Africa   123

5. THURSDAY: Vino Under the Volcano   167

6. FRIDAY: A Smoldering Liquid Tango   201

7. SATURDAY: A Storm of Pleasure in Every Port   235

8. SUNDAY: La Vie en Rosé en Provence   279

Drinking My Words: Closing-Time Comments   317

Acknowledgments   325

Index   329

A NOSE FOR A BARGAIN

Opening Thoughts

THE QUESTION I'M asked most often: "What's your favorite wine?" My answer: "The one someone else pays for." The second question I'm asked is, "Can you recommend a great wine that costs less than $5?" Answer: "Not unless all you want is a wet tongue."

When I'm not in a smart-ass mood, my answer to the first question depends on what I'm eating, who I'm with, and what the occasion is. But I never forget price. The reality is that wine from regions such as Tuscany, Bordeaux, and Napa Valley have become too expensive for most of us. Yet we still want that fleshy fruit pleasure that wine gives us rather than settling for tasteless plonk.

Tasteless plonk, of course, brings to mind memories of homemade wine. When I was a student, I eagerly dipped a boy-band mug into a bathtub filled with "shablie." After I graduated, I covertly doused the already well-watered fern at a friend's house with her "True Love Chardonnay." Years later, after I became a wine writer, I thought that my Château de Haute House Hooch days were over. Alas, they were not.

Occasionally, dinner hosts serve their own homemade concoctions and lock eyes with me expectantly. I usually try to escape with half-spoken comments such as, "This is a delightful wine" out loud, and then under my breath, "if I were shackled in Kingston Penitentiary." Or I might say, "This has a smooth texture," mentally adding, "making it an acceptable antiseptic to clean a chest wound before knife surgery in the Brazilian rain forest." Had I written a fancy-pants tasting note, it would have been: Under an initial layer of rotting roadside tomatoes, I detect nuances of a burning Fiat tire floating on a lake of rancid olive oil. Pair this wine with nasty divorce settlements or grand jury appearances.

Somewhere between Super Tuscans and vinous Tang crystals, there are delicious wines that we can still afford. But while most people believe that they can taste the difference between a wine priced at $5 and one at $50, it gets trickier when the difference is between $15 and $30. And since most of us would prefer to shell out $15 rather than $30, one of the missions of this book is to demystify wine pricing in relation to quality. Some regions have natural advantages that make winemaking inexpensive, whether that's climate or cheap land and labor. Other regions are still establishing their reputations and must keep their prices low to be competitive with better-known wines.

So why even bother searching for today's great cheap wines? Why not just be happy with whatever glass of vino is in front of you? Well, most of us don't drink just for the buzz: we want better taste experiences. Many nostalgic hedonists recall our first good wines; their taste can transport us back to a beach, a first apartment, a small bistro. Some people spend their lives trying to re-create the intensity of that first taste. But because our palates mature as they age, the wine has to be much better as we get older to achieve a peak experience.

My nose for a bargain was honed early in life. I grew up on the

East Coast with my mother, who separated from my alcoholic father when I was two. Money was tight, and we moved from one town to another frequently as she took up teaching posts at various elementary schools. We lived in rented trailers and basement apartments. I wore bread bags in my leaking boots, and we rummaged through the piles of secondhand clothing at a store called Frenchies, delighted when we found something our size. At night, we joked that we were going "to mattress" since our beds didn't have box springs or legs. Our weekly treat was to walk down to the local bowling alley on Friday evening and buy a chocolate sponge cake. In the morning, I'd look for lost change on the sidewalk.

So I know there are good deals and great experiences to be had if you're willing to search for them. As a mongrel taster, I know that even inexpensive wine is one of the most complex natural substances we consume, with more than a thousand compounds that contribute to its fragrance. The human nose can smell more than two thousand aromas, some at minute concentrations (think of a single drop in the equivalent of three Olympic-sized swimming pools). So with all the varying smells and their intensities, there are millions of unique combinations. In wine, such complexity is a stunning triumph of diversity, but like music, all the elements have to work together or the result is just cacophony.

Rich, layered experiences hold our attention, whether they're books, paintings, or wines. Our minds grapple to understand them as our senses play along their touch points. But who says that only expensive wines can be complex? I've tasted many inexpensive wines with flavors and aromas that lingered long after I swallowed, giving my mind time to wheel back and forth over my sensory impressions. It's simply snobbery to suggest that only pricey bottles have the unexplained magic that leaves us reaching for the words to express what we're smelling, tasting, feeling.

As I discuss these issues in this book, my views will be influenced by the type of writer (and drinker) I am. Some critics pride themselves on their "objectivity" and don't use first-person narrative. Not me. I'm neurotically personal, prone to tangential digressions and Bridget Jones–like overreactions. I fall in love too easily with people, places, and wines.

While some wine critics are afraid of vulnerability and intimacy with their readers, for me, these are the foundations of trust. I openly admit that I like to drink wine—and I like the buzz. I have personal preferences, and I make mistakes. In these ways, I am like my readers, and I don't hold myself at a professional distance from them. We all share a glass around the kitchen table, even if it is virtual. That's how today's "experts" operate: with candor and closeness that's as informal as your next tweet on Twitter or post on Facebook. That's also why I get about two hundred emails a day from my website readers at www.nataliemaclean.com.

My goal isn't to dumb down wine, because I think it's endlessly fascinating. I believe that it can be complex without being complicated. But some people misinterpret my approach. One website of male critics invited me to join as an afterthought just before launch, thinking that they needed some estrogen balance. I remember the mock-up screen they emailed to me. The men were described as respected, thoughtful, analytical. My description? I was fun and lively; in other words, the good-time wine gal there to provide blond relief in a sea of black stubble.

I was a competitive Highland dancer for fifteen years, placing fifth in the world championships behind four men from Scotland. Highland dancing is one of the few sports in which men and women compete with each other without restrictions. Traditionally, these dances were the preserve of military men who performed them as physical training drills to prepare for battle. The names of these dances still speak to that legacy: Sword Dance, Sailor's Hornpipe, Highland Laddie, and Wilt Thou Go to the Barracks, Johnnie.

Years later, my MBA class was more than 80 percent men. When I graduated, I joined a computer company as the marketing manager. At techie trade shows, I was sometimes mistaken for one of the "booth babes," models hired to draw prospective male buyers into the demo area. And now here I am writing about wine. That said, many of my strongest supporters have been men, not least my husband, Andrew, and my son, Rian. And I've never regretted being one of the few women in the room—it's a competitive advantage to be underestimated.

I guess I'm drawn to these fields because I've always been a geek of one sort or another, which goes along with being socially awkward and shy. I bond with other geeks who share the same passion; it helps me make connections that don't come to me naturally. That obsessive-compulsive hunger for one thing also keeps me from rusting.

Still, I have a terrible tendency to interrupt other people's thoughts (even my own). I often say awkward things that just hang in the air like moldy laundry. I frequently trip over my own cleverness and have to recalibrate back to humility. My sense of adventure and my short attention span combine to make me vilely allergic to the comprehensive, encyclopedia-style approach to wine. I'm a sucker for a good glass of vino—and an even bigger fool for a great story about it. I just think that you should know what you're getting into with this book.

We wine writers tend to be obsessive souls. How else can a person stay fascinated throughout a career with just one drink? Compare us to food writers: Over their lives, they'll encounter thousands of ingredients and ways of combining and cooking them. Wine, by contrast, is just fermented grapes. But it engages our primary senses—smell, taste, touch—in a way that is both hedonistic and cerebral.

That's why I've spent the past several years traipsing around the world, visiting wineries, tasting their offerings, and searching for the world's best cheap wines: one terrific bottle for each night of the week, plus an extra one for Sunday lunch. It's been an unquenchable journey to learn about new people, new places, and new wines. The narrative is as familiar as Arthur's quest for the grail and as naive as the little bird's plaintive search for the affirmative in *Are You My Mother?*

Inevitably, the emails will flood my inbox demanding how I could possibly leave out this region or that producer. But somehow, the subtitle "147 Cheap Wines to Drink Before You Die" just didn't seem as catchy. In each of the eight regions I explored, I visited between thirty and forty wineries, and I've tasted thousands more wines from each place. Still, I don't claim to have found all of the world's best value wines; I've just selected a handful that I heartily recommend. I hope you'll also find, as I did, that the search is as pleasurable as the answer—and that just a taste will leave you thirsting for more.

BEYOND THE ADVENTURES

THIS BOOK EXPLORES the subject of wine in a way that's relatively timeless, a whirlwind tour of the history, geography, and people who make it and drink it. It's as much a travelogue and memoir as it is a guide to wine. For those of us with a pragmatic bent, I've also added a takeaway section at the end of each chapter under the title "Field Notes from a Wine Cheapskate" in which I include the following:

- **INSIDER TIPS:** A summary of some interesting (and obscure) bits of wisdom that I gleaned from my travels.

- **WINERIES VISITED:** I feature about three wineries per region, sometimes fewer. These generally represent only the highlights of my visits to each country, but are selected based on where I found the most fascinating places and characters along with the best value wines.

- **BEST VALUE WINES:** The list of "value" wines that I tasted on this trip doesn't include the vintages for each wine, since they may no longer be available. However, these wineries are consistently good producers, so the odds are that their latest vintages will be as tasty as those I enjoyed. While I also tried a number of pricey bottles to get the full scope of each region and to anchor the value range, I haven't included them in this list. Rather, this is a brief guide to good labels from producers you can trust. Although it's impossible to select just one winner from so many terrific wines in each region, I have put an asterisk (*) next to the wine that I'd pick first for my own dinner each night.

- **TOP VALUE PRODUCERS:** This list comprises more great value producers from the region, beyond those I visited for the book. Some producers have other brands or labels that I've listed separately.

- **TERRIFIC PAIRINGS:** I've included only a few highlights of what I consider good pairings for selected wines in each chapter. (If these whet your appetite, I also offer thousands of wine and food pairings in my Drinks Matcher tool, www.nataliemaclean.com/matcher.)

- **RESOURCES AND RELATED READING:** I've included a short list of books, websites, and blogs, both of specific relevance to the wines discussed and to the region visited.

The world of wine is constantly changing, with new vintages, techniques, and producers coming onto the scene every year. So rather than trying to update this book as rapidly as things change, I publish a website that covers, among other topics, reviews of bottles in stores now, updates on the latest news in the wine world, and what your fellow drinkers think of the wines they've tried recently. Read the book for the adventure stories and then visit these web pages:

- My picks of top-value wines from each region in liquor stores now, including my tasting notes, scores, bottle shots, and food matches. You can create your own shopping list: www.nataliemaclean.com/winepicks.

- The website addresses, contact information, pictures, and other information for the wineries in this book, including my list of top-value producers at the end of each chapter, in this Worldwide Winery Directory: www.nataliemaclean.com/wineries.

- Recipes for the dishes I enjoyed along the journey, contributed by the winemakers and winery chefs, all paired with the local wines: www.nataliemaclean.com/food.

- A food-and-wine matching tool that you can use to find pairings for any dish. You can also post it on your own website or blog: www.nataliemaclean.com/matcher.

- A photo album of pictures from each chapter of the landscape, winemakers, and food: www.nataliemaclean.com/book.

- Suggested questions and discussion points for book clubs, along with tips on organizing an informal wine tasting for your group: www.nataliemaclean.com/book.

- My blog (www.nataliemaclean.com/blog), Facebook (www.facebook.com/natdecants), and Twitter (www.twitter.com/nataliemaclean), where I post updates on my latest travels, wine-tasting events, and other news.

- Mobile apps for iPhone, iPod Touch, BlackBerry, Droid, and other smartphones, with all of the information above: www.nataliemaclean.com/mobileapp.

I'd love to hear from you. Please email me at natdecants@natalie maclean.com when you have a moment, and we'll raise a virtual glass together.

Cheers,
Natalie

UNQUENCHABLE

ONE

SUNDAY

The Wine Wizards of Oz

"Watch out for the snakes," my friend Robyn said when she heard I was going to Australia.

The what?

"Nine of the ten deadliest snakes in the world are in Australia," she replied, proud as a quiz show contestant.

I changed the subject to our dinner plans.

Now, as I fly over the Barossa Valley, Robyn's comment comes back to me. I squint down at the vast dry biscuit of russet earth but don't see anything slithering on the ground, and I comfort myself with my usual self-delusions that snakes don't eat grapes.

The Barossa Valley is just forty-five minutes northeast of the city of Adelaide, located on the south coast. It's Australia's best-known wine region, and produces its most iconic wine: shiraz. The grape actually originated in the Rhône Valley of France, where it's called syrah and has been growing since 500 BCE. It's usually the leading grape in the blends of wines such as hermitage and Côte Rôtie. Although shiraz and syrah are the same grape, various wine-producing regions have chosen one name or the other. Australians went with shiraz, a variation on the original name they had for these vines—scyras—that was easier to pronounce, whereas California tends to use syrah because many feel their style is more European.

Shiraz thrives here on the planet's most arid continent because the vine is so vigorous that it needs hardship to produce concentrated wine. What little rain falls in the Barossa evaporates quickly, and temperatures can average in the high nineties for weeks on end. Shiraz transforms these dry furnace conditions into the lyrical, liquid voice of this sun-drenched land.

This "overnight sensation" began in 1832, when a progressive governor, James Busby, planted the first scyras (shiraz) vines in the country in the Hunter Valley near Sydney. He believed that local wine would be less intoxicating than the rum that the early settlers, mostly convicts and gold rush speculators, brought with them.

However, the Barossa Valley was mostly settled by Lutheran families, led by their pastors who had fled religious persecution in Silesia, in what is now part of Poland. Each family received a grant of thirty acres, and many started planting shiraz vines around 1842. Ownership was stable through the generations, and so these are among the oldest shiraz vines in the world.

Winemaking in Australia has continued uninterrupted ever since, thanks to several factors. Unlike North America, the Aussies never implemented Prohibition, and the continent's isolation spared most Oz vintners from having to replant acres of vineyards lost to the vine louse phylloxera that destroyed both North American and European vineyards in the 1800s and 1900s. However, Down Under wines weren't always popular or even good. Between the 1960s and the 1980s, they were mostly sweet and fortified—connoisseurs described them as tasting like alcoholic jam in an oak box. Their dubious quality was parodied in a Monty Python skit that featured Eric Idle, surrounded by men in cork-fringed hats, describing the "Château Nuits St. Wagga-Wagga" as smelling like a "kangaroo's aahmpit."

Today, however, with modern refrigeration and other advances, Australia has harnessed the heat and makes spectacularly tasty wines at incredibly low prices. Producers there don't have to fight cold and mildew as they do in cool climates. They're also incredibly free from the government regulation that restricts many European countries, such as France and Italy, from using certain grapes or making different blends. That allows Australian winemakers to use the grapes from the region that fared best in a particular vintage so that their wines are consistently good and low priced. Even most New World countries don't draw on grapes as far afield as do the Australians—it would be like labeling a wine as coming from "Western North America."

As a result, these wines have jumped to the number one or two market position in many countries. As a Scot who comes from generations of hard-drinking penny-pinchers, this pleases me immensely. It means that I can buy four bottles rather than one. It also means that I can pass off these wines as being much more expensive than they really are when giving them as gifts or serving them at dinner parties. Let me be clear: being cheap is in my DNA, but I'm also a hedonist after great taste. These are usually opposing forces, but that's easily solved if you travel around the world for five years and taste 15,267 wines. (I've done that so you don't have to.)

I'm also starting with Australian wines in this book, especially the robust shiraz, because it's ideal for a Sunday dinner of roast beef or meat lovers' pizza: comfort wine for comfort food. If you're like me and skip the introduction in books, let me say quickly that this is how I'm organizing these chapters: I start with a wine for Sunday dinner, progress through each day of the week, and end with one for Sunday lunch. The Barossa Valley is home to many of Australia's best producers fit for the Sunday table: Peter Lehmann, Grant Burge, Yalumba, Penfolds, Wolf Blass—and yes, those friggin' snakes, I remind myself as I jump into my rental car and, absurdly, lock the door.

A few hours later, as I cross the manicured lawn of the Wolf Blass winery, it occurs to me that many people don't realize there actually is a man after whom the winery is named. They think of Wolf Blass as another brand character, like Duncan Hines or Betty Crocker. But just as there is a Calvin Klein and Ralph Lauren, there's also a Wolf Blass—and no marketing team could ever invent a man so colorful.

He's barreling toward me now, trailed by an entourage of paid optimists. "Aren't you a supreme cookie!" he exclaims, beaming up at me as he grabs my hand and forearm with both of his. Well into his seventies, Wolf's a trim five-foot-three with mischievous dark eyes and pepper gray hair. He has the energy of a man half his age and twice his height. He wears one of his trademark bow ties (and has seven hundred of them, I'm told): a fire-engine red number that matches his banker's suspenders and arm band. He doesn't let go of my arm as he steers me over to the Wolf Blass museum, his worried PR people in tow. (Their boss is known for his stream of unedited thoughts about wine, money, business, friendship, sex, and success.)

Wolfgang Franz Otto Blass was born on the move. In 1934, in the German state of Saxony, his mother barely made it through the hospital doors before he arrived. Even as a child, "Wolfie" was a natural performer, though much of his childhood was grim. Inside the museum, Wolf stops in front of a black-and-white photo of three stone-faced children—himself and his two brothers. Growing up in postwar East Germany was "a bloody nightmare," he tells me. There were few jobs and less money.

"People were so desperate, they traded their watches for bread,"

Wolf explains, adjusting his Rolex. "I became a street fighter whose main concern was getting tucker." That's Australian for *food*, and I'm starting to tune into his carefree mangling of German and Australian, which comes out as a matey drawl in the middle and ends with a militant clip. Germany produced him, but Australia made him.

"Mother told me, 'Go into agriculture; at least you'll get something to eat,'" he says. "So I started to apprentice at the winery of a friend—he was a tyrant, you know, a real Nazi! But I learned inch by inch. Took me three years, very slow. Best terrible experience of my life."

Working with wine was his ticket out of Germany. "I wanted to get away, overseas, anywhere. So I went to France. I don't like the French." (One publicist looks uncomfortably at another one.) "But I learned how to make sparkling wine in Champagne."

In 1961, he jumped at a job offer from Penfolds and immigrated to Australia with a few hundred dollars in his pocket. "I was a bad employee because I always thought I could do things better than management could." After a few years, he became a traveling consultant to a number of wineries before opening his own in 1973.

"In those days, I did it all: I made the wine, I sold the wine," he says, as we look at a photo of Wolf in his early twenties, with a slicked-back ducktail haircut, sitting on the hood of a convertible. He became known as much for the way he sold his wine as for the way he made it. At baseball games, for instance, he'd chat with the television cameramen, telling them he'd be in the crowd with his winery sign. Every time they focused on the sign, there was a case of wine for them.

"So the ball is hit out of the park. It's a home run—up, up, up . . . everyone's watching it except the cameraman because he's found my sign. Bloody cunning!" he says approvingly at the memory.

He also used to have himself paged over the intercom system at airports so that shoppers in the duty-free stores would hear the name Wolf Blass, and he'd conduct impromptu wine tastings on planes with captive audiences. He was one of the first in the industry to realize that the winemaker is integral to the marketing of the product, the human face of the wine.

"People do business with people, not products. They want to put a face on the bottle. I went to every bloomin' state, every black-tie dinner, every bloody radio station," he says, his eyes twinkling like stage lights. "In one speech, I told them I didn't think Australian wine was worth more than $10. I told them, 'I'm going back home: you don't deserve good wine!'" But his chronic dissatisfaction for the status quo made him stay and create his first namesake wine priced at $15.

"I can't stand to lose," he says, as we walk over to a large glass cabinet filled with his trophies from wine competitions. Critics of Australian wine shows say that just about every wine gets a medal, and the heftiest ones win these sensory weight-lifting contests. However, Wolf believes that the competitions have raised the overall quality of Australian wine. Winemakers often share their knowledge at the gatherings, allowing the industry to fix faults and improve techniques.

In the early 1970s, Wolf was frustrated by a losing streak with his wines. A friend advised him to ask the judge's advice (rather than punching him out). The judge taught Wolf how to adjust his palate to "the winning formula." His new approach helped him win the country's top winemaking prize, the Jimmy Watson Trophy, three years in a row, in 1974, 1975, and 1976—a record never equaled before or since.

In his acceptance speech, Wolf declared that his wine could "make strong women weak and weak men strong. It's a bloody aphrodisiac: I can prove it because I'm testing it on myself!" His comments were in the newspapers the next day. After his third Jimmy Watson Trophy, he and winemaker Chris Hatcher celebrated late into the night and woke up together in the same hotel room the next day, much to their manly chagrin, even though they were fully clothed.

"Without proof of success at the wine shows, I would have been a nobody. No medals, no job," he says, clearly moved by his own words. He has little patience for producers who don't enter their wines into competitions, but complain about them. "That's like having a racehorse in the paddock and never racing it. If you're not in the competition, you shouldn't comment on those who are."

In his private tasting room, he's now pouring us a sample of that "winning formula": a blend of cabernet sauvignon and shiraz. Power and elegance dance in the glass: Fred Astaire shiraz and Ginger Rogers cabernet. Wolf believes that blending is a large part of Australia's success in the international wine market, since it offers the flexibility to choose the best ingredients. Australia is also famous for its "GSM" blends: grenache for lift and fruitiness, shiraz for body and flesh, and mourvèdre for spice and structure.

"We are consistent year after year. Consistency is quality. It's like the signature dish of a restaurant: you want it to be the same every time you go. It creates loyalty. We make wines the consumer likes to drink—they buy the brand. Maybe the wines aren't for fanatics; they might find them too . . . symmetrical. But we are an extremely safe brand, consumers depend on us. It's a big responsibility when there's seventy million bottles with your bloody name on them."

I can tell that this is a spiel Wolf has delivered many times to many audiences as he rolls on enthusiastically. "I'm proud of our success: we get down people's throats! Too many precious winemakers think commercial success means the wine is no good. But what's no good is to be a loser. Manchester United: seventeen times champions. Bloody beautiful!

"Shiraz is all about full, fat flavor. You can't have high-acid wines that are a commercial success: people won't drink the bloody stuff. The everyday punter doesn't understand it," he says with a significant rise of his eyebrows, as though we've come to a mutual unspoken agreement.

"Shit. Don't write that."

The senior PR woman gives me an apologetic what-can-you-do smile. I return her smile as sweetly as I can.

Wolf changes the subject as quickly as a river finds a path around a boulder, moving on to his marketing innovations, such as his different label colors to distinguish each wine. "Most people didn't know their bloody grapes, and they didn't go into the wine store describing the grapes they wanted. They'd say I want the Wolf Blass yellow label or gray or whatever." The yellow label was inspired by the yellow jerseys of the Australian football team; gray was for the wolf; red came from a trip to China, where it's a lucky color; and green was "for the Irish." Black is reserved for the company's best blended wines, and platinum is for its flagship Barossa shiraz.

Consumers responded enthusiastically: his $17 Yellow Label Cabernet became the bestselling red wine in North America, at least until Casella Wines' $12 Yellow Tail Shiraz hopped onto the scene in 2001. It became the most successful wine launch in North American history, selling more than a million cases in the first year. Today, annual global sales of Yellow Tail are about twelve million cases compared to six million for Wolf Blass.

Yellow Tail was part of the "critter craze": cuddly creatures on wine labels designed to make wine more accessible and fun, such as Crocodile Rock, Little Penguin, and Cat Amongst the Pigeons. Other countries also launched their own brands: French Rabbit, France; Monkey Bay, New Zealand; and Wolftrap, South Africa, among many others. Such labels are easy to remember when you want to buy that delicious purple lizard wine again. More important, they appeal to women, who buy most wine—and who, apparently, are suckers for a cuddy little creature.

"Yellow Tail did a great job of soaking up the oversupply of grapes in Australia," Wolf observes. "If it gets people into the wine category, then it's a good thing. But they pinched my yellow!" he adds teasingly.

The idea of color coding is based on Wolf's close observations of the female mind: "My marketing was always driven toward women because I love women—I married four smashing crackers! The beer companies ignored women, the puffs," he says cheerfully, pouring a glass of his Red Label Shiraz Cabernet Sauvignon.

"I call this wine the leg opener," he says with a sly grin.

I look down at my notebook.

"Well don't bloody write that down!"

As I divert my eyes to the wine I'm sipping, it's clear that his wine does have a loosening effect, even though my legs remain firmly crossed. His blend, dominated by shiraz, is full and lush on the mid-palate, with a mocha-coffee character that backs off the spice and pepper. I can just taste the blackberry hint of cabernet at the tip of my tongue, which is quickly flooded by fleshy plums before I swallow. Clearly, Wolf's outsized personality is not solely responsible for his success: the broadsides are backed up by wines that are pretty damn good.

Shiraz, Wolf claims, shouldn't have a dominating flavor: "It's a winemaker's wine, like chardonnay. It can be whatever you bloody well want it to be. But it's also powerful and needs American oak because it's creamier and sweeter than French oak. Putting shiraz into French oak is like stuffing a fat man into a lace corset. American oak is also half the price of French oak—the bloody French!—which is important when you have to compete on price. My motto is 'no wood, no good.' But you need to know what you're doing; you need to be a timber expert. I'm going to buy wood from forests near Chernobyl so I can make glow-label wines.

"Shit! Don't you print that now."

I smile. The PR woman smiles.

"Leave that out."

I smile again.

"These wines have great drinkability. They take the mickey out of the French," he says, pounding his fist on the table, then leaning toward me to push his words in. "If you're paying $2,000 for a bloody bottle of bordeaux, you need to get your head shrunk."

Wolf takes another sip of the wine and turns more reflective: "The boom we experienced in the last decade only happens once in the history of an industry. Now we have to fight to hold on to that leadership. We don't have competitors on quality, only on price. Germany paid the price for selling cheap wine in the 1970s. We have to be careful not to turn into style merchants who want to make wine into liquid fast food. We wouldn't survive the bulk market . . . tall poppy syndrome . . . someone will eat our tucker!"

Wolf Blass took his winery public in 1984, and then it subsequently merged with several others, increasing in size and value until the beer giant Fosters bought the company in 1989. Fosters's wine division is now called Treasury Wine Estates. Today, Wolf Blass winery exports 70 percent of what it produces. Wolf himself, no longer running the company, is now its brand ambassador. What's his official title these days?

"Troublemaker," he says, grinning. "I can say anything I want now because I can't get sacked. My job is to go around the world and sell my Australia. This wine is Australia."

And after all these decades of experience, what does he think the industry needs to do? "We need to go to Asia . . . they're very thirsty over there. There are too many wineries in Australia, too many amalgamations; 60 percent is controlled by five companies. We need more boutique wineries, more small operators, more cellar-door sales.

"And we need to use our natural advantages: we need to convince people around the world that Australia is a great place for a vacation. It's not ripping overcrowded, like Napa Valley, and you don't need a bloomin' letter of introduction to get into the wineries, like France. You can speak English, the wines are cheap, the food is great, the land is beautiful."

And for Wolf personally? "When we do bottle signings, I get mobbed," he says, winking at me over the rim of his glass. "Yeah, I'm a bloody legend, but I'm not dead yet. I'm fit, my mind still works, lots of sex—it's all good."

PERHAPS THE ONLY thing more mind-boggling than meeting Wolf Blass is driving in Australia. Not only am I on the "wrong" side of the road, but the steering wheel is on the passenger side. I keep signaling with my windshield wipers. In Adelaide, I could follow the car ahead of me; but after an hour of driving out here to wine country, I'm disoriented. I turn a corner hidden by eucalyptus and gum trees, and find myself head-on with a tractor. Fortunately, it's going so slowly that I can swerve out of its path and continue on my way to Penfolds.

There I meet Peter Gago on a ramp in front of the barrel cellar— a slim man in his early fifties in an understated gray tunic and designer pants. He looks more like an art gallery owner than Penfolds's chief winemaker, whom I'd expected to be in wine-splattered overalls. Peter's title is actually "custodian," embracing a wider role than simply winemaking. His off-season road trips would leave a rock band exhausted—a recent tour involved twenty-six cities over ten weeks.

Penfolds was founded in 1844, making it older than many European wineries. The original vine cuttings from southern France were planted for medicinal purposes: a physician who had emigrated from England, Dr. Christopher Rawson Penfold, wanted to make wine for his patients. Predictably, more and more locals sought the "wine cure" for an increasingly wide range of ailments. Demand soon outpaced production, and Dr. Penfold decided to give up medicine and make wine full-time.

The business prospered for decades, and after the good doctor's death in 1870, his widow, Mary, ran the business for another fourteen years. Penfolds remained in the family until part of its stock was sold in 1970. Then, in 2005, the winery was bought by Fosters, which also owns Wolf Blass.

Peter joined the company twenty-two years ago, after graduating from oenology at the prestigious Roseworthy College of Agriculture at the University of Adelaide. He invites me to tour the cellar before we taste the wines, opening the large door with balletic grace. Inside are long rows of massive dark oak barrels, twelve high and fifteen feet in diameter. "We are the world's largest boutique winery," he says in a soft Australian accent with polished finishing-school diction. The winery produces 2.5 million cases a year and is one of the country's largest exporters.

There's a small plate on one of the barrels, bearing the name of Helen Keller. "When she visited the winery in 1948, she was fascinated by the texture and girth of this vat," Peter explains, brushing his fingers against it. "Someone told her its height, and she took less than a minute to correctly calculate that it held 10,774 gallons of wine."

A previous Penfolds winemaker pioneered the use of oak in Australia. Max Schubert joined the company as a messenger boy in the early 1930s and over two decades rose to become winemaker. In 1949, he went to Spain for a month to learn sherry-making techniques, since at the time, Australians who didn't drink beer mostly drank fortified wines. On his way home, he stopped in Bordeaux, tasted the local wines, and noticed that producers there aged their wines in oak barrels. He realized that oak was the ideal cradle for unfortified wines to develop the structure they needed for aging.

When he got back to Australia, he experimented with a small batch of red wine. Since he hadn't planted any bordeaux-style grapes, such as cabernet sauvignon or merlot, he used the local shiraz, then mostly the base for port-styled wine. After the wine had fermented, he didn't have any French oak, so he used American casks. He positioned the wax-coated wooden closures called bungs at the twelve o'clock position and topped the barrels up regularly so that the wine wouldn't oxidize. A small percentage of the wine slowly evaporates through the wood—it's whimsically called the angel's share.

Max drained the clear wine from the sediment that had settled out of it at the bottom of the barrel to a new barrel, a process called racking. He then aged the wine another eighteen to twenty-four months in oak for a tight-weave flavor and structure—a warp and woof of tannin and fruit. He named the wine Grange Hermitage, in honor of Grange Cottage (Mary Penfolds's home in England) and the French wine syrah (known as hermitage in the Rhône region).

However, at that point, the wine was merely his personal project. When he unveiled his creation to the senior management at Penfolds in the early 1950s, they were less than impressed. The dry style of wine, with a hint of oak, didn't suit their taste or that of their customers, they believed. They didn't understand that the wine would soak up the oak over time and that they wouldn't taste it directly, just as you don't notice the structural beams in a beautiful house when it's finished.

Grange became proof that senior management often doesn't know what they're doing. They issued Max a direct order on company letterhead to cease production, or he would be fired. Fortunately, Max was convinced of the wine's potential, didn't listen to his bosses, and kept making the wine in secret from 1957 to 1959. These are now called the Hidden Granges and are coveted by collectors around the world.

Grange is also proof that wine critics often don't know what they're talking about. When the wine was first launched, they said it tasted like crushed ants. But in 1962, Max entered his 1955 Grange into the Sydney Wine Show, where it won the gold medal. Penfolds senior management relented and asked Max to restart production (unaware that he had never stopped).

A decade later, more and more winemakers adopted Max's approach and started using oak and creating a dry style of wine. Today, Grange is the world's most expensive shiraz. (The Hermitage part of the name was dropped in 1990 before the French could protest that the name belonged to them, as much as names like Champagne and Bordeaux do.) The starting price of Grange is $500 a bottle when it's released every May 1. One bottle from 1951 recently sold at auction for more than $50,000.

Hang on, this doesn't sound like a wine for a cheapskate, even a choosy one. Well, the brilliance of Penfolds is that they established their reputation at the high end of the price scale. Then, over time, the company diversified into a wide range of wines with lower price tags, though they still had the signature flavors of the flagship wine.

The entry-level wine, Penfolds Rawson's Retreat, starts at about $12, followed by the $15 Koonunga Hill, the $20 Thomas Hyland, and then the pricier Bin numbered wines (128, 138, 28, 407, 150, 389, 707), the St. Henri, the Magill Estate, the RWT, and finally, Grange. The Penfolds style trickles down through all the tiers. Other Australian brands, such as Rosemount and Hardys, also use "ladder brands" to move their customers up the product line. Personally, I'm happy to stay on the lower rungs, where the price-quality ratio of these wines is terrific.

Like Wolf Blass, Peter believes that American oak is well suited to shiraz because the wood's wider grain can support the rich flavors of the grape. Still, not all American oak is the same. Peter explains that its character differs depending on how it's seasoned. When oak staves are first cut, the wood is still green and full of tree resin, so the barrels made from it would impart green, dill pickle flavors to the wine. Many barrel coopers leave their wood slats outside for several years, allowing the rain and sun to naturally leach out the resin and dry the wood before making them into casks.

The wood staves are set around a small fire, but not touching it, in order to make them pliable enough to be shaped into a barrel. A high-temperature toasting releases estuary compounds in the wood—notes such as coconut and vanilla—whereas lower temperatures may impart aromas of chocolate and coffee. Whatever the technique, Peter says, the essence of the flavor should be "oak-derived" but not quite oak. "It's interesting that many Americans didn't like the taste of their own oak until they tried Australian wine" he observes.

When tannin is balanced with the fruit of the wine, it acts like acidity, as a mouth scrubber with its drying astringency. This leaves your palate refreshed for the next bite of food rather than fatiguing with the same taste. Tannin is terrific with fatty foods, cutting through their richness, and in turn, the food smoothes out the wine. The combination is exhilarating: the food brings down the roughness of the wine, and the wine brings up the different flavors in the food.

As the only animals who cook our food, we humans have grown to love a broad range of foods and flavors. Many of us have also developed a liking for the smoky flavors derived from the hardwood originally used to cook our food, especially oak. In wine, oak adds complexity with non-fruit flavors, such as vanilla, smoke, caramel, and cedar.

However, too much oak in a number of other Australian wines I've tasted obliterates the taste of the wine, much like dousing everything you eat with ketchup or salt. These "termite specials" club your palate until it's numb, assaulting you with flavors and tannins. If the death of elegance had a taste, this would be it. They don't even pair well with food except perhaps wild buffalo—if it's still alive.

"At Penfolds, we blend most of our wines, both the grapes and the regions," Peter explains. The signature Grange, for instance, is a multiregion blend in American oak, but it's protected stylistically in the market by RWT, a shiraz that's from a single region, the Barossa, and finished in French oak. "Blending diminishes the troughs, so the style isn't on a roller-coaster ride from year to year," he says. "Winemaking is a culture of renegades—we love a difficult year! But we don't want our customers to have to deal with it. We want our wines to be dependable for investors, collectors, and everyday drinkers."

Consistency is a controversial benchmark for wine quality: many vintners feel a wine should reflect the individual vintage. It's also at odds with the efforts of the industry group, Wine Australia, to market the differences between the country's more than sixty wine regions. It's a thin red line to walk because some drinkers don't want wine that's indistinguishable from one region to the next, while others don't want French-styled complexities imported to the country that's made wine so accessible.

Peter is less concerned with such philosophical debates and more focused on creating good wines at Penfolds—he's most comfortable when talking about that. "Aiming for ripeness is like confusing information with intelligence," he asserts. "We don't chase flavor: we create structure first; then flavor follows and fills in the structure.

For us, cabernet is usually the bridesmaid to shiraz. When you taste cabernet on its own, it's long and lean because of those drying tannins. However, when those structural tannins are fleshed out with shiraz flavor, the wine becomes full and balanced. After the richness of shiraz on the mid-palate, you feel that fresh lift of cabernet just before you swallow. This gives our wine longevity—it's why the 1953 Grange is drinking so beautifully now. Just because the tannins feel silkier in our wines doesn't mean that they can't age."

The famed Penfolds longevity is also the result of another of Max Schubert's innovations. He realized that the heat of Australia's climate in many of its regions ripened the grapes to such a degree that their sugar was high and their acidity low. Acidity protects them from bacterial infection. Without this natural protection, Australian winemakers often had to throw out up to a third of their production every year. Max realized that if he could stabilize the wine to the right level of acidity and pH, it could have the potential to age for decades. His solution was to "correct" the finished wine by adding a small amount of tartaric acid, a substance that's already naturally in grapes.

This move attracted the criticism that Max was manipulating the process too much and making a "chemist's wine." In France, the corresponding controversial activity is chaptalizing, which means adding a little natural grape sugar to the fermenting wine to increase its body and alcohol. This is done mainly in cool climates, such as northern European countries, where the grapes don't get sufficient warmth to fully ripen in some years. Obviously, that's never the issue in Australia's warm regions, like the Barossa. Increasingly, though, winemakers on both sides of the ocean are learning how to best work with their grapes in the vineyard to get enough sugar and acidity rather than having to add them afterward.

Peter shows me around several large open vats made of concrete. They're empty now because the harvest took place about two months ago in April, so the new wine is already in barrels. Australia is in the Southern Hemisphere, so its seasons are the opposite of those in the North. The open vats are a highly aerobic method of winemaking, which doesn't simply refer to how hard the winemakers work (they do) but to exposing the wine to oxygen. Several times a day during fermentation, Peter does what he calls "rack-and-return": the juice is drained from the bottom of one tank into another tank and then splashed back over a grate to aerate it. The skins sink to the bottom of the tank as the must is drained, and then the must is pumped back over the skins. The skins gradually rise to the top again as the juice extracts more flavor and color from them, conditioning the wine for long-term aging.

The culture of innovation remains widespread in Australia: the country publishes more research papers on technology than any other country, led by scientists at Roseworthy. Penfolds's own history of innovation didn't end with Max Schubert. In the early 1960s, winemaker Don Ditter named the newest wine Bin 707 after the Boeing 707, one of the most advanced aircraft of the time. In 1997, the vintner before Peter, John Duval, created RWT, which stood for Red Winemaking Trial—the name was supposed to be a temporary one for an experiment with aging Barossa shiraz in French oak. When the trial turned out to be successful, the name stuck. Peter also experiments on a variety of winemaking aspects, including his 2011 launch of the Coonawarra Bin 169 Cabernet Sauvignon matured in French barrels, as the stylistic foil to the American oak-aged Bin 707. However, he is wary of depending on either oak or technology too much.

"Technology can make your wines too squeaky clean," he cautions, as we walk out of the cellar. "They can be pasteurized beyond personality. We need to have technology in Australia to drive down our costs because we're too distant from cheap labor to help pick the grapes and make the wine, the way that California and Europe can.

But technology can't tell you what to do—just how to do it more efficiently. Tradition influences us just as much."

Peter's never far from the tradition of Penfolds: his office is in the old Magill Cottage, the Penfolds's original home, which still stands beside the cellar. Inside the timbered cottage are sepia-toned photos of Mary, Christopher, their children, and their grandchildren. There are yellowing deeds and land certificates and leather-bound books. Peter takes me to a small room where we taste the wines. It's fascinating to taste both history and modernity as a gathering essence in the glass. The modestly priced Rawson's Retreat, Koonunga Hill, and Thomas Hyland are all exceptionally well-made for the price. There's a sheen to the fruit that seduces you, and a lusciousness in the taste that makes good on the promise.

The St. Henri is lighter bodied than the Grange, but with the same fruit intensity. It's fermented in large 385-gallon vats that are fifty-five years or older, so it has little oak character or oak tannin. The flavors unfold in my mouth like a peacock tail, growing wider and more varied as I taste.

Peter pours me the higher-end offerings. RWT offers concentric circles of pleasure: fleshy blackberries roll around the outer circles of flavor, deepening to a dark, concentrated core of hedonism. There's an elemental interplay of liquid, air, and wood that's built for aging. By contrast, Grange is an expansive darkness of licorice, black olive, and graphite depths. The first sip is big, and then it builds in your mouth. It's a cumulative wine that swells and engulfs your senses like the musical signature of Ravel's *Bolero*, becoming more pronounced, more exciting, the more you taste it.

As we taste the wines, Peter and I chat about the winery's recorking clinics, constituting what must be the best after-sales service in the wine world. Penfolds invites customers to bring their Penfolds bottles older than fifteen years to selected venues in cities around the world. Peter opens the wines under argon, a protective inert gas cover, then samples a tiny amount to determine if the wine is as it should be and without faults. If it is good, the bottle is topped up with a few ounces of the same wine but from the latest vintage, which isn't enough to change the taste or the wine's integrity for resale. Then it's resealed with a stamped cork and a new capsule, and Peter signs a certification label on the back. This seal of approval boosts the wine's value: bottles sold at auction often fetch more than they otherwise would with this updated guarantee of quality.

"The clinics are a great way to meet our customers, and almost every bottle has a story," Peter says. "One man found a bottle of Grange behind a park bench in the city. Another customer took a bottle with him when he climbed up Kilimanjaro. Recently, a young woman brought in a bottle from 1951 that she had inherited. But when we opened it, we found that it was filled with tea! Her grandfather must have enjoyed the wine decades ago, then recorked it."

Over the past twenty years, more than a hundred thousand bottles have been checked for their quality. "We've found less than 2 percent have been faulty. Still, we do advise many people to drink the wine soon," Peter says. "That's the biggest mistake people make with all wines: keeping them too long in the cellar."

I enjoyed attending a recorking clinic in Toronto; it was like a wine version of the *Antiques Roadshow*, with lots of surprised and happy customers. As I watched Peter listen attentively to an elderly woman, both of their hands on a bottle with a yellowing label, I couldn't imagine a better title for him than custodian.

As I DRIVE along an old dirt road, through the gaps in the wattle and gum trees, I spot some kangaroos hopping through the brush. A few of them stop and stare at me curiously, looking as soft and unreal as stuffed toys. This magnificently strange country makes me feel like *Alice in Wonderland*—and not just because of the Down Under notion of falling through the rabbit hole and finding everything reversed. It's the sensory playfulness and abandon here that I love: the odd, joyful jumble of color and flavor and aroma.

My mind wanders back to my favorite part of the Lewis Carroll story: "She found a little bottle . . . and round its neck a paper label with the words 'Drink Me' beautifully printed in large letters. . . . Alice ventured to taste it, and finding it very nice (it had a sort of mixed flavor of cherry-tart, custard, pineapple, roast turkey, toffee, and hot buttered toast), she very soon finished it off."

I wish Alice were with me now—we'd share a bottle of shiraz. She'd describe it perfectly but not take the tasting too seriously. We'd laugh when she'd recall how the Red Queen and her guests "put their glasses upon their heads like extinguishers, and drank all that trickled down their faces; others upset the decanters and drank the wine as it ran off the edges of the table."

I swim back up to reality when I spot the old stone Henschke winery nestled amid a tangle of trees and bushes. True, Henschke wines are not cheap, but they do offer great value compared to many other wines of their quality. And I can't resist going off the path occasionally for the sake of a tasty nip. I'm prone to tangential digressions, but I've never regretted being remarkably inconsistent: it's led me to fascinating people and interesting stories. If you're looking for consistency, try the *Oxford Companion to Wine*. If you want adventure, let's go . . .

I'm here to meet Stephen Henschke, the great-great-grandson of the original founder. He's a compact, scholarly looking man, dressed in an Oxford shirt and Dockers. His quiet, serious manner amid this wild plant life reminds me of a botany professor on a remote expedition. He meets me in the winery's small reception area and gives me a brief history of the family business. Its founder, Johann Christian Henschke, was a buggy maker and farmer when he came over from Silesia on a ship of Lutheran farmers in 1868 with his wife and five children. Only he and two of his children survived the journey. But he worked hard on his grant of land, saved money, planted vines, married again, and had eight more children.

The Henschke winery has stayed in the family over the generations. Johann's great-grandson, Cyril Henschke, went to Oxford University as a Churchill Fellow, and then worked with Max Schubert at Penfolds during his viticultural training. Like Max, Cyril was also an early proponent of dry table wines in the 1950s. He had the foresight to develop his vineyards and bottle his wine rather than sell his grapes in bulk to larger companies, as most growers did. Stephen, Cyril's middle child, studied botany and biochemistry at Roseworthy. There he met Prue Weir, who was studying zoology and botany. Ten days after they graduated, they got married and moved to Germany. Stephen enrolled in the renowned Geisenheim Wine Institute, while Prue audited classes and worked at the Geisenheim Grape Breeding Institute.

When the couple returned to Australia in 1978, they started making wine on the family farm, which they inherited when Cyril died. However, they had a huge inheritance tax to pay to the government. "We were penniless," Stephen recalls. "Those were long days and nights. Most winemakers know that you're only as good as your current release. But it was very motivating to be fighting for your home as well as your business."

Their big break came one day when a major British importer dropped into the winery and asked for more of their wines. He thought their style was more French than Australian and would sell well in the U.K.—provided they left the word *shiraz* off the label. They did, relying instead on their vineyard names, and sales built steadily. Today they produce forty thousand cases a year.

Stephen takes me to the back office to meet Prue, who's sitting at a large oak desk covered with stacks of papers, books, envelopes, and charts. Her pencil moves rapidly down a long list of numbers that looks like the ledger of a 1950s general store. She glances up when Stephen introduces me, says hello in a whisper, then goes back to her numbers. She has the same dazzling sapphire blue eyes of the late Princess Diana, as well as her shy manner.

"It's going to be a cracking afternoon," Stephen comments.

"It should be raining," Prue replies.

Indeed, there hasn't been rain for four months. Dry weather was ideal for the harvest, but now the vines need rain to develop their leaves and shoots in preparation for the growth cycle. There's also the Murray River to worry about, since it's the main source of water for many wineries here. I stand there awkwardly for several moments until I think to ask Prue what's happening with the river. She lights up at the question, clearly more comfortable with science talk than with small talk. "The river is almost dry," she says. "Not quite the drought we had in 2007 but dangerously close."

She explains the environmental problem: "In the 1970s, thousands of trees around were pulled out to make way for vineyards and farmlands. Those deep roots were natural desalinators; their constant absorption of moisture kept the water table low. Without them, the water table rose, pushing up layers of salt and saline water that had been distributed lower down through the soil strata. This sterilized the topsoil, turning vegetated areas into sand bowls and making the groundwater too salty for the vines to thrive. Most Henschke vines are dry-farmed rather than irrigated. This forces the roots to search deeper for moisture, thereby exposing them to a wider and deeper soil volume, as well as making them less vulnerable to droughts."

Prue is active in a number of land preservation groups in the country, and water conservation is at the top of their agenda. All wineries today need licenses to get a water allocation from the Murray River or any other water catchment, but these are a lower priority than drinking water. Back in 2007, the river fell so low there was no water left for the wineries, and the region's crop was down by about 70 percent over the previous year. One solution that's been proposed is to build a desalination plant in Adelaide, but that will cost $1.2 billion, so it will be some time before that happens.

"When you have a basic knowledge of plants and agriculture, you can see what the land will be like in ten, twenty years," Prue tells me. "I feel a responsibility to use that knowledge to convince others of what we need to do now."

Prue and Stephen have replanted 30 percent of their land with indigenous vegetation to try to reestablish the natural balance and water table. They've planted native grasses and cover crops between the vine rows; these grasses harbor beneficial insects, such as ladybugs and wasps, that feed on the insects that eat the grapes, such as vine moths.

"The cover crops are also helpful because vines can't draw up flavors from the rock," Prue says. "The clover and lichen allow a healthy mycorrhiza fungi to grow around the roots of the vines. These break down the minerals in the soil into micronutrients so that the plants can absorb them and produce sugars and carbohydrates for healthy fruit. It's a natural system of viticulture."

The grasses don't take much moisture from the vines because they're sparse and have shallow roots. The couple also protect their vineyard's precious moisture by putting down a straw mulch, which has the added benefit of keeping the worms active, those natural tillers of the soil.

After Prue explains this, she goes back to her figures, and Stephen takes me on a quick tour of the winery. It's clean and orderly, though tiny compared to Wolf Blass and Penfolds. It's much older, too: the last renovation seems to have been done around 1870. Large blackened wood beams span the ceiling over rough-hewn concrete vats that show years of pockmarks.

At Stephen's suggestion, we leave for the vineyard. I follow him out to his truck, open the door, and find myself about to sit on his lap—I'm still not used to the driver-passenger seat switch here. As we drive down the bumpy road, I comment on the fragrant light blue haze in the air. Stephen explains that it's eucalyptus oil from the trees. Researchers at the Australian Wine Research Institute have found that the airborne compounds in this oil settle on and seep into the skins and leaves of red grapes and are responsible for that faint mint flavor that's often in Australian red wines. These compounds don't affect white wines as much because they're made with little to no skin contact.

Stephen stops the truck and pulls a leaf from a wattle tree as gently as a parent removes a Band-Aid from a child's elbow. He crushes it between his fingers and hands it to me. It smells like a forest of green flowers. He stops the truck several more times to show me different leaves and berries, rattling off the Latin names of half a dozen species. These plants are lucky to have such a good friend.

As we trundle along, the fiery evening sun is on the horizon ahead of us. Slowly, a black spire comes into view, trying to pierce the red balloon above it. This turns out to be the community's original Lutheran church, built in 1860 and called Gnadenberg—German for "Hill of Grace," after which the Henschke vineyard surrounding it is named. Stephen pulls up in front of the church, with its chipped headstones and a stone angel that looks sad to have lost her arms. This is all that's left of what was once a thriving village, apart from some ruins of a few former homes and an old schoolhouse. After the last teacher moved away a century ago, the town couldn't persuade another one to come to such an isolated spot. So the families moved away one by one, and eventually the town was no more.

The vineyard is a thin slice of eight acres at the confluence of two dried-up creeks that have contributed an astonishing variety of soil types. The red-brown earth gives a fruity character to the grapes, the sandy loam adds a perfume lift, and the heavy black soil and tight red clay impart a robust, masculine character. These vines have become scavengers here, sinewy but strong, and always in survival mode, working hard for their nutrients and water. Against the surrounding countryside, they look like a small island of green in a sea of red dust.

These vines have grown here since the settlers planted them before phylloxera destroyed most European vineyards in 1856, more than 150 years ago, and I wonder how many hands have touched and tended these vines since then. Stephen calls them "the grandfathers." They are the reason that he asked me to stand in a tray of antibacterial solution before we left the winery, to ensure I didn't bring any diseases into the vineyard on my shoes. It reminded me of the same reasonable precaution they took at the Louvre when the Mona Lisa was finally put behind glass.

"These vines were planted before the motor car was invented; they've seen two world wars, a global depression, and many droughts. They can take whatever nature throws at them. We don't have any old châteaux here, but we do have living history."

Stephen and Prue's single-vineyard approach is the antithesis of Australia's multiregion blending but not at odds with it. To me, it seems more in tune with what the medieval philosopher Duns Scotus called *haecceitas*, or "thisness." The fashionable term in the wine industry today is "somewhereness," essentially the English translation for the traditional French concept of terroir. It refers to the specific place where the wine is grown and made because it's particularly suited to that place. This wine couldn't be made anywhere else because the memory of the land hasn't been erased.

Age is a virtue in grapevines, Stephen explains. Larger trunks mean better management of sugars and carbohydrates. "The spindly young ones are always in a hurry to ripen their fruit, but they're all talk—they can't keep their acids up," he says. "It's only when a vine hits twenty that something changes: the taste and texture of the grapes become more balanced, and the wine they produce throws you more texture. The old vines take their time and let the flavor rise and develop slowly in the grapes. Less talk, more wisdom."

As I watch the red fingers of the setting sun touch the gnarled crevices on these vines that have weathered so much, I think of the stoic Lutheran doctrine: "Here I stand. I cannot do otherwise." We walk deeper into the rows, and some of the vines start to lean toward each other, like old men holding each other up on a park bench. They look so wizened that it's hard to believe there's something still alive in their core. Stephen calls this the vineyard within the vineyard. These vines aren't vigorous, and they produce less fruit every year, perhaps only a bottle per vine compared to three to four bottles per vine for the younger ones. But what glorious wine that one bottle is! Later, when I try some of it over dinner, I can taste the subtly spiced fruit, which that has the texture and zing of acidity but is more nuanced. The pepper and wintergreen notes are gone, replaced with rich, dark blackberry-mulberry aromas.

"Controlled neglect is how we keep the plants strong," Stephen says. Every year, one vine in a hundred dies of natural causes, old soldiers dropping out of the annual veterans' march. However, in the truest sense of estate planning, Prue has a fifty-year succession plan that involves taking the best genetic material from the vines and propagating it in her nursery before replanting. She no longer buys any outside plant material. While she and Stephen now have the scientific proof that these old vines produce extraordinary wine, it was simply Cyril's good intuition that kept him from pulling them up in the early 1970s when the government paid growers to replant more marketable cabernet.

Off in the distance, I can hear the soft lowing of cattle between the tinkling of their bells. Surprisingly, I can also hear someone laughing a few rows over—I thought Stephen and I were alone in the vineyard. When I ask him about this, he laughs, too, and explains that I'm actually hearing a kookaburra, the Australian kingfisher bird. Unlike the North American loon, whose haunting call sounds like a lunatic (hence the name), the kookaburra's sound is a dead ringer for human laughter. It makes the vineyard a happy place to be.

A more familiar bird, a magpie, lights on a post near us and warbles with all its might from its tiny chest. "They're beautiful creatures," Stephen says. "They eat the grubs and insects that would damage the vines." As the sun sets, the magpie flits on from post to post, until it's lost from sight against the black shapes of the gum trees and the vines that seem to huddle closer together in the darkness.

Suddenly, after a day of feeling too hot, I get a cold shudder up my back. The nights here along the mountain ranges of the Barossa, a thousand feet up from the valley, have a piercing freshness to them, with a risk of frost in the winter. That's why the vineyard is dotted with several large electric windmills that go into action whenever the nighttime temperature dips toward freezing. Their rotating blades create a circular wind that can reach up to twenty miles an hour, and inverts the layer of warm air that sits above the cold air. This brings warmth closer to the ground, helping to melt the frost.

As Stephen and I get back into the truck, he explains, "Our climate sets the intensity of our wine. In the 1970s, we tried to make European wine with lower levels of alcohol, but it just ended up being wishy-washy. We have to accept that our style means a lot of color, flavor, and richness. Barossa wines are always slow to mature because in the extreme heat, the vine shuts down to protect itself. But that's a good thing because it results in a greater depth of flavor in the fruit."

After a quiet period, he says something that surprises me, given how hard he and Prue work. "Wine makes itself if you let it," he observes. "A winery is not about fixing things. You can only make the wine that the land will give you."

The night is clear and crisp, the moonlit sky marbled with a few wispy clouds as we drive to dinner at a small resort called the Louise. Its outstanding restaurant, Appellation, is unapologetically wine-centric. When we get there, Prue has already arrived, and we join her at a table for a delicious meal to showcase the local cuisine and the Henschke wines.

For our first course, we enjoy a creamy chowder of oysters, accented with spring onions and chervil. The Henschke Eden Valley Riesling is a perfect foil for the soup: it starts with floral grace and then fills out with aromas of grapeseed and lemon-lanolin. The Eden Valley is only an hour away from the Barossa, yet its climate is dramatically cooler. Although Australia is best known for its reds, the country also produces spectacularly refreshing white wines in the cool climate regions, such as Eden Valley, Mornington Peninsula, Victoria, Yarra Valley, and Tasmania. Neighboring New Zealand is known for its zesty sauvignon blanc, but Australia's white specialties are riesling and chardonnay.

As we eat, I love listening to the catch-and-release play of Stephen and Prue's conversation, reminding me of the poet Rilke's "deep calling to deep." The world of science and plants brought them together; now theirs is a marriage of two fine intellects. They're interested in everything; they wrap themselves in curiosity. Out the window, we see clusters of stars dancing, and they debate which constellation it is.

They seem to have experimented with every aspect of winemaking: vine genetics, grape types, yeast strains, barrel woods, toasting methods, maturation periods, tannin structures, and soil compositions. "We take one sliver of a subject and do minute variations on the same experiment every year, such as a small change in harvest temperature or a drainage elevation," Stephen says. "We are micro-winemakers."

A prime example is Prue being one of the first in Australia to use Scott Henry trellising, a method of training the vines so that the grapes get more sun exposure. This results in fewer herbal and green notes in the wine. I ask Prue why she doesn't graft some of the dying old vines with the new phylloxera-resistant stock to save them. "Grafting on rootstock can save a vine's life, but it can shorten it, too, like an elderly person who gets a hip replacement," she explains. "We have to understand the vineyard health and energy forces to foster the best of its precious genetic material."

Our second course arrives: a dish of juicy local corn-fed chicken, with thin slices of *lachsschinken*—cold-smoked loin of pork—tucked in the middle. Pork has long been a staple in the Barossa, ever since the settlers brought with them their love of sausages and schnitzel. The locals say that the only bit of the pig that escapes the pot is the squeal. The pork gives the chicken a wonderful smoky note, which is enhanced by the glaze of fried butter, diced garlic, and fresh sage leaves. It's perfect with the white wine blend in the Henschke Tilly's Vineyard Semillon, Chardonnay, and Sauvignon Blanc. The wine is a sun field of aromas: clover blossom, daisies, and green apples.

Both wines we've enjoyed so far have a screw cap. As no-nonsense scientists, Stephen and Prue hold no romantic notions about corks. They were among Australia's earliest adopters of screw caps. Wine corks, made from the bark of cork trees in Spain and Portugal, have been the traditional closure for wine bottles since the 1600s. They were a great improvement on the previous method of a cloth and rope around the bottle opening. However, natural bark corks can contain a chemical compound that can taint the wine. Even a mild case of cork taint strips wine of its expressive aromas, and a severe one makes it smell like moldy cardboard. Screw caps, however, don't have that problem.

"Often, you need to drop your suspicions and just try something," Prue says. Stephen explains that wine ages better under a screw cap than a cork, letting very little oxygen into the bottle. It's the same principle as a large-format bottle, such as a magnum: the lower wine-to-oxygen ratio helps it age more slowly, which helps to better integrate the elements, such as fruit flavor, acidity, and tannin.

Screw caps are also up to a thousand times less likely than corks to allow the wine to become tainted. Still, the Henschkes acknowledge that many consumers prefer the traditional option, so they're experimenting with Vino-Lok glass stoppers, which have the same benefits as screw caps. "They're a great placebo for cork," Stephen says. "They look gorgeous and let you play with elegance, yet they're easy to open and won't ruin your wine."

Ah, here comes our first red wine of the evening, their Mount Edelstone Shiraz. The name is derived from the German word *edelstein*, meaning "gemstone." Made from ninety-year-old vines, Edelstone is full of fruit with just-squeezed juiciness that tapers into fine tannins, like the tinkling top notes of a piano concerto. It finishes with just the right sweep of acidity to prevent its lushness from becoming too heavy. It's that lift at the end that makes you return to this wine.

Some say that you should "eat" shiraz with a fork because it's so hefty, but Prue doesn't think that wine should be a meal on its own. Shiraz is a succulent wine, she believes, that goes best with tender meat dishes. That's why we're drinking it now as our third course arrives: a croquette of lamb with a salad of curly endive and Barossa bacon. The lamb comes from Hutton Vale, which abuts one of the Henschke vineyards. The animal is a cross-breed between Merino (grown for wool) and Suffolk (grown for meat). It has a richer flavor than the lamb I've had in Europe, America, or even New Zealand because of the pasture grasses the sheep eat here.

Our endive salad is garnished with strongly smoked bacon—yet another tribute to the ethnic heritage of the Barossa. Smoked foods are a cornerstone of the cuisine, though with a distinctly Australian twist. Unlike German meats that are smoked over European hard-woods, the woods here are from red gum and acacia trees. The result is spectacular, and the smoky bacon fills every corner of my mouth with flavor. It pairs beautifully with the wine's lashings of dark plums and fleshy berries. I drink lustily, giving myself permission to love shiraz again and all its fleshy goodness after a streak of drinking mainly Burgundian pinot noir. Saturated fruit flavors flood my mouth and pool around my taste buds before slipping down to deeper pleasure centers.

The Henschke shiraz would pair well with other hearty fare: I imagine that it would encase rare roast beef, then pierce and soak Yorkshire pudding. My rule of thumb is that when the weather is cold, drink wines from warm regions, like Barossa shiraz or Argen-tine malbec: they produce full-bodied, high-alcohol wines that pair well with robust dishes and warm you up when it's chilly. When it's hot, drink wines from cool climates, such as German or Canadian riesling. These regions produce lean, more acidic, lighter-alcohol wines that are great refreshment when it's warm and pair well with lighter dishes.

"Shiraz is a gorgeous freak of nature; it's our signature," Stephen says. I couldn't agree more, but my mouth is full. "The North American palate has an affinity for shiraz, with its sweet, spicy, lush flavors. Compare that with cabernet, which is far more astringent and drying, a chalky sensation that often has a strong oak component," he adds. "You can only drink so much of it. By contrast, shiraz has an incredible generosity of flavor and vivacity because we lead with fruit, not forests. You want to drink something from a grape, not a tree."

Next we try the 1986 Hill of Grace, and I recall the ghost village around the vineyard. Drinking it makes me feel like a tourist of time. The silky tannins make it taste sensuously slippery. It also has a lengthened lingering; it tastes like more. Stephen says it's also delicious when young. "Never believe anyone who says a wine doesn't taste good now but will in ten years," he warns. "They're conning you. A good wine should taste great when you open it and even better ten years on."

As we enjoy our next course of a breast of Eden Valley pigeon in a semolina and pea puree with their shiraz, Prue and Stephen reflect on their industry: "We did a great job of convincing people that Australian wine is cheap and cheerful," Stephen says. "We made consumers comfortable with our category. But the dangerous thing is that people get used to you being one thing and then they don't want you to change.

"Big brands like Jacob's Creek spill more wine in a year than we make," he comments wryly. "They're good anchors for the category, like a department store in a mall, but we need to personalize our wine now. We need more midsized boutique wineries like Peter Lehmann, Brown Brothers, Yalumba, and Henschke to tell the story of Australia at the grassroots level. A place gives you a sense of belonging; a story gives you a sense of familiarity."

In Stephen's opinion, the biggest threat to the future of Australian wine is not other New World countries like Chile and Argentina.

It's actually the traditional winemaking countries like Italy, Portugal, and Spain. "They've got the distribution channels, the cheap labor, the developed vineyards—and, above all, a strong history of place."

As our waiter brings us our dessert, a Riverland lime and lemon tart, Prue expands on Stephen's vision with a more personal note: "More than anything else, we need to complete the cycle of the previous generation and prepare for the next one," she says. The Henschkes have three children: their eldest, Johann, twenty-six, is already a qualified winemaker; Justine is studying marketing at the University of Adelaide and helps with public relations at the winery; and the youngest, Andreas, studying engineering at the university, helps in the vineyard during his vacations. "Sometimes, it seems like an enormous task," she adds. "But making wine teaches you that the end is always the beginning."

Field Notes from a
Wine Cheapskate

So you've breezed through the first chapter, and now you ask: "How's this going to help me find a good bottle of value-priced wine for Sunday dinner?" This is probably because you skipped the section entitled "Beyond the Adventures" near the beginning, but no matter. Although most of the wines I discuss in this book are widely available, I know that you won't be able to find every one of them at your local liquor store.

So at the end of each chapter, I'll give you my cheat sheet of tips that I've picked up from my travels to help you find great wines from each region, as well as other terrific producers. Visit my website at www.nataliemaclean.com to get the latest reviews of wines in stores now.

INSIDER TIPS

- Look for wines from warm regions, like the Barossa Valley. Often the cost of production is cheaper because winemakers aren't battling disease, rot, and weather as much as cool-climate producers do. Therefore, there's less crop loss and lower costs for production. It's no coincidence that six of the eight regions in this book are warm climates. (Niagara and Germany are cool climates.)

- When it's cold outside, drink wine from warm regions, and when it's warm, go for those from cooler climates. You'll drink the full-bodied, soul-warming styles that are comforting in the winter and the lighter, more refreshing ones in the summer. The bonus is that these wines also complement the dishes we eat in the different seasons.

- Twist and shout when you see a bottle closed with a screw cap! No longer does a screw cap necessarily mean that the wine is plonk. Many good producers are using this effective closure to protect their wine. The bonus is that no special equipment is needed to open your bottle.

WINERIES VISITED

Henschke: www.henschke.com.au
Penfolds: www.penfolds.com.au
Wolf Blass: www.wolfblass.com.au

BEST VALUE WINES

Henschke Eden Valley Riesling

Henschke Tilly's Vineyard Semillon, Chardonnay, and Sauvignon Blanc

Penfolds Koonunga Hill

Penfolds Rawson's Retreat

Penfolds Thomas Hyland

Wolf Blass Red Label Shiraz Cabernet Sauvignon*

Wolf Blass Shiraz

Wolf Blass Yellow Label Cabernet Sauvignon

*My first pick for my own Sunday dinner.

TOP VALUE PRODUCERS

The following list comprises more great value producers for the region, beyond those I visited for the book. Some producers have other brands or labels that I'll list separately. For example, Clancy's is made by Peter Lehmann Wines. You can find the website addresses for all of these wineries in my online Worldwide Winery Directory at www.nataliemaclean.com/wineries.

You can also find my most current reviews of these wines on the site, with prices, scores, tasting notes, food matches, recipes, and bottle shots at www.nataliemaclean.com/winepicks.

Angove	d'Arenberg
Banrock Station	Elderton
Brokenwood	Evans & Tate
Clancy's	Gemtree

Grant Burge

Kilikanoon

Leasingham

Lindemans

McGuigan

McWilliams

Mitolo

Peter Lehmann Wines

Pirramimma

Robert Oatley

Rosemount

Saltram

Shingleback

St. Hallet

Thorn-Clarke

Tyrrell's Wines

Wakefield

Wyndham Estate

Xanadu

Yalumba

Yering Station

SUNDAY DINNER FOR A WINE CHEAPSKATE

I've posted recipes for the dishes that we enjoyed at Appellation, the restaurant at the Louise resort, as prepared by executive chef Mark McNamara, at www.nataliemaclean.com/food.

*Barossa Corn-Fed Chicken and Smoked
Pork in a Garlic and Sage Glaze*

Butter-Poached Chicken

Chicken with Fennel Bulb and Sunchokes

Creamy Oyster Chowder and Scallions

*Striped Bass or Tilapia with Red Wine
and Thyme-Infused Glaze*

*Breast of Pigeon or Squab with
Semolina Gnocchi and Pea Puree*

Lamb Croquette

Lime and Lemon Tart

TERRIFIC PAIRINGS

Shiraz and syrah both create rich, robust wines with a smooth texture and signature aromas of spice, pepper, clove, and licorice leading, followed by dark fruit such as raspberry, plum, and black cherry, as well as truffle, earth, violets, vanilla, smoke, sandalwood, cedar, cigar box, earth, and leather.

Shiraz and syrah pair well with many meaty, robust dishes.

Aged cheddar	Meat lovers' pizza
Barbecued beef ribs	Meat or game casseroles
Beef or chicken fajitas	Peppercorn steak
Bison steak	Roast beef
Brisket	Roast goose
Grilled or braised lamb	Smoked pork chops
Grilled vegetables	Spicy sausage
Hamburgers	Squab
Meat loaf	Venison stew

RESOURCES

To learn more about Australian wines and shiraz:

James Halliday Australian Wine Companion by James Halliday
Heart and Soul: Australia's First Families of Wine by Graeme
   Lofts and James Halliday
Crushed by Women: Women and Wine by Jeni Port

Wineries of Australia: www.nataliemaclean.com/wineries

Wine Australia: www.wineaustralia.com/australia

Wine Australia USA: www.wineaustralia.com/usa

Australian Wine Society Ottawa: www.awsottawa.com

Australian Wine Society Toronto: www.aws.ca

Australian Wine Society Calgary: www.members.shaw
.ca/auswinecgy

Australian Wine Appreciation Society Vancouver: www.awas.ca

South World Wine Society Vancouver: www.southworldwine
.com/aboutus.html

RELATED READING

The following books, while seemingly unrelated to the main subject matter of this chapter, provided some enjoyable reading before, during, and after my travels:

Alice's Adventures in Wonderland by Lewis Carroll

The Selected Poetry of Rainer Maria Rilke by Rainer Maria Rilke

Oscar and Lucinda by Peter Carey

TWO

MONDAY

The Unbearable Lightness of German Riesling

BELOW THE MOUNTAIN road on my left, the slope plunges down a half mile to the river. Grapevines cling to the weathered rock with white-knuckled nerve. As I drive through Germany's Mosel Valley on this honeyed September morning, I can see the medieval homes and churches of Wehlen. The village's watercolor reflection on the river slowly divides on either side of a barge and re-forms behind it. Here, at the world's northern edge of viticulture, they create a wine with the weightless intensity of white lightning: riesling.

For thousands of years, the Moselle River has shaped this valley, first in one direction and then in another, unable to make up its meandering mind. Its three-hundred-mile journey starts in the Vosges Mountains of Alsace, flowing into Germany via Luxembourg and then joining the Rhine to the west. While the Mosel area is only the fourth largest of Germany's thirteen wine regions, more than half the country's riesling grapes are planted here. And while several other areas are also famous for riesling, those from the Mosel float above them all in their ethereal blend of aroma, delicacy, and steely concentration.

That's what makes German riesling ideal for Monday night dinner: it's low in alcohol, so it's a gentle way to start the week after indulging on Saturday and Sunday; the bonus is that you won't fall asleep on the sofa at seven p.m. when you're trying to catch up on email. Plus, the wine goes well with the less fussy dishes we have after a busy day at work, such as grilled chicken or fish, creamy pasta, Indian or Asian takeout, or a simple salad.

Riesling is a tough-skinned little berry that likes to fume all day, then calm down in the chilly nights. So it loves the confluence of climate and geology here in the Mosel. Its vines can withstand winter freezes as low as −13°F, cold enough to kill less-hardy plants between growing seasons. The precipitous rock walls cradle the vines from the coldest winds racing overhead. As the ancient river wore down this valley over millions of years, it deposited minerals and uncovered the Devon blue slate. Slate is a rock that fractures easily with extreme variations in temperature; it covers the ground here like thousands of discarded arrowheads. That makes it excellent for drainage—essential for growing flavorful grapes in a wet climate. The unyielding rock challenges the vines to survive. Their roots often have to slither aboveground until they can fight their way down through craggy fissures, often groping ten feet or more in the stony layers to find sustenance. Riesling thrives on suffering. I like that in a plant.

Slate also slows vegetative growth. Even the trees planted along the ridge have a tighter grain than those in less acidic soils. So the grapes accumulate their flavors slowly. (In warmer regions, riesling hurtles headlong into ripening, and the resulting wine tastes like watered-down chardonnay.) But here the grapes' depth of taste is akin to small, wild tomatoes rather than those bland, supersized, fertilizer-fed ones. In fruit, as in people, complexity is built under difficulty. The rock's porous crystalline structure helps it to trap heat in the day and release just enough to the vines at night. The result is a barely possible wine from a small indent on the planet that's on the same fiftieth parallel as Krakow, Winnipeg, and Mongolia.

Over the centuries, vintners have discovered how to extract the best from this harsh land. They've planted the vines angled to soak up warmth from the low northern sun and light reflected from the water. The river also circulates warm air up between the vines like a balmy tide. The vines, two-thirds of the way up on the mountain, get just the right amount of warmth to make wines of prickling excitement. They're part of a thirty-mile stretch through the heart of the region, known as the Mittelmosel (middle Mosel). The vines lower down get too much heat, while those at the top don't get enough to make the finest rieslings. And yet even these wines are priced at a fraction of those benchmark wines in other great regions, such as Bordeaux and Tuscany. Both history and fashion have kept riesling's prices in the bargain range.

Some of the best rieslings here, and throughout Germany, are made by a family named Prüm, which has lived in Wehlen since 1156. I start with this winery to calibrate my palate for the less-expensive wines I'll taste later in the trip. In my opinion, bargain wines aren't worth drinking if they're completely blown away by the top producers. I am choosy even if I don't want to pay for it. And as a true cheapskate, I wouldn't miss the opportunity to taste these wines for free.

The winery that Johann Josef Prüm founded in 1911 is now run by his grandson, Manfred Prüm. A lawyer by training, eccentric winemaker by choice, Manfred is also famously private. No one outside the business has ever descended into his cellars. I've pestered in vain to be permitted the privilege, but at least Katharina Prüm, the eldest of his three daughters, has agreed to meet with me.

The family's Victorian manor house is tucked into a narrow strip of land between the river and the mountainside. Looking up at the emerald hillside across the river, I can see the ten-foot sundial that Manfred's great-great-uncle built into the rock face in 1842. It gave workers a strong sense of the time—and presumably all the work they had to finish before going home. The German word for "sundial" is *sonnenuhr*, and this vineyard, Wehlener Sonnenuhr, is named after it.

Walking around the Prüm house in search of the front door, I almost run into an elderly man with a thick shock of white hair and ruddy cheeks. An old family vineyard hand, I think, as he doesn't seem to understand when I ask him for directions. Then he smiles, gently takes my arm, and guides me to the entrance. I ring the bell and turn to thank him, but he's gone.

Katharina Prüm looks like a young Jane Seymour, dressed in a cashmere turtleneck, tweed jacket, riding jodhpurs, and leather boots. I follow her past the mounted antlers and tusks in the hallway—relics of Manfred's successful hunting of wild boar and deer—and into a dark-paneled drawing room. The sun streams through the tall windows, burnishing the gold frame on the portrait of her great-grandfather Johann Josef Prüm, known to wine fanatics as JJ.

Katharina is the fourth generation in her family to make wine, and she's expected to succeed her father and her uncle Wolfgang. "As a child, I didn't want to become a winemaker, but I loved being with my father in the vineyards," she reminisces. "My deepest wish was always to be with him, to smell the grapes, to walk beside him tasting them."

Like her father, Katharina studied law, completing a doctorate at Münster University as well as a certificate in American law. Her focus on the United States landed her an internship in Tulsa, Oklahoma. While there, she hosted tastings of her family's wines for American importers and retailers. Although her father had been forced to leave school to run the family business when his own father died, it was Katharina's choice to return to the winery when she graduated.

"It's helpful to leave your home and your village for a few years to see the world," she says. "The backgrounds of the people who go into the wine business are so varied: artists, lawyers, doctors, real estate agents, and so on—this industry collects people who love life. After a while, I knew I'd come back. I think about all the previous generations who gave their energy and time to these vines. Their memory lives in them."

After a meditative moment, she suddenly perks up, grins, and reaches into the cooler at her side. "Now, let's have some fun!" she says, pulling out a bagged bottle and pouring some wine into two glasses. Oh hooray, a blind tasting. There's no better way for a vintner to expose self-proclaimed wine experts than to play guessing games with them using their own wines.

When I raise the glass to my nose, my heart drops. This wine reeks of rotten eggs, burned matches, and animal sweat. How on earth can this be wine from one of Germany's most coveted estates? Why does it earn scores of 99 and 100 from the critics? And what do I say now? Katharina's eyes are locked expectantly on mine.

"Hmmm," I say, closing my eyes and breathing deeply. I'm wondering which animal's sweat I smell. "I'm not quite sure I can put my finger on exactly what I'm getting here," I murmur, playing for time.

"Well, I hope you *don't* like it—at least not yet," Katharina says, laughing. "This is from last year; we just bottled it, so what you're probably getting is the sulfur. I wanted you to taste our whole range, though, so you could see how the wines develop."

I laugh, releasing my usual nervousness. The young Prüm wines are tightly wound, feral creatures, with forbidding aromas of yeast and sulfur. They're often described as "backwards" because they don't reveal their rich fruit and finesse until after at least five years of aging. The family favors longevity over accessibility, tradition over innovation.

Katharina and I move on to sampling the next riesling, which shimmers like a gold leaf. This wine reels me in with an electric interplay between fleshy fruit and racy acidity. Prüm wines, while never the boldest, are among the most exciting in their ephemeral vibrancy. I lick my lips, savoring its tangerine fragrance. It's refreshing in a world awash with vanilla, oak, and jam. (In life and in wine: too much foreplay is frustrating and too quick satiation is boring.) We often confuse light body with lack of taste.

"It is fascinating to live with wine," Katharina observes softly. "Every day, the wines become a little more expressive. To work on one thing for months, you must have discipline, but it is also peaceful, meditative work. After fermentation, we work hard to do nothing," she says, smiling. "We just try to keep the wine stable."

Every time wine is moved, even for filtration or pumping, it loses some of its freshness and purity. So the Prüm bottling line is a mobile unit that's brought to the wine, rather than the other way around. The wine is further coddled with a gravity-flow system rather than a mechanized one. All these measures, plus the use of wild yeasts, which create sulfur by-products as they metabolize, as well as the sulfur the winemaker adds, help the wine retain its acrid smell. That's a good thing for wines designed to age, since sulfur, like the tarry tannins in young red wine, allows the wines to mature slowly, though it makes them a bitter mouthful when young.

The Prüm's famously frigid cellars slow fermentation from the usual two to four weeks to three months or more. The chill also gives the wine a light spritz because a little carbon dioxide remains in them. The wine ferments in stainless steel tanks rather than in oak, which works better for vines grown on stone. The grapes move from rock to metal; both preserve freshness. Barrels are better for wine from heavy soils, such as the clay in Chile and California. The open-grained wood allows a little oxygen in, giving the wine more texture and heft. But riesling doesn't need power any more than angels need muscle.

Riesling has a robust longevity that goes back almost two millennia. Like all vines, riesling is a weed, originating in Germany during the Middle Ages. Well before that, the ancient Romans first cultivated vines here for some 450 years. The remains of their pressing houses are scattered along the Moselle. In 371 CE, the poet Ausonius wrote about winemaking in this valley in his poem "Mosella." In medieval times, the monks tended the vineyards, and then the aristocracy took them over when Napoleon secularized the holdings in the early 1800s.

During this time, exports were steadily increasing throughout Europe. In 1845, Queen Victoria, who was married to a German, her beloved Prince Albert, coined the term *hock* for riesling, which became her favorite wine after she drank it in the Hockenheim region on the Rhine River. ("A glass of hock keeps away the doc.") Soon after, hock became *the* white wine of aristocratic British dinners, joining the select company of bordeaux, the red also known as claret, and port, the postprandial drink.

Although generations of winemakers have cultivated riesling, it remains the most naked of wines, never blended with other grapes or wines in Germany, and rarely combined with riesling from neighboring vineyards. In some other countries, wines labeled as single varietal are still allowed to have other grapes in the blend. A Californian cabernet sauvignon, for example, can actually contain as much as 25 percent merlot in the bottle. And unlike nonvintage champagne, riesling from different years isn't blended, so there's no compensating for one bad year with a few good ones. It's also not aged in wood to add oaky flavors, nor does it undergo malolactic fermentation, in which harsh malo acids naturally present in the wine are converted into softer lactic acids. That's why riesling is considered a wine of purity, a liquid mirror of the vineyard—and of winemaking mistakes. Small flaws are magnified in the bottle. That's why more and more producers are now using screw caps to avoid the taint that corks can easily impart to such a transparent wine.

Like Prüm, many leading estates focus exclusively on riesling. However, they may make ten or more of them from different vineyards, different parts of the same vineyard, different styles, or different quality levels. Prüm's pickers sometimes make fifteen or more passes through their vines in the fall, combing them to select only fruit at peak ripeness and sorting them by hand. The grapes are fermented in small batches to preserve subtle differences. In fact, the eight-gallon tanks often used for riesling look like milk cans in comparison to the gleaming fifty-foot ones in other regions that are always part of a tour (even though when you've seen one tank, you really have seen them all).

"Some vintners have an image of the wine they want to create, but we just take the wines nature gives us," Katharina explains. She pours me another glass, her large brown eyes alive with mischief. "So what is this?" she asks.

Since our last glass was her most basic wine, a riesling kabinett, it's not a terribly astute guess that she's gone one step up. "Riesling spätlese?" I ask tentatively.

"Yes, but what year?"

The fruit aromas are still fresh in this one, but without the heavy sulfur residue. "Could it be 2002?"

"It's 2004. It has a good line," she says simply. "Clear and elegant."

We taste through a range of vintages and styles as the sun shafts through the emerald bottles on the table. (Mosel bottles are green glass; those from the neighboring region of the Rheingau are brown.) Katharina uncorks a bottle of Wehlener Sonnenuhr Riesling Auslese Long Gold Capsule. It delivers a mouth-shock of ripe apricots, finishing with a haunting lemon smoke. There's also the elusive exhilaration of a dream about running a marathon that makes your heart pound, even though you haven't left your bed.

"This reminds me of the wonderful 1893 vintage," she says, as though she remembers picking the grapes. I love the way she can telescope time—a hundred years is nothing when your family has been making wine for centuries.

"We can't rest on our history, but you should still taste it in the wine," she says as we say good-bye.

Leaving the house, I look up at the high windows and spot the man I met earlier. Before I can wave to him, he's gone. Later in my trip, paging through a book on German wines, I find his photo and realize that I did meet Manfred Prüm.

No one could be less elusive or more vocal than Ernst Loosen of the Dr. Loosen wine estate, the next vintner I meet. Ernie loves to enthuse about German wines and to rail against the country's restrictive wine laws, which are among the toughest in the world. Compared to the Prüms, he and his family are relative parvenus: they've owned their Mosel estate for only two hundred years. Also unlike them, Ernie isn't shy. He's part of a small international cadre of winemaker rock stars that includes California's Randall Grahm and Italy's Angelo Gaja—men known as much for their opinions as for their wines. The British wine writer Hugh Johnson observed, "Ernie Loosen has brought the Mosel and its rieslings into the twenty-first century with a bang. He thinks worldwide, as few German vintners have done."

Ernie studied viticulture at Germany's renowned Geisenheim University, but he had no intention of taking over the family business. He was just there to appease his father, even though Loosen senior had treated the winery as a sideline to his real work as a lawyer and politician. At Geisenheim, Ernie and his roommates "didn't get up before noon" and skipped most of the lectures. Still, he managed to graduate in 1981 and then went on to pursue his true passion at the University of Mainz: archaeology.

When his father fell ill a few years later, his mother talked about selling the winery. Ernie decided that he would run it. Before doing so, he embarked on a self-directed tour of some of the best estates in Europe and North America to understand what makes a wine great. The journey taught him to respect local traditions as it broadened his perspective globally. One of the most important things that he learned was from Olivier Humbrecht in Alsace, who showed him whole-cluster pressing—the grapes are pressed in full bunches, not crushed individually—to retain fresh fruit flavors. Ernie, in turn, introduced this technique in the Mosel.

When he started managing the winery in 1987, Ernie realized that his family's benign neglect of their vineyards had actually been a bonus. Back in the 1970s, they had ignored the fashion to rip out old riesling vines for more productive, less flavorful grapes. As a result, his mature vines, some now 120 years old, produced tiny amounts of concentrated fruit. They were still on their original rootstocks, having escaped the phylloxera blight that ravaged so many of Europe's vineyards in the late 1800s. The destructive aphid can't survive in much of the Mosel's rugged terrain. Ernie had the two things he needed most: old vines and great dirt.

He made some radical decisions, one of which was to hire his college classmate Bernhard "Bernie" Schug as winemaker. He also decided to slash yields, to use organic fertilizers instead of chemicals, to let the grapes ripen longer on the vines, to hand-select them at harvest, and to treat the wine gently in the cellar. In these matters he was ahead of his time, but his employees weren't happy with the new hands-on approach: it meant more work for them. They walked out in the middle of the 1987 vintage.

"I could either apologize to them so that they'd return, but I'd never be able to control them," he tells me later. "Or I could just ignore them. If I fired them, I'd have to pay expensive severance fees. So I called their bluff. Best decision I made."

After this hurdle, he had to identify which vines he owned, since the family holdings were fragmented into more than 160 parcels of land scattered among other producers' vines. A consummate pragmatist, Ernie decided to simply wait until everyone else had finished picking so he could tell which grapes were his. His tactical decision turned out to be a brilliant strategy. That November was warm and dry, perfect for ripening 67 percent of his late-hanging grapes to the highest quality, while most other estates had only 1 percent at that level that year. He still picks later than most producers, hoping that even after bloating September rains, the weather will warm and ripen the grapes just that little bit further.

Ernie's next big obstacle was his own father, who was reluctant to give him credit or control of the winery. Several months after they agreed on a lease, his father wanted to increase the payments that he received from Ernie because the doctor on the label referred to him, not to his son. Ernie reminded him that his new wife had graduated from medical school: "She's the doctor on the label."

I'm meeting Ernie at the pretasting for the Grosser Ring Auction in Trier, Germany's oldest city. Founded in 16 CE, it still has the noble ruins of Roman amphitheaters and imperial baths. The annual auction, which attracts serious collectors from all over the world who buy the Mosel's rarest wines, helps set the prices for all the rest. This free-market approach would probably have been scorned by Trier's most famous native son, Karl Marx. However, he did write sympathetically about the difficulties facing local producers in the 1800s. Grape pickers unite!

As I make my way through the chattering, clinking crowd, I spot his hand first, stabbing the air enthusiastically above the cluster of people around him. Then I catch sight of the tousled gray curls, gold-rimmed glasses, and waistcoat. He reminds me of a radical classics professor I once knew: irreverent, witty, outrageous, and still on fire with his subject, especially when he finds attentive students.

"A great wine begins in your head," Ernie says to the group. "But of course, the measure of a great wine isn't where it begins but where it ends—in your glass!"

The man is still a tornado of energy, whose vortex is propelled by travel, talk, and drink. The group doesn't disband until the bell rings for the auction to begin, and I finally get the chance to introduce myself. "Ah, Natalie, good!" he exclaims. "We'll talk after the auction. Lots to discuss!"

Four hours later, it's a relief when the auction is over. Ernie has invited me to taste his wines at his home this afternoon. As we walk to the parking lot, he launches into his manifesto: "Many wines are big and fat and that's it, you know, but riesling is strong and delicate at the same time. It has many facets, like a diamond, depending on when and where you taste it and what you're looking for."

As we jump into his burgundy Porsche SUV, its interior all spotless cream leather with bird's-eye-maple woodwork, he doesn't pause in his dissertation. "When cabernet and chardonnay grapes get riper, the wines get more flavorful," he says as he peels out of the garage. "But riesling isn't like that. Quick ripening just makes it awkward. It demands spot-on viticulture."

As we hit the Autobahn, his explanations—and the Porsche— accelerate. "There are thirteen distinct regions in this country, you know, so we don't talk about German wine, we talk about Mosel riesling," he says, hitting the steering wheel, making the SUV swerve a little into the opposite lane. "I am fascinated with the differences!"

I am fascinated with the oncoming traffic. Fortunately, another passionate gesture gets us back over the line into safety.

"When I drink Mosel riesling, I want to *smell* the blue slate soil that formed the fruit. I want to *taste* the memory of the old vines, and I want to *feel* the rain and the sun that year," he declares. "Without all of this, wine is just another drink."

Mosel rieslings are sculpted from acidity rather than from alcohol, so they need some sweetness to soften their taut lines and to flesh out the fruit flavors. Producers stop fermentation when it's only about two-thirds complete to preserve the grape's natural sweetness, which also results in a relatively low alcohol level of 7 to 8 percent.

In fact, riesling's versatility from puckeringly dry to succulently sweet can be a handicap. The wine can surprise novices who open a bottle expecting a dry taste and instead discover a dessert wine. By contrast, chardonnay is always made in a dependable dry style, so drinkers have a better idea of what they're getting. Dependable, of course, doesn't mean good, just consistent.

Ernie shifts gears literally and figuratively: "We understand the difference that soils make because we can see them: slate, quartz, limestone, clay, and so on. But it's hard for most people to imagine the microclimate around the vines or the drainage conditions below them. Yet these factors have a profound effect on wine. Technical analysis doesn't tell you those things, only tasting does."

Ernie doesn't seem to be a man who lacks marketing savvy; his wines are now sold in fifty-nine countries. Other Mosel vintners might wonder why he bothers with tiny islands in the South Pacific or outposts in the frozen north, but he views global distribution as a sound sales strategy. He jokingly refers to his missionary work as "The Rocky Horror Riesling Show." He is also one of the organizers of the Riesling Rendezvous, an annual summit in Washington State that draws vintners, wine lovers, and writers from around the world.

"When others gave up, I kept going, giving tastings even when it was just for two old ladies in a hotel ballroom," he says, laughing. He believes that these grassroots efforts are the only way to return riesling to its rightful place as the queen of white wines. But don't get him started on the marketing success of liebfraumilch in the 1970s.

"It almost destroyed Germany's image," Ernie growls, knocking the rearview mirror askew with a dismissive wave. The wine had a harmless genesis back in the 1800s. *Liebfraumilch*, medieval German for "blessed mother's milk" or "milk of Our Lady," was first made on former convent grounds near Wittenberg, where Martin Luther was purported to have nailed his manifesto to a cathedral door to start the Protestant Reformation. Back then, liebfraumilch was a high-quality wine of limited distribution made by the Valckenberg family. But the quality declined over the years, helped by the infamous German Wine Law of 1971.

The bright idea was to introduce *grosslagen* (large or collective wine-growing sites) to simplify wine labels. The plan was to expand the definitions of the most prestigious vineyard and village names from precise boundaries to areas of hundreds of miles. This would give a commercial boost to many wine cooperatives and small growers. The rules were open to abuse because high quality was equated only with ripeness. Suddenly, it was all about sugar, so these wines simply increased their sweetness without balancing acidity or flavor. The obscure hybrid grapes used were so vigorous they often collapsed the vines under their weight.

Liebfraumilch brands such as Blue Nun and Black Tower killed riesling's reputation just as Mateus killed dry rosé, Beaujolais nouveau the age-worthy Beaujolais crus, and white zinfandel the red kind. Decades later, top German producers are still trying to shake that cheap-and-sweet image from the drugged-out 1970s.

"Blue Nun and Black Tower don't represent a region or a style," Ernie mutters. "They're Coca-Cola brands. Even *cru bourgeois* wines are still typical of Bordeaux—the French never gutted their reputation as we did."

However, these wines fed on the zeitgeist of North Americans who were new to wine and wanted something sweet to wean themselves from martinis and spirits. The wines were perfect with shrimp cocktails and hot-dog canapés. In the late 1980s, a backlash against cheap, sweet wines began and has continued ever since, as North Americans developed a taste for drier, more complex wines. Drinkers moved on to wines made in Australia, Chile, and California, and began asking for their wines by grape name.

"No one wanted to hear about riesling when I started. It was all chardonnay, you know?" Ernie says, looking at me and shrugging. I shake my head vehemently, hoping he'll watch the road again.

At its peak in the 1970s, Blue Nun was selling more than 35 million bottles a year worldwide, and Black Tower around 12 million. By the late 1980s, sales had fallen to less than half of that. Sales have since recovered, and the two brands remain Germany's top-selling wines. Like specters emerging from the Black Forest, they both have assumed a new form. The companies now use riesling grapes, and their sugar content has dropped, though they're still more "fruity" than average. (That's the term wine companies prefer today rather than the S-word, which is bad for sales.) They've also started to make red wines. Black Tower blends pinot noir with the German hybrid grape dornfelder. The red version of Blue Nun (Purple Novice?) uses merlot grapes from the southwest of France.

They've updated their look as well. The iconic stone-crock-style Black Tower bottle, a re-creation of a Roman wine vessel, has been slimmed down and the label simplified. Both the Blue Nun's robe and her bottle have been changed from brown to blue. The old girl herself got a makeover, too, going from frumpy to fit—less Sister Wendy, more Julie Andrews. And unlike traditional German wines with long, difficult names, Blue Nun and Black Tower are easy to say in a liquor store or restaurant.

"Why do we have to throw *all* those damn terms on our labels?" Ernie exclaims.

With their indecipherable gothic script and nomenclature, interpreting most German labels is a Wagnerian exercise. Hugh Johnson once commented that he was surprised that no one had ever endowed a university chair in German wine labels. Ernie's own view is that basic wines should print only the estate name on the front label, and all other information should go on the back.

He also thinks that marketing-driven brands, with no connection to a particular grape, style, or place, do nothing to help Germany. In his view, more and more people "don't want to drink anonymously anymore. They want to know about the wine, where it came from, who made it. The specific is knowable, but the generic is not. One is artisanal, the other is mass culture."

In pursuit of that goal, he believes that the top German estates should follow France's example and produce second labels—a more economical version of their best wines. Château Mouton-Rothschild, for example, produces Le Petit Mouton and the even lower-priced Mouton Cadet. This top-down philosophy makes a lot of sense.

"For years, we led with the cheap wines, and now we need to focus on the best estates to reestablish our reputation," he tells me. "Look at France: Château Margaux sets the image, and the basic wines benefit. Most people can't afford the great estates, but they can still buy a small piece of the Bordeaux prestige with the bourgeois wines."

At last, we pull in front of his vine-covered home, high on the bank of the Moselle River just outside the town of Bernkastel. Inside, the library overlooking the river is lined with sagging bookshelves, photographs, maps, and awards. A pitted oak desk in one corner is strewn with papers, notebooks, and old vine cuttings. We sit at the dining table and he pours me a glass of Dr. L Riesling. Even his wines—gutsy and opulent—are a stark contrast to the delicacy of J. J. Prüm's, yet both have a crystalline clarity. This one begins with wild field flower aromas, then offers the snap-and-attack of limes and green apples.

The next wine he pours, his Ürziger Würzgarten Riesling Spätlese, glides to the back of my mouth so quickly that it brings to mind the term *seamless integration*—one that some critics use to describe such wines. To me, it's just slippery-good. *Würzgarten* means "spice garden," and I can smell the faint notes of nutmeg and cloves that give the wine its name. These vines grow in red volcanic soil that gives even white wines exotic aromas of red berries rather than the green apple and lime notes associated with blue slate.

In fact, most Mosel rieslings tend to have citrus aromas, such as lemon, lime, and grapefruit, whereas wines from the neighboring Rheingau are chiseled from yellow stone-fruit notes, like apricot, peach, and Anjou pear. In the warmer region of the Pfalz, rieslings have aromas of dark yellow fruit, like mango and papaya. However, all those flavors can change with the temperature of the growing season. In cooler years, they all lean toward tart citrus fruit and green apples; in warmer vintages, they achieve riper tropical-fruit notes.

As we continue tasting, he brings out his Wehlener Sonnenuhr Auslese, which, like Prüm's interpretation of this vineyard, fills my senses with tangerine radiance. Although the wine is sweet, its filigreed acidity gives it a clean, refreshing taste. It finishes like a sunset that throws slashes of purple, red, and amber across the sky.

"We need riesling back on stage," Ernie says as we sip the wine. "But single estates are too small to carry the message alone." Like Burgundy, most producers here are small because the inheritance laws are based on the Napoleonic code, introduced in the early 1800s. When a father died, the estate was divided equally among male offspring. The result, over two hundred years, was that vineyards were divided among ever-greater numbers of descendants, becoming ever-smaller parcels of land. Today, the average vineyard size is just seven acres. Many winemakers view themselves as gardeners, tending their tiny plots with the attention usually paid to roses and hollyhocks. In contrast, Bordeaux châteaux often own thousands of acres because inheritance passed solely to the eldest son under the law of primogeniture.

While Ernie explains this to me, we taste his Erdener Prälat Riesling Auslese Long Gold Capsule from his most prized vineyard. He owns less than four acres of this treasured plot, nestled into a curve of the Moselle where the warmth of the sun and river are concentrated. The grapes for this voluptuous riesling are picked last, giving the wine a heady richness and length that chardonnay can only dream of. It's also a subtle wine, with a finesse that occurs to you only after the second or third glass. It reminds me of evenings when I settle into a good book, race through the rolling narrative, and then look up at the end to realize that it's morning.

I ask about the story behind its unusual name. Prälat refers to a Christian prelate in 1066 who was captured and held for ransom by robber barons in a castle on the hill. Like many entrepreneurs, the villains misjudged their market: no one was willing to pay the ransom. So they dumped the goods, throwing the abbot off the steep cliff to his death into what is now the Prälat vineyard. Local legend says that the soil is still stained with his blood. In fact, the earth is naturally rust colored from the underlying red slate. But as Ernie tells me poker-faced, it does produce "a bloody good wine."

Many believe that the resurgence of riesling began in 2001, spurred by one of the greatest vintages in a quarter century. Those wines were heralded by sommeliers, retailers, and writers around the world. The famous American critic Robert Parker published his first big report on German riesling that year. Since then, North American sales of riesling have jumped 49 percent, making it one of the fastest-growing categories of wine, along with the other fresh, unoaked white wine from Italy, pinot grigio.

Despite this, riesling remains an insider's wine. Wine drinkers love to ignore the writers who keep recommending it. Of the 19.5 million acres of all vineyards worldwide, riesling is just half a percent.

Ernie sighs and looks out at the glittering river. "This riesling renaissance everyone talks about isn't going to start in Germany. The New World will lead it. But once people are hooked on the wine, they'll come back to us. We are riesling's spiritual home."

* * *

LATER THAT EVENING, after saying good-bye to Ernie, I'm driving along a country road through an ancient forest. As my stomach grumbles, my mind turns to the questions about food-and-wine pairings that my readers often email me.

"What should I drink with Pacific salmon?"

Try a crisp riesling, I usually reply.

"How about an Indian curry?"

Have you thought about a slightly off-dry riesling to balance the heat of the spices?

"What goes well with fresh salad greens and a lemon vinaigrette?"

A citrusy riesling would be perfect.

"Herb-rubbed chicken?"

You can't go wrong with a riesling.

Did I mention that riesling is incredibly versatile? The wine is like the foam cuisine: an ethereal essence of flavor. We drink it with some of the foods that are toughest on wine, such as sauerkraut, bratwurst, and Wienerschnitzel. (Maybe the Germans *had* to invent such a resilient wine just to match their traditional cuisine.)

Riesling doesn't get clobbered by rich dishes because of its steely acidity, but it also pairs well with delicate dishes because of its low alcohol and subtle flavors. In our modern health-conscious society, more and more people are turning away from the problems plaguing meat production, such as unsanitary and inhumane factories, steroids, animal diseases, and fear of cancer. Instead, we're eating lighter foods, like salads, vegetables, and seafood, and we prefer spices and herbs for flavoring rather than butter and salt. All these choices are natural partners for riesling.

The magic ingredient that enables riesling to be such a vinous chameleon is acidity. I avoid using the word *acid* in my tasting notes because of its unfortunate connotations of drinking battery acid or sucking on lemons. But the natural acidity in riesling is both harmless and beneficial. It gives the wine lift and refreshment; it's the cool wind that tempers the heat of alcohol. If alcohol in wine is depth, richness, and power, acidity is zest, vitality, and youth. Acidity is the prickling excitement that gets your juices running, your mind wheeling. Imagine a salmon steak from the grill with no lemon juice to brighten the smoky char. Whenever you squeeze lemon juice on food, drink riesling with it. (But if you slather butter on the dish, try chardonnay instead.)

As I round the last forest bend in the road, I see the lights of Rüssels Landhaus St. Urban, the companion restaurant of St. Urbans-Hof winery, glowing in a clearing. I've been dying to visit this bistro for its modern German cuisine that has evolved well past the heavy dishes I mentioned earlier. In fact, this country is now second only to France in its number of Michelin-starred restaurants. Yet because there are very few German restaurants in other countries compared to the number of French and Italian establishments, we're not as familiar with this country's cuisine and wine. As well, many people travel to France and Italy on culinary holidays, but far fewer choose Germany.

This evening, I'm looking forward to chatting with Nikolaus Weis, the third generation of his family to run the winery originally founded in 1947 by his grandfather. Before taking over the family business in 1997, Nik studied at Geisenheim, then apprenticed in California, Champagne, and Niagara. His winery, St. Urbans-Hof, is named after the patron saint of wine producers, the third-century St. Urban, also known as Pope Urban I. The restaurant is run by Nik's sister, Ruth, and her husband, Harald Rüssel, who are maître d' and chef, respectively. As I enter the warm, cozy restaurant that smells of simmering sauces, I'm greeted by Nik, a handsome thirty-five-year-old, who clearly enjoys a good meal.

"Shall we start with a glass of riesling?" he asks playfully, as we sit down at a table with two chilled glasses of St. Urbans-Hof Kabinett. "It's a peerless aperitif, the only wine to drink in the morning," he adds. "It satisfies your blood sugar without making you drunk."

Wine in the morning? Nik is my kind of man. But he's not the first to propose such a civilized start to the day. Thomas Jefferson, who visited Germany in 1775 before going home to pen America's Declaration of Independence, described the rieslings as the "best breakfast wines."

I'm loving this riesling, a bewitching bouquet of freesia and lilacs. It's a slender wine but incredibly flavorful, with just 7 percent alcohol. I comment on this, and Nik agrees. "We are happy with each percentage of alcohol that we *don't* have to put in the bottle. People no longer drink aperitifs and ports in restaurants because they're concerned about the calories and the drive home."

Ruth and Harald, an attractive couple in their thirties, come out to greet us. If I don't mind, they say, they'd like to prepare a surprise menu this evening of local game and fish, homemade breads, fresh vegetables, and fruit from their garden. I don't mind.

Our aperitif riesling goes beautifully with the first course: breast of wild duck with poached duck liver, sautéed figs, and a sherry-vinegar jelly. "Riesling cuts through the fat in the duck and lifts up a heavy dish," Nik says, moistening his lips.

The wine works just as well with savory game birds and braised meats, which are often accompanied by a sweet garnish like jelly, chutney, or berries. Riesling's own sweetness, Nik explains, adds piquancy rather than heaviness, making the wine taste more alive.

The natural sugar amplifies the wine's fruity ripeness. Sweetness is as much the signature of riesling as bubbles are of champagne.

The next kabinett Nik and I drink comes from the famous Ockfener Bockstein vineyard, another steep, rocky slope, with slate that leaves a bluish powder on your fingers. Nik still uses viticultural techniques introduced by the Romans two thousand years ago, like trellising his vines on single poles rather than on horizontal wires between posts, as is done in other countries. The vine canes are tied to the pole in the shape of a heart, which gives the grapes more exposure to the sun and makes them easier to pick. These leafy hearts look like rows of Irish valentines. Grapes are then handpicked into shoulder-mounted baskets so they're not damaged.

Our next wine, the Piesporter Goldtröpfchen Riesling Spätlese, is a bit sweeter and dances with our second course: belly of pork and goose liver on noodles, with nuts and apple-vinegar sauce. Nik starts to talk about sugar and riesling, a subject that provokes debate and frustration for many vintners here.

"We're the only country in the world to put our sweetness front and center on the label," he says. "Château d'Yquem doesn't list the grams of sugar on its label. We created our own problems by focusing on that aspect. Describing a wine solely in terms of its sweetness is like describing a woman just by her height and weight—it doesn't give you a sense of the complete person."

Sweetness, like acidity, is necessary for complexity. The main source of sweetness in wine is the natural sugar in ripening grapes, which increases with more warmth and hang time. Grapes for the best wines are picked over a six-week period to capture just the right degree of ripeness for each particular wine style. The second source of sweetness is the cheapest and most obvious, when the vintner adds sugar, a method called chaptalization. This process, permitted only for the most basic wines, is used when grapes fail to ripen enough to balance their acidity. Top estates, such as St. Urbans-Hof, Loosen, and Prüm, don't use this method at all. That's because sugar, like oak, can mask faults or lack of taste in inferior wine.

German rieslings often get an unfair rap for cloying sweetness, even though many "dry" New World wines actually taste sweeter. Take Californian chardonnays, for example. Some of the more popular brands don't have the acidity to balance their residual sugar, ripe fruit, and creamy oak notes. The same applies to high-alcohol wines, which taste sweeter than they really are because alcohol gives the impression of sweetness even though it actually has no flavor. So, we talk dry and drink sweet.

"With riesling, sweet can be good, dry can be good," Nik observes. "But completely dry chardonnay sucks."

Riesling, with all its complexities, is often overshadowed by the more obvious charms of chardonnay, the world's most popular white wine. Chardonnay is the pliable good-girl of the wine world, adapting to the winemaker's hand and absorbing the barrel's flavor. Oak is the sensory counterpoint in wines that don't have much acidity. Just as many people who eat hot-buttered popcorn actually like the taste of butter more than the corn, many of those who love chardonnay actually love the taste of oak, butter, cream, vanilla, and smoke.

"It's just mean to put a California chardonnay beside a German riesling in a blind tasting," Nik says. "Their robust flavors overwhelm rieslings. We call them U-boats."

For me, the difference between the two wines is their comparative ranges. Riesling is a quivering wine of potential energy that reminds me of opera diva Sarah Brightman singing pop tunes. She barely pushes her voice, yet what thrills me is knowing that her range stretches far beyond what I hear. Conversely, many chardonnays remind me of breathy pop stars who have to whisper the high notes.

That's why there's been a growing pendulum swing against chardonnay called ABC (Anything But Chardonnay). Of course, not all chardonnays fall into this stylistic camp. Chablis, unoaked chardonnay from northern Burgundy, shares riesling's nervy vivacity.

However, it's not just the unaffordable benchmark wines that should be considered great, whether it's riesling, chablis, or pinot noir. As Nik points out, "Relevance is an aspect of greatness. It's important to have a wine that you can make a part of your daily life rather than having to save it for special occasions. Affordability is part of that."

Entry-level German wines are labeled QbA (*Qualitätswein bestimmter Anbaugebiete*), meaning a quality wine that has enough character to taste like its growing area. The best rieslings are labeled QmP (*Qualitätswein mit Prädikat*), meaning a quality wine of special distinction. Like it or not, the Germans categorize their finest wines not by vineyard or region, like the French and Italians, but according to the grape's sweetness when picked. So prädikat wines are "predicated" on six levels: *kabinett, spätlese, auslese, beerenauslese, trockenbeerenauslese,* and *eiswein.*

The greater the ripeness, the higher the wine is ranked. But this designation only refers to how sweet the grapes were at harvest, not necessarily how sweet the wine will eventually taste. Vintners can still ferment their grapes to complete dryness. You need to learn your prädikats to understand German wine the way you learned your multiplication tables for basic math. Quit moaning; just do it.

Kabinett (*kah-bee-NEHT*) rieslings, like the delicate, dry one that Nik and I started with this evening, are made from fully ripened grapes. "Kabinett" originally referred to the locked cabinets in which the most valuable wines were cellared. These wines go well with light dishes, such as sole, trout, sushi, salads, smoked salmon, and mild curries.

The next level up is spätlese (*SHPAYT-lay-zuh*), meaning "late harvest." These grapes are picked at least a week after the main harvest is finished, so the wines have a hint of sweetness and are more full-bodied than kabinetts. Legend has it that the spätlese style was created by accident in 1775. Back then, a courier on a fast horse took an annual sample of the grapes to the Prince Abbot of Fulda to get his approval to begin the harvest. But that year the prince was late in giving his consent. By the time the "Spätlese Rider" returned, the grapes had overripened.

So rather than lose both the harvest and their heads, the vintners decided to pick the grapes anyway. To their delight, these sublimely rotten grapes created a new luscious style of wine that was a hit at court. In subsequent harvests, they experimented with leaving some grapes on the vines for longer and longer periods. Goethe, author of *Faust* and a man who surely knew how easy it is to sell one's soul for greatness, was an avid fan of these sweeter styles. In 1814, he wrote in his diary, "The excellence of the wine depends upon the site, but also upon the late harvesting."

Nik and I are now enjoying our third course of codfish in a potato-pumpkin broth with white onions and mushrooms. His Piesporter Goldtröpfchen Riesling Spätlese goes beautifully with the dish. We also drink this wine with the next two courses: pikeperch with chin of pork, bacon-mashed potatoes and chicory with orange-cardamom gravy, and then (you didn't think you were done yet, did you?) red mullet with chickpeas, polenta, and beans in a carrot-thyme sauce.

Our sixth course—sweetbreads on fig couscous—dances with our third wine, Ockfener Bockstein Riesling Auslese, redolent of ripe apricots. Auslese (*OWS-lay-zuh*), German for "select," are rieslings made from selected bunches of late-harvested grapes. Often, they've started to overripen, becoming affected by the desirable mold

Botrytis cinerea, or noble rot (*edelfäule* in German). The mold attacks the grape skins, dehydrates the fruit, and concentrates its sugar and flavor. This natural chemical transformation in the grape gives the final wine a lovely orange-tinged honey flavor. Germany's most famous dessert wines are touched by botrytis, as are Bordeaux sauternes (like Château d'Yquem) and Hungary's tokaji.

"The ugliest grapes give the best juice," Nik says, showing me a bunch he's brought from the vineyard. The leathery, furry berries don't look good enough for horse feed, but he tells me that the fruit will yield five different wines. The bitter botrytis taste finds its balance in the wine's honeyed notes, creating a savory character that works with hearty meat dishes, like the one we have next: a nut-encrusted saddle of deer, accompanied by dumplings and quince in a pepper gravy. Savory dishes like venison demand mature rieslings, since the sweet and sour element of the meat and plum or raspberry sauce requires a wine that has intensity of flavor but isn't obviously sweet. That's why mature rieslings also pair with hearty meat dishes. It's easier to match a white wine like riesling with most meats than it is to pair most robust red wines with fish.

When we get to beerenauslese (*BEAR-rehn-OWS-lay-zuh*), or BA for short, we're into the dessert wines. These are made from individually selected grapes (*beeren*) that are shriveled and fully affected by botrytis. Nik's Leiwener Laurentiuslay Riesling Beerenauslese pairs well with the Dawson apricots in aspic with Guanaja-chocolate cream and Tahitian-vanilla ice cream.

Balancing the wine's luscious texture is less a flavor than a faint tingling sensation, like I used to get as a child from Lick-a-Maid powder. Winemakers call it minerality, a trait imparted by the slate and other rocks in which the vines grow. It's as much a texture as it is a taste, but it shouldn't be confused with the aroma in mature riesling called petrol. Plants don't metabolize minerals as they do organic material, so grapes grown near roads, for example, don't produce wines with lead in them despite all the gasoline fumes they're exposed to. However, put white roses in blue-colored water and they absorb the color pigments that tinge their petals blue. The minerals in slate also dissolve in water. That's why mineral water has a more distinctive taste than filtered water. Think of it like drinking water that's gushing fresh in a mountain stream and running over the rocks.

Nevertheless, some people confuse minerality and petrol, despite the fact that most winemakers here despise the latter. The P-word is almost as verboten as the S-word. Others use the descriptors kerosene, motor oil, or gasoline. I wondered at first if these nuances were imparted from the country's famous Autobahn. And after this morning's drive, I was convinced.

Nik certainly doesn't look happy when I ask him about it. "Petrol says oxidation at best, contamination at worst," he observes. "Who wants to drink either one?"

While some drinkers and critics think petrol is a good aroma, many consider it a flaw. The aroma often develops when certain compounds in the wine oxidize, usually the result of a short, hot growing season with too little water and too much nitrogen fertilizer. As the grape tries to protect itself against environmental stress, it produces organic compounds that smell like linseed oil. Other critics say that gasoline aroma is just a matter of perception: drinkers also confuse it with dried fruit notes or the butterscotch-toffee character of mature residual sugar.

Riesling's ability to age is another aspect of its greatness. The British wine writer Jancis Robinson called them "whites for eternity." Riesling's acidity survives on its residual sugar, enabling the wines to live longer than most whites and even many reds. They can easily age for five to ten years; and the great ones, for twenty-five years or more. Chemically, riesling's molecules bind together to become longer flanking chains. New ones are created and others are destroyed in a gloriously silent battle within every bottle. The result is a long, smooth, open wine.

"The things that last have greatness, whether it's a novel that still reads well after a hundred years or a wine that drinks well after thirty," Nik says. "We all want the secret of youth, but the real secret is how to age well."

During a brief respite between courses (gasp), we enjoy a small glass of Nik's icewine. Eiswein (*ICE-vine*) is made from grapes of beerenauslese sweetness that are left on the vine in winter until frozen and picked at 18°F or colder. What little water the grapes still have in them is left on the press, so what's extracted is highly concentrated fruit flavor.

Icewine was actually discovered in Germany, by accident, in 1794. Vintners were preparing for the harvest when an unexpected early frost froze the grapes on the vine. The vintners pressed them anyway and were delighted to learn that the resulting wine was not only drinkable but exceptionally sweet and delicious—thanks to the concentration of sugar in the frozen dehydrated grapes.

Trockenbeerenauslese (*TROK-ehn-BEAR-rehn-OWS-lay-zuh*), or TBA, means "dry berry selection," for the individually selected grapes in this wine that have completely shriveled to raisins from botrytis. This wine encases our last course, an exquisite dessert of wine-poached vineyard peaches with a verbena-mousse ice cream. TBA wines are the richest, rarest dessert wines of nectared depth.

Mentally, I compare this wine with Château d'Yquem, also made from 100 percent botrytis-affected grapes, but the sauterne has more alcohol and less acidity than TBA wines. For the true hedonist who wants to prolong pleasure, TBA is your wine. You don't tire of it quickly. That's why many people enjoy it with foie gras at the beginning of a meal; it's lighter than the traditional sauternes and, hence, less filling and less inebriating. In fact, through extensive research, I've discovered that the only dishes that clash with riesling are rare steaks (the wine lacks tannin for the meat's juicy proteins to latch on to) and cotton candy (for pete's sake, you're at the fair so have a beer).

Now that dinner's over, Nik and I keep ourselves from falling asleep at the table with a spirited discussion on how the country's wine labels are a metaphor for the German soul. "Why should our labels be easy to read when our wine was so hard to make?" Nik jokes. "Should Thomas Mann's *Magic Mountain* be condensed to make it more accessible? We Germans love complexity."

I can tell. Unlike France's relatively stable bordeaux classification of 1855, the changes to Germany's prädikat system since 1971 would bring a senate inquiry to its knees. The problem was that the new classifications were both too vague and too generous (political) in awarding top status. They also didn't replace the existing system but simply added more layers of confusion.

However, Nik makes a good point: "Burgundy is even more complex, but wine lovers make an effort to understand it because the wines are so great. Germany deserves the same effort." At least riesling is labeled with the grape, whereas Burgundy's pinot noir isn't. And often there are many owners of one Burgundian vineyard whereas there are more German estates owned by just one family.

Today, the best riesling producers agree that a national classification of vineyards is the only way to escape the chaos of the sugar cult. However, they're not waiting for the country's wine laws to change. Many have started to brand-name their own wines to guarantee quality, such as Loosen's Dr. L Riesling and Nik's Urban Riesling.

The International Riesling Foundation, formed in Washington State in 2007, has proposed an even simpler Riesling Taste Scale. It designates wines as one of the following: dry, off-dry, medium dry, medium sweet, and sweet. The power of such voluntary guidelines is not only that they're easier for consumers to understand but also that they can be universally applied to rieslings from many regions and countries.

Closer to home, Nik feels that riesling should be the only wine made in the Mosel. Until 1988, making red wine here was actually illegal, but now the government allows up to 10 percent of production to be red. He also believes that wine should be made on only the south-facing sites, and yields should come down. The poor-quality growers get three times as much wine from a vine as the better-quality ones do.

"I have riesling in my blood," Nik says, smiling. "Every generation reinvents winemaking from the way their parents did it—we just do what our grandfathers did. We're trying to get back to where we were, but it might take another generation to do that—or a century."

A FEW DAYS later, I'm driving beside the Moselle as dazzling shafts of sun burn through the morning fog. I've tasted an impressive array of wines this week, both from the Mosel and from other regions: Fritz Haag, Willi Schaefer, Egon Müller, Zilliken, Christoffel, Dr. Pauly-Bergweiler, Dr. Bürklin-Wolf, Selbach-Oster, Schloss Vollrads, and Robert Weil. All were remarkable in their own way but share an effortless vitality.

Now I'm on my way to visit Bernkasteler Doctor, one of the

country's best vineyards and certainly its most storied. Founded in 1291, Bernkastel is an opera-set village of half-timbered houses, window ledges filled with flowers, narrow cobbled streets, courtyard fountains, and a medieval clock tower. High above the town, a crumbling castle is a black shadow against the sky.

Nine vineyards can put Bernkastel's prestigious name on their label, but the most famous is the Doctor. This tiny vineyard clings to the cliff that soars up behind the village, where eight acres are sheltered from cold winds by the Hunsrück Mountains. The south-facing vines soak up reflected warmth from the sun, the river, and the town's slate roofs.

The Bernkasteler Doctor vineyard earned its name in 1630, when the Prince of Trier, Archbishop Bohemund II, fell gravely ill while visiting the village. He declared that the person who saved his life would be granted any wish. A local winemaker gave the cleric a flask of his wine, which resulted in a miraculous recovery. The archbishop granted the man's wish to call the vineyard "the Doktor" for its curative properties. The wily vintner knew that its value would soar with such a name.

A few decades later in 1650, Christoph von Söetern, the owner of the vineyard, decided to create a storage vault for his wine inside the mountain. There were no machines or explosives back then; the 210 feet of slate rock was all dug out by hand. Today, the cave still has 90 percent natural humidity and a temperature that stays at 50°F in summer and winter. It's perfect for wine storage.

The vineyard passed from owner to owner until 1900, when local brothers Carl and Julius Wegeler bought the largest parcel of it for an astronomical sum. For every single vine, they paid roughly the price of a horse—some one hundred goldmarks, or $29. But their enormous investment paid off. The vineyard's wines have long commanded Germany's highest prices. The 1959 Wegeler Doctor Spätlese, for instance, sold for $10.25, whereas the 1959 Pétrus went for just $7.95. Such was the wine's prestige that Dr. Konrad Adenauer, a chancellor of Germany, gave fifty bottles to President Eisenhower during his state visit in 1962. Today, the Doctor vineyard is the highest-priced piece of agricultural land in Germany, and its grapes cost three times as much as those from vineyards on either side of it.

In 1957, Carl Wegeler's great-grandson Rolf retired and handed over the family's 148 acres of vineyards, including the Doctor, to his oldest daughter, Anja. Until then, her interests lay more in commerce. She had taken a master's of business administration at the University of Trier. There she had met her future husband, Tom Drieseberg, while he was completing his PhD with a thesis on the rituals of eating and drinking as cultural indicators. They married, both worked briefly in the consumer products industry, and then Rolf suggested that they take over the estate.

I meet Tom in front of the Wegeler home. He's six-foot-three with laughing periwinkle blue eyes and a friendly manner. He claps me on the shoulder as we shake hands. With him is winemaker Norbret Breit, a shorter, more compact man who looks down shyly when I say hello. I follow them into a long, rectangular room above the wine cellar, its arched ceiling made of blackened old-barrel staves. The large open window is filled with the green sunlit hill, and children's voices drift up from the courtyard below.

We all sit down at a long oak table, and Norbret brings out glasses and several bottles. Tom pours the Bernkasteler Doctor Kabinett Riesling. "This wine challenges you to pay attention to it," he tells me. I don't find it a challenge to pay attention to this wine at all. A citrus zing runs up the sides of my mouth, softened by a spring drizzle of ripe peaches. The wine opens my senses, first making my mouth water. Then as I breathe in deeply, its aromas travel upward, lifting my eyebrows and perfuming my mind.

"You must come out to meet this wine," he says. I'm already there, in the glass.

Next we try the spätlese, which has the fragile intensity of Chagall stained glass. Its flamboyant fruitiness suffuses the room the way the jeweled light from the artist's pane does a church. As *Slate* editor Fareed Zakaria once observed, "This is what God drinks at five o'clock in the summer."

For Tom, the wine calls to mind a dinner in the Caribbean. "It was perfect with the marinated mahi-mahi I had on the beach in the Grand Caymans once," he recalls. "But maybe that had less to do with my wine and more to do with being on a beach in the Grand Caymans."

The next wine Norbert pours is his beerenauslese. The room fills with nectarine, peach, and honeysuckle. Then we taste the trocken-beerenauslese, a smoldering wine of honey and clementines. It has a disturbingly attractive aroma, like a field of flowers with a snarling undergrowth. The wine's luscious texture seeps into all the crevices of my mouth and coats the back of my throat.

Distractedly, I confirm if I heard them correctly: do they make 110 cases of this wine a year? Both men look at each other and burst into laughter, slapping the table. Apparently, I've told a good one.

This is the Doctor's most expensive wine; a half-bottle sells for $400 (though mature vintages at auction command thousands). They produce just ten cases in a good year. To make a mere half bottle, it takes one worker a full day to pick ten pounds of these grapes, which have to be the ripest and most succulent.

Tom recalls a memorable moment with this wine while he and Rudi Wiest, his American importer, were dining in Las Vegas. The two men enjoyed challenging each other, and that evening Tom offered to eat a spoonful of wasabi without bursting into flames or tears. Sushi fans know that wasabi, the bitter flavoring herb often called Japanese horseradish, is much hotter than jalapeño peppers. Its heat is generated by compounds called isothiocyanates, which create intensely hot nasal vapors. Rudi took him up on the dare, expecting fireworks. Then he watched in disbelief as Tom ate the wasabi without batting an eyelash, following it with a mouthful of his riesling.

What Rudi didn't know was Tom's secret weapon: osmosis. Riesling, a thicker, higher-density liquid, enveloped the wasabi and mixed with a thinner liquid, his saliva, generating more of it. It effectively protected his palate because the heat compounds weren't able to attach to his tongue and throat. The key, Tom emphasizes, is not waiting more than a second or two after eating the wasabi to drink the wine. "You don't want to miss that deadline," he says, smiling.

Although employees were initially wary of the "son-in-law who has a PhD," the winery thrived under the young couple's management. The family invested more than $3 million to modernize the cellars. And in 1993, Tom hired Norbert, whom Tom describes as "a fantastic sparring partner."

Now the two seem to finish each other's sentences. Tom observes, "It's the German love of precision that makes us work with a grape that creates so many styles. We want to know exactly what we can produce depending on what we do with it." Norbert agrees. "You can trim riesling to the essence you want from it. It's such a personal wine that where it grows and who makes it matter deeply."

Are there any tricks to working with riesling? I ask.

"Time," Norbert says. His placid farmer's features give away nothing and take in everything. "You can tell people a lot about riesling, but finally they just have to taste it."

As we sit silently smelling our glasses, the open window reminds me of the May morning after a party in my first apartment. I woke up to a slender-sloped bottle of riesling, half full, on the window ledge. The lace curtain brushed over it and back again in the breeze. Its aroma of lime and nectarine mingled with the white cherry blossoms outside and drifted over the sheets.

"Let's go see the vineyard," Tom suggests. The three of us pile into his old van and drive up a steep path that would tire a mountain goat. At the top of the vineyard, the air is crisp and cool. From up here at the curve of the Moselle River, you can see the grandest sweep of vineyards in Europe. As far as you can throw open your arms to fill your lungs with mountain air, there are vine-draped slopes to the south and to the west.

However, just looking straight down at the rows of vines almost gives me vertigo. I try to imagine what it's like for the Polish immigrants who work here. Flatland vineyards can use machines to harvest the grapes and need only about two hundred hours of labor per acre a year. But growing cliff-face riesling demands thirty-five hundred or more grueling hours hiking up and down carrying a hundred-pound basket of grapes while strapped to cables. As Tom notes, "We practice sustainable viticulture, but to be organic would require slaves."

So what's the first thing you do in the spring, I ask him?

"We remove the bones of the workers who didn't make it through the fall harvest," he quips.

From the back of the van, Norbert takes a chilled bottle of the 1982 Bernkasteler Doctor Riesling Spätlese. The glasses mist over as he pours the wine. We clink them together and look out at the green shadows across the hillsides. The wine opens with expansive aromas of lemon and honeysuckle edged by a streak of smoke. The valley opens beneath the fog, which rolls up like a sleeping blanket to reveal the silver braid of water.

I'm infused with a desire to tell someone how beautiful this valley is, how glorious the wines are, but I don't want to move. Fortunately, I don't have to. Wine is the voice of the soil; without it, the land would be silent. Norbert's soft voice breaks in on my reverie, as though he's read my thoughts.

"I love this place," he says quietly.

Field Notes from a
Wine Cheapskate

INSIDER TIPS

- Look for labels that have illegible gothic script and impossibly long names that are difficult to pronounce in the liquor store (or anywhere else). Few people can read them, so they don't buy the wines, and demand doesn't push up prices.

- Wines that had a bad reputation several decades ago are behind the eight ball in trying to reposition themselves as good quality producers at reasonable prices.

- Low-alcohol wines are often your most versatile food-wise because they can go with so many lighter dishes that we enjoy today without overwhelming their flavors.

WINERIES VISITED

Dr. Loosen: www.drloosen.com
Johann Josef Prüm: www.jjpruem.com

St. Urbans-Hof: www.urbans-hof.de
Wegeler: www.wegeler.com

BEST VALUE WINES

Dr. Loosen's Dr. L Riesling*
St. Urbans-Hof Kabinett Riesling
St. Urbans-Hof Riesling
St. Urbans-Hof Urban Riesling

*My first pick for my own Monday dinner.

TOP VALUE PRODUCERS

Anselmann	Karl Erbes
August Kesseler	Kloster Eberbach
Balbach	Kruger-Rumpf
Balthasar Ress	Lingenfelder
Becker-Steinhauer	Pfeffingen
Black Slate	Reichsgraf von Kesselstatt
Carl Reh	Reinhold Haart
Darting	Schloss Johannisberg
Dr. Fischer	Schloss Reinhartshausen
Dr. Hermann	Schloss Schönborn
Dr. Pauly-Bergweiler	St. Antony
Geil	Studert Prüm
Josef Kollmann	Zilliken

MONDAY DINNER FOR A WINE CHEAPSKATE

You'll find Ruth and Harald Rüssel's recipes for the meal that's similar to the one that Nik and I shared at www.nataliemaclean .com/food.

Pork with Sweet Potato Salad, Lentils,
Smoked Salmon, and Crawfish

Terrine of Beef

Pike Perch (Zander) in an Orange Cumin Broth

Sauté of Veal Kidneys and Heart Sweetbreads

Wrapped Venison Knuckles and Nut Escalope

Potato Ravioli and Sweetheart Cabbage

Semolina Gratin

TERRIFIC PAIRINGS

Riesling is a light, vibrant white wine that often has aromas of apricot, peach, wet slate, minerals, and flowers. It's incredibly versatile with food because its styles range from bone-dry to intensely sweet. Here are some of my favorite pairings:

Dry, Kabinett, and Spätlese Riesling

Cheese: Brie, Camembert
Chicken korma

Chicken: fried
Chicken: lemon or citrus sauce

Curries: mild or medium
Duck liver pâté
Fish: barbecued or
   planked
Indian and Thai dishes
Pizza: cheese, vegetarian,
   Hawaiian
Planked salmon

Risotto with butternut squash
Salad: Caesar or green
Shellfish: crab, lobster,
   mussels, oysters
Smoked trout
Turkey: roast, soup
Vegetarian dishes

Auslese, Beerenauslese, Eiswein/Icewine, and Trockenbeerenauslese Riesling

Biscotti
Cheese: Stilton, Muenster, Gorgonzola
Curries and spices: medium or hot
Fruit-based desserts: flan, tart, cobbler
Toffee pudding

RESOURCES

For more information about German wines and riesling:

The Wines of Germany by Stephen Brook
Riesling Renaissance by Freddie and Janet Price
Wineries of Germany: www.nataliemaclean.com/wineries
Wines of Germany-Canada: www.germanwinecanada.org
Wines of Germany USA: www.germanwineusa.com
International Riesling Foundation: www.drinkriesling.com
Riesling Rendezvous: www.ste-michelle.com/winery/
   rieslingRendezvous
The Germany Wine Society: www.germanwinesociety.org

RELATED READING

The following books, while seemingly unrelated to the main subject matter of this chapter, provided some enjoyable reading before, during, and after my travels:

The Magic Mountain by Thomas Mann
The Tin Drum by Günter Grass
Faust Part One by Johann Wolfgang Von Goethe

THREE

TUESDAY

Helicopters, Hawks, and Hellacious Ladybugs

UNDER HEAVY GUNFIRE, we run for the chopper. Gray clouds roil overhead as the wind whips our faces. The ground man signals us to scramble in but then stops and waves for us to turn around. As we do, we're blinded by white flashes.

We're not being fired at, though: it's just the smiling tour guide snapping photos of us. The shotgun blasts are automatic "bird bangers" to scare birds away from the fields of Niagara grapevines around us.

This isn't Baghdad, but it is war.

The enemy—massive in numbers, cunning, and beady-eyed— weigh less than two ounces each: the European starling. These birds travel in black clouds of peckish delight, swooping down to strip vineyards clean of the fruit in a few hours. They're especially partial to grapes at this time of year, just before harvest, when they're sweet. Hence the bird bangers, which work like an exploding barbecue on a pole. A propane tank inside the cannon-shaped drainpipe ignites a tiny spark plug at odd intervals, firing the gas out through a long barrel that amplifies the sound. This works for a while, until the birds get used to the sound. I've seen them perched saucily on top of a cannon, barely fluttering as it goes off.

"The other choppers have left; let's get out of here," I yell for no apparent reason, other than having watched *Black Hawk Down* too many times. I'm about to take an aerial tour of Niagara with Martin Malivoire, whose pinot noir is a favorite of both starlings and wine lovers. Pinot noir is also my favorite red wine; I often give pinot noirs from various producers the highest scores, even though wine critics aren't supposed to allow their personal preferences to influence their "objective" analysis—hogwash. I stopped being objective the day I was born.

Pinot noir is difficult and expensive to make. That's why it's often pricey, with benchmark wines from Burgundy, France, starting at $60 a bottle and going up to several thousand dollars for legends such as Domaine de la Romanée-Conti. However, pinot noir from Niagara is a relative steal, often just $25 to $35 a bottle. It's a gorgeous wine that packs a lot of flavor yet isn't heavy and alcoholic—I think of it as riesling's red twin, though they're completely different grapes. But this makes pinot noir perfect for Tuesday night dinner.

My thoughts are jolted back to the chopper as we lift a hundred feet straight up into the air, then zoom like a crazed bumblebee over the patchwork of farm fields below. At one point, the chopper tilts almost onto its side, and I wonder if the ground man remembered to lock the full-sized window—all that's between me and the ground below.

Flying over Niagara is a meditation on landscape: horizon-reaching rows of vines, weather-scarred farmhouses, wispy peach trees, antiques stores, roadside fruit stands, and limestone bluffs that plunge down to the shimmering waters of Lake Ontario. By now, in mid-October, most vineyards have turned shades of yellow and brown, like a spice cabinet, but some are still summer green. I ask Martin about this, and he grins. "Bright green at this time of the year isn't natural," he explains. "Those vineyards have had a little chemical help."

The chemical help comes in the form of fertilizers, fungicides, pesticides, and other applications. Farming in Ontario is tough; growing wine grapes is even harder. Vintners battle mildew, leaf disease, and pests. Martin doesn't use any synthetic chemical treatments on his vineyard; Malivoire Winery was the first commercial organic winery in the region.

As we bank over the Niagara Peninsula, I can see almost all the triangular arm of land where the Great Lakes meet. The name Niagara comes from the Iroquois word *Ongniaahra*, meaning "point of land cut in two." Niagara is defined northward by Lake Ontario, southward by Lake Erie, and eastward by the Niagara River, reflecting silver and gray below us. We scout up the river until we reach Niagara Falls, the raw power of unstoppable nature. More than six million cubic feet of water a minute plummet 180 feet over the cliff edge, the equivalent of 85 million bathtubs full of water. Its rising spray is shot through with rainbows.

The falls sit on the Niagara Escarpment, a massive ridge of fractured limestone, dolomite, shale, and sandstone that stretches for a thousand miles south to New York and on to Wisconsin and north to the Canadian Shield. This particular section is where the escarpment shifted and lifted up between Lake Erie and Lake Ontario, creating the faster water flow.

This shrugging shoulder of land is actually the upthrust shoreline of the Jurassic sea that retreated eighty-three million years ago, long before the Ice Age. Now the ridge divides the Niagara Peninsula, creating a series of protected slopes and nooks that trap the moderating airflow from Lake Ontario. The lake, eight hundred feet deep in some places, acts like a giant water bottle, slowly releasing stored summer warmth in the fall to help ripen the grapes and in the winter to help protect the vines from icy death. The moderating effect of the lake and escarpment is limited to the Niagara Peninsula, which is why you don't see vineyards in Toronto or Hamilton.

More than twenty million people a year visit Niagara Falls, so why do comparatively few of them drive twenty minutes north to Niagara-on-the-Lake? Granted, it doesn't have the gold-trimmed souvenir ashtrays, wax museum, and casino gambling, but it does offer beauty, history, and culture. British Loyalists settled here at the end of the American Revolution. The last battle between Canadians and Americans, during the War of 1812, was fought at Fort George. Today they stage battles and mock displays there. The internationally acclaimed Shaw Festival features the works of Irish playwright George Bernard Shaw and his contemporaries.

I recalled Shaw's wit as I considered the challenges for local vintners. He once observed: "The reasonable man adapts himself to the world; the unreasonable one persists in trying to adapt the world to himself. Therefore all progress depends on the unreasonable man." Winemakers here must be exceptionally unreasonable, not to mention unusually stubborn, to brave the climate: humid summers that can cause rot and mildew, rain right before harvest that can bloat the grapes and dilute their flavor, and winters that can kill the vines. As one vintner told me, "You can lose the whole field—and a year's work—in an afternoon."

What doesn't kill you makes you stronger, right? True for humans, maybe. For grapes, no. Grapes thicken their skins to protect themselves from winter cold. This can mean too much tannin without enough balancing fruit ripeness. For years, Ontario wines were made from winter-hardy Labrusca grapes, like concord and white Niagara. They produced nasty little wines that were then fortified with brandy to make them drinkable. Their alcoholic strength earned them the nickname "block and tackle" wines because after drinking them, you could tackle anyone. In the sixties and seventies, Canadian wine went through a grim cheap-and-sweet zoological period, featuring wines named Baby Duck, Gimli Goose, Fuddle Duck, Pussycat, and so on. Bright's wine, founded by pioneer Thomas Bright, was uncharitably dubbed Bright's Disease.

Things started to improve with the 1988 Ontario Wine Content Act, which banned Labrusca grapes in table wines. That same year, the Vintners Quality Alliance (VQA), an appellation system for Ontario wines similar to France's AOC and Italy's DOC, was founded. The VQA designation guarantees that wines are grown and produced in Canada to certain standards. Another spur to better winemaking was the 1989 Canada-U.S. Free Trade Agreement, followed by the 1994 North American Free Trade Agreement. These initiatives prompted a renewal of the wine industry: the government phased out protectionist taxes on foreign wines and gave vintners subsidies to plant better-quality European grapes.

Today, the Niagara region is home to some of North America's most exciting wineries, such as Malivoire, Tawse, Flat Rock, Coyote's Run, Le Clos Jordanne, Featherstone, Lailey Vineyard, and Inniskillin—the first commercial winery to open after Prohibition. Founders Karl Kaiser and Donald Ziraldo are credited with bringing international recognition to Canadian wine, after their vidal icewine won France's 1991 Grand Prix d'Honneur in a blind tasting against more than four thousand of the world's best wines.

The icewine story is a particularly Canadian one, associated with this country as much as snow, ice rinks, hockey, parkas, and maple syrup. Other countries make it, too, but Canada, with its consistently cold weather, has long since surpassed them in both volume and consumer awareness. At its best, icewine tastes like an incoming tide of pleasure. Vibrant notes of apricot, mango, peach, clementines, honeysuckle, baked apples, and quince are all suspended in a gossamer haze of sweetness.

Canada now sells some $45 million of icewine a year, accounting for more than half the country's wine exports. Seventy-five percent of it is made in Ontario, and the rest in British Columbia, Quebec, and Nova Scotia. Half bottles sell for $50 to $80. The high price tag is because it's an expensive and risky wine to make. Most icewine is made from the vidal grape, which has winter-hardy skin and aromatic intensity. Some vintners also use the more elegant riesling, with its lovely tension between acidity and sweetness. Harvesting in January can mean losing up to 60 percent of the crop compared to the fall, as the grapes are more prone to damage from both weather and pests. The surviving grapes are picked at temperatures of 17°F or colder, usually at night. When these frozen vinous pellets are pressed, they yield only 15 to 20 percent of the juice of unfrozen grapes. One year, this icy fruit broke a two-ton wine press at Inniskillin.

The largest buyer of Canada's icewine is Asia, where it's considered a luxury—which may be why most fakes come from Asia. Some of the knockoff wine labels are creative with both geography and spelling, such as "Chilliwacko, Ontario" (inspired perhaps by Chilliwack, British Columbia), "Snow White," and "Elixir of the Gods from Torontow"—the latter bears a picture of Whistler, a British Columbia ski resort more than five thousand miles west of Toronto.

That Inniskillin icewine win turned Canada's snowy image into both a boon and a bane. It helped the reputation of Canadian wine change from plonk to quality. This, in turn, encouraged the growth of Ontario wineries, which have jumped from 18 in 1989 to 140 today. The wine and grape industries are now worth $550 million and provide some seven thousand jobs. However, the international triumph was for a niche dessert wine, and the country has been struggling to shake that typecast role ever since. That's why I've decided to focus on pinot noir while I'm in Niagara. It's the wine that I believe is the most exciting for this region, and it will change the world's perceptions of the Grape White North. As one winemaker remarked, God made cabernet sauvignon, but the devil made pinot noir. I'm here to drink some black magic.

When the helicopter drops Martin and me at Malivoire Winery, I'm relieved to be on terra firma again, even though my stomach is still circling above Lake Ontario. As we came in to land, I was curious about a series of giant tin canisters lying on their sides. It turns out that's actually the winery: they're buildings made from large semicircular sheets of corrugated steel, like the Quonset huts the British built in World War I as barracks.

"We built this winery out of found objects," Martin explains with gee-whiz enthusiasm. "Some of the corrugated steel sheets came from a local building that was being torn down. They're light and fast to assemble, and the design mimics the curves of the hills." It also follows the gravity-flow design of the winery: as the cylinders descend down the hillside, the juice flows through them for various stages of the winemaking process. This treatment is gentler than mechanical pumping, and it results in better wine.

The other parts of the structure were scavenged, too: the rocks and pediments are "blaster's mistakes" from a local quarry, and the wood beams are telephone poles rejected by Ontario Hydro. "We need to think more about our energy footprint," Martin says. "Thinking about human time and energy ultimately leads to thinking about how you spend your life."

In his case, the answer is very productively. Martin recently retired from a successful career as a movie special-effects producer. Some of his best-known films are *Quest for Fire*, *Porky's*, *My Big Fat Greek Wedding*, *Hairspray*, and *Fly Away Home*. A native of Oakville, Ontario, it was while filming *Trapped in Paradise* in 1993 that he fell in love with the Niagara region. In 1996, he and his partner, Moira Saganski, an investment banker, built a home here and bought eighty-six acres of vineyards. At first, they sold their grapes to local winemakers. But when Martin tasted one of the resulting wines, he wasn't impressed. That prompted him to try making wine himself, though the experiment was short-lived.

"I followed a winemaking book step-by-step—and that was the first and last time I ever made wine," he says, laughing. "The next year, I hired a winemaker." But even Martin's failures seem to succeed: his wine won a gold medal in an amateur competition. After that, he and Moira built the winery in 1998 and devoted themselves to serious winemaking.

I'm keen to talk to Martin because he's one of Niagara's best producers of pinot noir. Known as the "heartbreak grape" for its racy taste and finicky nature, its siren call lures winemakers into its rocky shoals when they'd be safer on the shores of chardonnay, cabernet, and merlot. Niagara is heartbreak central when it comes to this wine. The grape got its name for its tight bunches shaped like pinecones (*pineau* in French). This reduces air circulation around the grapes, which increases their susceptibility to rot and mildew. So you'd think that it would be the last choice for Niagara with its cool, wet climate. In the winery, it's susceptible to bacterial spoilage called *Brettano-myces*, euphemistically described as smelling like a barnyard.

However, winemakers keep going back to it like a bad boyfriend who is dangerously exciting. Pinot noir loves living on the edge: regions right at the last margin for growing grapes often excel because the grapes don't overripen and become alcoholic and flabby from too much sun. Still, the fruit has incredible depth of flavor. The escarpment is loaded with the fossils of ancient microscopic marine animals and seashells, giving it a calcium-rich composition similar to the famous soils of Burgundy and Champagne. As a result, Niagara pinot noir has a mid-Atlantic style that combines the fleshy fruitiness of Oregon with the brooding earthiness of Burgundy.

Given these challenges, I'm surprised that Martin farms organically, without even a little chemical help. Partly, that's a reaction to having tried it once: during his first harvest, he sprayed his crop with a commonly used chemical. Its airborne drift into his winery caused him heart palpitations for several months. "There was no question about our approach after that," Martin says.

Until the 1950s, there was no such distinction: most crops, including wine grapes, were grown without synthetic pesticides and fertilizers. Crops were at the mercy of diseases and pests, so farmers had no choice but to wait until nature recalibrated itself after the blight died out with its food source, the crop.

Then along came the so-called green revolution, with chemicals perceived as the modern way to farm. This was aided by the phosphorus and nitrogen left over from World War II. These chemicals seemed to offer problem-free fields, and for two decades, they ruled agriculture in North America and many other countries.

In the 1970s, the backlash started. Consumers began to worry about the domination of big agribusiness, the harm to the environment, and the long-term effects of chemical dependency. A growing back-to-the-land movement, along with the hippie culture's yearning for self-sufficiency, strengthened public desire for "natural" food. Ever since, modern concerns—genetically modified foods, mercury poisoning, mad cow disease, and fast food—have all contributed to the organic momentum.

What does *organic* actually mean when applied to wine? There are two answers to that because making wine is a two-step process: first you grow the grapes, and then you make the wine. There's a distinction between "wine from organically grown grapes" and "organic wine." Organically grown grapes must not have any synthetic fertilizers, pesticides, herbicides, fungicides, or soil fumigants used on them.

However, organic farmers can still use chemicals that are derived from naturally occurring substances. Some of these organic chemicals also come with worker protection warnings. And which is more virtuous: organic sulfur, which is mined and consumes a lot of energy, or synthetic sulfur, which is a by-product of petroleum distillation? The issue isn't simple, even though our desire for "natural" farming is. As Martin points out, how far do you want to go with organic? Should the winemaker wash his hands with organic soap?

Organically made wine takes this a step further; not only were the grapes grown organically, but the wine itself must also not contain any of the five hundred or so additives available to winemakers. That includes not having more than ten parts per million sulfites— the salts of sulfuric acid—a common food preservative that prevents the wine from spoiling after fermentation.

Sulfites are harmless to most people, though some asthmatics are allergic to them. More important, there's no avoiding sulfites, because they're a natural by-product of fermentation. They exist naturally in many fruits and vegetables as well as in fruit juices, jams, baked goods, salad bars, and bottled mineral water. A single glass of orange juice has more sulfites than a whole bottle of nonorganic wine. Organic wine tends not to travel well or keep long because it doesn't have much sulfur. Therefore, it's wine made from organically grown grapes that you see in the organic section of most liquor stores.

For wine lovers, there's no evidence that organic wine is any better for you than nonorganic, or that it will reduce your risk of cancer, heart disease, or other illnesses. In blind taste tests, many experts perceive no difference between well-made organic and nonorganic wines. (And no, drinking organic wine won't reduce your hangover.) Having said that, though, my instinct is that farming methods do make a difference. Wine is an expression of the earth where the vines grow. If that earth is rich and alive with microorganisms and insects, rather than being a chemical wasteland, that's got to affect the health of the vines, the taste of the fruit, and the quality of the resulting wine, even though the difference may be subtle.

Martin agrees. He also believes that organic farming is not just more sustainable but also cheaper in the long run, with its lower dependence on fossil fuels and expensive synthetic chemicals. He thinks that many farmers, including winemakers, will eventually be forced to maintain their prices, even if the cost of oil goes up, in order to compete with organic producers. Plus, he says the organic approach is part of an overall commitment to quality. It requires a deeper understanding of the vineyard and a greater vigilance. Problems must be detected early because organic fixes take longer to work.

"The world will become healthier out of sheer necessity because organic foods will become the cheaper choice," he observes. "The simpler we make our business, the easier it is to run."

Organic also fits with the new fashion for fresh and local with the popularity of the hundred-mile diet and sustainable agriculture. Why not the hundred-mile cellar? Organic wine sales have been growing at 20 percent a year compared to about 5 percent for nonorganic-certified wines. "It's like the peach industry," Martin explains. "Years ago, they had to change from canned to fresh peaches because no one was eating canned fruit anymore."

Malivoire met the stringent requirements for an organic designation from the Canadian Food Inspection Agency in 2004; however,
he still doesn't put that fact on any of his labels. I ask him why not.
In a word, he says, consumer perception. Most drinkers already think
of wine as a natural product, though they're likely less influenced by
knowledge of the winemaking approach and more by those leafy
pictures of vineyards on labels and in ads. So although they may seek
out organic versions of lettuce, tomatoes, or beef, they don't think
to do so for wine.

Martin isn't alone in his caution; many wineries hesitate to pro-
mote their organic designation. Most consumers buy wine for its
taste and quality; the organic part is just a bonus. As well, organic
wines have an unfortunate history. In the past, they were perceived
(often correctly) as being poorly made and prone to going bad quickly
because they lacked preservatives. More important, many vintners
don't want to lock themselves into one mode of production—just in
case there's an unexpected attack of pests or rot that requires emergency chemical treatment. If a winery had to remove the organic
designation from its label, it would be awkward to explain why to
its customers. And if a winery produces several wines, and not all
are organic, that declaration on one label could reflect poorly on the
others. For all these reasons, only a small percentage of wineries that
are certified organic actually market that fact.

One of my favorite parts of Martin's organic approach is his ladybug strategy, which is why many of his bottles feature a cheerful
little red beetle crawling across the label. To combat destructive
insects that have a taste for grape leaves, Martin releases thousands
of ladybugs into his vineyards. The ladybugs are selective about what
they eat, whereas insecticides destroy every bug in their path and
leave a vineyard more vulnerable to pest attacks the next year.

But wait, didn't ladybugs taint Niagara wines a few years ago? After wines were barreled or bottled for the 2001 harvest, many winemakers noticed an odd smell of rancid peanut butter. A number of wineries, including Malivoire, pulled their affected wines from store shelves that year.

Eventually, they traced the problem to an Asian species of ladybug, quite different from the indigenous five-spotted ladybugs. Farmers in the southern United States had introduced the bug to feed on the aphids that were plaguing their pecan trees and soybeans. The problem began when these ladybugs migrated north, following the aphids, and became a seasonal pest in wine country. Swarms of these beetles amass whenever a cold snap is followed by an Indian summer. They hibernate in the grapevines, which offer both food and warmth as winter approaches.

When the affected grapes were picked and crushed, these stowaway ladybugs emitted a foul fluid called pyrazine that smelled like rancid peanut butter. The smell also has a dampening effect on the wine's natural fruit aromas, similar to mild cork taint. Wine tolerance for this type of beetle is low; more than four beetles per four-ton bin can ruin the entire harvest. Martin, though, is philosophical about the problem: "It's just Mother Nature doing her thing, and we're the ones who have to adapt."

The good news is that early-ripening grapes, such as sauvignon blanc, provided the first warning about the problem. Martin and other vintners largely addressed the issue before it affected pinot noir and other later-ripening grapes. Vintners have also learned how to deal with the pests: spraying the vines with certain chemicals, harvesting at night when the beetles aren't active, shaking them out by hand when picking the grapes, and sorting the grapes before crushing them. The sorting table at Malivoire starts with a heat blower to blow off intruders; then the grapes travel along a vibrating belt to shake them off, with workers picking them out; and then the grapes go past a final heat blower.

Martin has invited me back to his home for lunch. The house is a modern glass-and-concrete affair, designed by the late architect Andrew Volgyesi, that somehow fits in this forest setting. Large glass doors open onto a wraparound porch and bamboo garden. Inside is open concept, with big wooden beams supporting a twenty-four-foot-high ceiling and three fireplaces with sitting areas. In the center is a large open kitchen with a marble counter, a Wolf gas oven, and cabinets full of pots and wine glasses. Pumpkin soup is simmering on the stove, its spicy aroma warming the house.

"I started cooking in my filmmaking days to help me relax after a long day of blowing things up and killing people," Martin says, smiling as he stirs the soup. "With such a superficial job, I loved the reality of cooking: fresh ingredients, a glass of wine. It changes your whole focus."

He's an intuitive, shoot-from-the-hip cook, with a passion for cookbooks; more than five hundred of them line the shelves around the house. "Every recipe is a story," he says. "I'm not a classically trained cook, so I try to understand what the author is saying with the flavors in the dish."

He hands me a large cleaver to chop new potatoes in half, showing me how to make an even slice with a quick flick of his wrist. I am the world's slowest chopper, if you don't count also slicing your own fingers. But it feels natural to be working beside him as the conversation continues.

From the fridge, Martin takes out a tray of deboned quails that have marinated overnight in maple syrup. They were raised on a local farm. "I know the farmer, and that's important to me," he says. "They ran free and were happy. The ingredients on my plate are personal."

He salts the quails and takes them outside to the barbecue, where eleven cats circle and meow. Most of them are adopted strays; the oldest one jumped inside the filming truck ten years ago. The cats and I watch Martin hungrily as he slides the small birds on the barbecue, the flames leaping and sizzling around them.

"Entertaining in the country usually means sharing more of yourself with guests," he says. "When you have dinner together, you're likely staying overnight—it's not the drive-through visiting of the city."

When the quails are cooked, we go back inside. Martin ladles the steaming soup into freshly cut pumpkins for bowls. He's added chicken stock and chestnut puree to give it more savory richness. The soup tastes wonderful with several vintages of his Courtney Gamay, which offers superb instant gratification with its peppered raspberry and black currant notes. The fiery reflections in the wine are an antidote to the chilly fall air.

Gamay is a little lower down on the wine social scale, but Martin believes Niagara needs it to support the more aristocratic pinot noir. It's winter hardy and disease resistant and can be priced lower to fill out a product portfolio. "You need a dependable and affordable wine to make up for all the money you'll waste on pinot," he observes. He's even tried blending pinot noir with gamay. "We're too hung up on varietal purity," he says. "Pinot noir brings the complexity and silky texture, and gamay punches up the fruit and makes the wine more vibrant. As a winemaker, you need to keep your ego in your back pocket."

Alongside the juicy quails with their seared barbecue notes, we enjoy three vintages of Moira's Vineyard Pinot Noir. They flood the senses with fleshy aromas of damson plums and a core of stone-fruit acidity. Their smoky finish is a lovely match with the charred gamey notes of the quail. We also sample his estate pinot noir, which has a creamy texture and is pleasingly mouth-filling. "I don't want people to hit those tannins; it should have a velvet texture," Martin says.

As we finish the meal sipping on pinot, Martin grows reflective about his second career. "There are lots of times when I don't want to be in this business," he confesses. "We're trying to grow finicky fruit from a hostile land. But when someone tastes my wine and smiles or says they like it, that's all I need to keep going."

THE NEXT DAY, approaching Featherstone Winery, I can see a pepper storm of starlings flying over the vineyard. Husband-and-wife team David Johnson and Louise Engel have a passion for all things fowl. Before they became winemakers, they ran a gourmet poultry shop, selling tasty birds, from turkeys to quails. (That's where the "feather" comes from; the "stone" is the Niagara Escarpment.)

However, those hungry starlings that feed on the ripening grapes are no friends of David and Louise. That's why I'm going to meet their latest avian associate today, a Harris hawk that's trained to hunt those pesky birds.

In 1989, David started making wine as a hobby and won awards in amateur competitions. He began to spend less time at the shop and more in the cellar, eventually becoming certified with the Amateur Winemakers of Ontario judging program. In 1999, he and Louise sold the poultry shop and bought a farmhouse surrounded by twenty-three acres of vines on the Niagara Escarpment. The vineyard's lovely contours and rolling hills dip down to a small creek running between them. To the east is a rich stand of pine trees, and to the west looms the rugged rock face of the escarpment.

Louise Engel could be Peter Pan's sister, with her pixie haircut, impish grin, and compact frame that would be perfect for flying. I ask her about the harvest. "We *just* managed to pull this one out of the moat," she says. "After such a wet summer, we really needed those twenty-six days of sunshine. Could be a sleeper year, like 2008."

David comes out of the barn, taking off his heavy gloves to shake my hand. He looks more like an English professor than a winemaker, with steel-framed glasses and a serious expression. Louise tells him she's taking me to see the lambs—vital team members in maintaining the Featherstone vineyards.

David got the idea when he worked at Sileni Estates winery in New Zealand, where many wineries use sheep to nibble down the grass and unwanted vine leaves. ("This may have something to do with the fact that there are thirty-five million sheep and three million people in the country.") For larger wineries, the savings add up, especially since there isn't a ready source of cheap farm labor there. One New Zealand vintner, Peter Yealands, calculated that without sheep, he'd have to have seven tractors mowing his two thousand miles of vineyards a dozen times a year—at a cost of about $35,000.

"When I got back, we tried a few 'lambmowers' here," David says. The experiment was such a success that now about forty lambs arrive every July. Once they finish with the grass, they start eating the tender, young grape leaves that grow low on the vines. In the fruiting zone, where the grapes will eventually grow, the leaves must be thinned to give the bunches more sun exposure to ripen and better ventilation to avoid mold.

"Sheep are ideally suited to the job," David observes. "They can't reach high enough to damage the vine, and they're not interested in eating the unripe grapes. They graze 24/7, don't complain about the weather, and don't ask for days off. They also cultivate the soil, not just with their natural fertilizer of digested nutrient-rich grass but also with their hooves, which till the earth. That means less chemical fertilizer. Their environmental hoofprint is quite small."

There's even a vineyard tool called a sheep's foot for when the woolly kind isn't available. They eliminate the need for tractor mowing, which compacts the soil and reduces the biodiversity of the earth's natural microorganisms.

Raising vineyard-friendly lambs is now a niche market for some farmers, such as Cindy Deserioux, from whom David and Louise buy their lambs. Louise takes me to visit her postcard-charming farmhouse, where two dozen adult ewes run away to the pasture when they see us coming. Only the breeding ram, twice as large as the others, stands his ground and stares us down. "He's from Alberta and thinks he's hot stuff," Cindy comments.

The sheep are a low-slung breed descended from an ancient British mountain stock called Olde English Babydoll Southdowns. They're rugged, short-legged creatures that only grow two feet high at the shoulder, the perfect range for thinning vine leaves. Most are bred to be born in February and ready for work in July. Right now, in October, there are only two out-of-season lambs frolicking far out in the field, one black and one white. These babydolls are so damn cute, like bowlegged granny wigs. They're skittish around Louise and me, eyeing us with suspicion.

"Come here, girls!" Cindy calls in her sweet, motherly voice. If I were a lamb, I'd follow her anywhere. We move back and eventually they come bounding to the barn, where she feeds them.

At Featherstone, the lambs stay until the end of August, just before harvest. Where do they go then? ("Do you hear the lambs, Clarice?") David and Louise sell them to restaurants, where they finish their happy lives on plates matched with local wines. (Hey, it's the circle of life.) That's why Louise never names any of the sheep: "I'm never here when the truck comes for them."

Every fall, Treadwell Restaurant in the nearby town of St. Catherine's hosts a Featherstone Lamb Dinner. The menu celebrates the animals from snout to tail, featuring dishes like pickled tongue with lobster knuckles and celery root remoulade paired with Featherstone's Blacksheep Riesling, and then pan-seared liver with caramelized shallots and brown butter matched with the winery's Canadian Oak Chardonnay.

This is followed by a savory "odds and ends" (don't ask) shepherd's pie with whipped mashed potatoes and parsley bread crumbs served with the Cabernet Franc, stout-braised shank ravioli with confit shoulder and autumn ratatouille paired with the Gamay Noir, and a saddle of roasted lamb and garlic dauphinoise potatoes in truffled pan juices served with the Onyx Cabernet Franc Merlot. A selection of Ontario sheep's milk cheeses and homemade preserves paired with the Late Harvest Cabernet Franc caps the meal.

Back at the winery, Louise fills me in on the biggest problem she and other vintners face in this region: bird predation. It's estimated that North American farmers lose about $1.6 billion a year from birds and other crop predators. The Niagara grape growers association estimates that starlings destroy $15 million or 5 percent of wine crops a year. A flock of birds can strip clean several tons of grapes in a couple days, with a vintner's entire year's work sliding down those beaky little gullets. The fruit they don't eat they peck at and leave to rot on the vine.

Louise dislikes starlings. They're not even a native species but an import from England. In the 1870s, some idiot who was enraptured with Shakespeare decided to collect all the songbirds mentioned in the sonnets and release them in New York City's Central Park. The starlings fared best as opportunistic feeders and prolific breeders, and muscled their way into habitats across North America.

"They have no redeeming features," Louise says, her personal enmity showing. "They are parasitic rats with wings." She remembers

Thanksgiving 1999 with particular venom because "the friggin' starlings ate *all* our crop. That was when I became determined to do
something about it."

Modern technology has given vintners an arsenal of weapons to
fight the avian menace. Among the tools are advanced computerized
versions of the bird bangers that explode at random intervals so that
the birds don't get used to a pattern. Other wineries use "screamers,"
modified starting pistols that shoot firecrackers, and biosonic technology known as "squawk boxes," which broadcast distressed bird
calls. Then there are "terror eyes," balloons painted with the eyes of
predators; foil-glittering Mylar ribbons; reflective windmills; flapping
windsocks; and automatic guns that spray the vineyard with pebble
pellets. Some vintners (or their teenaged offspring) ride all-terrain
vehicles through the rows, dragging cans.

The problem with all of these approaches is that the birds quickly
adjust to most of the attempts used to scare them. For instance, they
learn exactly how far the automatic pellet spray reaches and stay just
outside its range, like an enemy outside the castle walls taunting the
besieged.

The most effective way to protect vineyards from birds is to drape
the whole property in nets. That works, though it's an expensive
solution, and they need to be replaced every five years. The nets also
make tending the vines more time-consuming. They can also cause
other headaches: after some birds became accidentally ensnared in
one local winemaker's nets, the provincial ministry of natural
resources fined him for "trapping birds out of season." (Fortunately,
the charges were dropped.) Most wineries use nets just for icewine
grapes, which are more vulnerable to birds because they must stay
on the vines until December or January. The precious (and pricey)
dessert nectar they produce justifies the expense.

However, Louise is about to demonstrate the one starling-repellent that really works. She introduces me to Amadeus, a Harris hawk with gorgeously sleek saffron plumage. She puts on a big leather glove and gently lifts him out of his wire pen in the yard. Louise is a licensed falconer who owns several hawks, though she's not required to have a license to own Amadeus (he's not an indigenous species). But she chose to get the qualification, enrolling in a two-year study program, to better understand him.

"Owning a hawk is a substantial year-round commitment," Louise says. "It's on par with owning and training a horse. They're not pets."

We start walking through the vineyard, Amadeus flitting ahead of us, from one trellis post to the next. I haven't been paying much attention to the background birdsong, but I notice that as we stroll along with Amadeus, the vineyard suddenly goes eerily quiet, as though every living thing has frozen into silence at the sight of a predator.

Hawks are trained entirely by the reward of food. Punishment is ineffective; unlike dogs, raptors couldn't care less about pleasing their owners and won't respond to a gruff tone of voice. Louise describes Harris hawks as the Ford pickup trucks of the raptor world: durable, dependable, and open to tailgating.

What about those little thieves that are his prey? Louise explains that the flocks that damage vineyards include both resident and migratory birds. The migrating birds start arriving in mid-August en route to their winter homes in corn and soybean fields in the southern United States. For those grackles, sparrows, crows, waxwings, and orioles, the Niagara vineyards make a lovely roadside diner. To encourage them to keep moving, Featherstone uses four propane bird bangers and a battery-powered squawk box, which sounds to me like a screeching bird hell. The bangers' only drawback is their effect on some tourists, who are convinced that the winery must be on prime hunting grounds and ask eagerly what's in season. (On the plus side, Louise quips, it's great cover if you ever want to get rid of someone during the fall.)

Niagara's year-round resident birds are mostly robins, starlings, and mourning doves that live in the woods bordering the farm's fields. Because the birds become accustomed to the bird bangers, Louise tries to prevent them from settling in, since they're much harder to remove once they establish themselves. That's why Amadeus is such a powerful "there goes the neighborhood" deterrent: his mere presence in the twenty-three-acre vineyard discourages them from settling in. Even if the hawk flies for just a few hours each day, he can establish dominance over the vineyard. However, when she doesn't fly him for a few days because of the weather or other projects, she notices that the bird activity increases again.

Some birds, such as robins, starlings, and mourning doves, are protected by federal law, so Louise needs a permit to hunt them even on her own property. She also needs a hunting license because a falcon is considered a weapon and must be registered like a firearm. Louise took the same course designed for hunters who shoot moose or deer with rifles. Hunting with falcons is a blood sport, which may be why only 10 percent of licensed falconers are women.

Louise tells me that when Amadeus does catch a songbird, he carries it to a tree branch, where he's hidden from other predators who might steal his lunch. He'll "mantle" his food, covering it with his wings while he eats. He plucks off the large feathers, then eats the whole bird—bones, cartilage, small feathers—in about twenty minutes. After eating, his crop (throat) swells visibly, and about twelve hours later, he casts up the indigestible feathers and bones.

Although he could snack on a starling a day, it's more natural for raptors to gorge three to four times a week and not eat in between. Captive raptors have their diets monitored vigilantly. Managing the bird's weight is critical: if he's too heavy, he won't bother hunting; if he's too light, he gets weak and unhealthy. Amadeus is weighed daily, and the result is recorded along with his food intake and weather. (When it's cold, he needs more food.) In the summer, his ideal flying weight is twenty-two ounces: if he gets just one ounce heavier than that, he loses interest in hunting, akin to the demotivational principle, such as too-high unemployment benefits.

Amadeus is part of David and Louise's commitment to both sustainable and organic farming. "We're not tofu-and-granola people, but this approach makes sense," Louise says. "I read a warning on a bag of synthetic fertilizer that said, 'Do not enter the vineyard for seven days after applying.' Well, we live here!" Instead, David spreads mushroom compost on the vineyard to help aerate the soil and improve its moisture retention during dry periods. This compost helps control weeds as well and reduces the need for herbicides. David plants cover crops of rye grass and radish to help control erosion and to enrich the clay with organic matter.

The couple also tries to minimize the winery's impact on the environment, using all of their resources efficiently, such as water and energy, and to use recycled and nonpolluting materials wherever possible. David stopped using insecticides in 1999. Instead, like Malivoire, he releases ladybugs and lacewings into the vineyard to control aphids. He releases pheromones to disrupt the mating cycle of the grape berry moth. By avoiding insecticides, the farm fosters beneficial insects.

While she's telling me this, Louise leads me into the tasting room. David joins us and pours us a glass of their Black Sheep Riesling, a medium-bodied wine with mouthwatering notes of melon, pear, peach, honeysuckle, lime, and tangerine zest. It would marry beautifully with spiced Thai cuisine, grilled salmon, and vegetarian dishes.

Next we try their chardonnay. Featherstone was one of the first wineries to use Canadian oak barrels to age wine. The trees are grown, harvested, air-dried, and milled near Ancaster, Ontario. Then the wood slats are shipped to California for coopers to make the barrels. It's the same species as American oak but with a tighter grain that supposedly imparts less oak flavor. Using Canadian oak on Canadian wines may make sense conceptually, but I find that the wood imparts a funky aroma, with an odd fennel aftertaste. Maybe it's just a matter of working out the toasting and cooperage methods.

We move on to several vintages of their pinot noir, my favorite wines. These bright young things wake up your mouth and enliven your senses. Pleasingly tart cherries dance across your palate, followed by a dazzling weave of truffles, rose petals, and spices. This wine would be perfect with a starling stew. (Four and twenty blackbirds baked in a pie would be better with their icewine.)

Next we try their cabernet franc, which dispels the misperception that Niagara can't make this wine without it tasting of bell pepper. Their rich version is loaded with ripe dark berries and mocha notes. A full-bodied, balanced flavor gives way to dried tobacco leaves and blackberries on the finish. This would be perfect with lamb and mint sauce—or perhaps with liver and fava beans.

As our wing-and-hoof visit draws to a close, I almost expect to hear the theme music from *Born Free* swelling behind us. However, the hawks and sheep are not some sort of stealth PR strategy; they're an integral part of the couple's approach to winemaking. Growing grapes can be a monoculture, so they like having the animals around to make the winery feel like a working farm.

"We want to get wine off a pedestal," Louise says. "That starts with our visitors seeing the vineyard for what it is: a grape farm."

* * *

IT WAS THE pop of a cork heard around the world. The results made headlines even outside the wine industry, with newspapers proclaiming "Chardonnay Shocker," "Transatlantic Upset," and "Tempest in a Wine Glass."

In 2009, an expert panel of fourteen sommeliers and wine critics gathered in Montreal to blind-taste and rank sixteen top Burgundian and Californian chardonnays—and, slipped into the lineup as a ringer by the organizers, one unknown from a Canadian winery. It was audacious even to contemplate a comparison. But when the results were announced, Le Clos Jordanne's 2005 Claystone Terrace Chardonnay from Niagara had bested all of the wines.

Journalists dubbed it "the Judgment of Montreal," after the similarly upsetting 1976 Judgment of Paris tasting in which French critics chose California's Chateau Montelena Chardonnay and Stag's Leap Cabernet Sauvignon over top French wines. This win helped to debunk the myth that Old World wines were inherently superior to New World ones. The story was later made into a film called *Bottle Shock*, featuring the splendid Alan Rickman who was ill-served with a mediocre script.

This morning, I'm on my way to visit the winery that put dry Canadian table wine on the map, just as Inniskillin had two decades earlier with dessert wine. However, finding Le Clos Jordanne is proving difficult. I drive up and down the Niagara highway several times before realizing that it's a large, green, windowless building—no iron-wrought gates, no cherub fountains, no scripted winery name.

Why is Canada's flagship winery hiding in an industrial warehouse? I get the full story later: the plans for the proposed temple of wine are still gathering dust in the offices of superstar Canadian architect Frank Gehry, whose builds have been described by the *New York Times* as "powerful essays in primal geometric form."

In 2000, Le Clos Jordanne's owner, Vincor—the Canadian company that also owns wineries such as Inniskillin, Jackson-Triggs, and Sumac Ridge—commissioned Gehry to design a building that would be part of the contoured landscape—not an easy task when buildings have hard edges. They hoped Gehry would do for Niagara what he had done for a Spanish winery, the iconic Marqués de Riscal, with its undulating rooflines that evoke the movements of a flamenco dancer.

Gehry's design for Le Clos Jordanne included a roof of billowing titanium ribbons to give the feeling of a cloud floating across the vineyards. Inside, floor-to-ceiling glass columns would reveal all aspects of winemaking. The goal was to capture the energy of the entire process in one visual sweep: sorting grapes, pressing them, fermenting the juice, racking the wine into barrels, aging the wine, and bottling it. It was the most ambitious project in Canadian winemaking history, a breathtaking concept—and so was the projected price of $30 million. That may be why the project came to a full stop in 2004, when steel and titanium costs started to soar.

Feeling like the guy who's come to read the meter, I pull open a metal door on the side of a building—and almost get forklifted into the air. I jump back as the driver reverses, the metal prongs sliding from under my feet to pick up the wine boxes instead. Inside the warehouse looks like Santa's workshop on Christmas Eve: people scurry in different directions, someone's climbing a ladder up a wine tank, trolleys whiz past, workers sort grapes at conveyor belts, engines rev and beep.

And look, there's Santa in the middle of it all! His hair is pepper-gray rather than white, and at six-foot-five, this jolly old elf is taller and leaner than the North Pole version. But with his merry red cheeks, brown button eyes, and warm smile, I know he's the man I'm looking for. Le Clos Jordanne's winemaker, Thomas Bachelder, comes striding across the room to say hello.

"Let's start in the vineyards," he says above the noise, as I follow him outside to the parking lot, where I hope to find his sleigh and reindeer. Instead, we climb into his standard-issue, mud-splattered winemaker's pickup truck. As we drive along the Niagara back roads, Thomas explains his winemaking approach.

"We're searching for the geography of flavor," Thomas says. "Let the vineyards express themselves. To do that, you need to get out of the way of your vines and just let them do their thing. You still have to watch them closely, but keep your paws off. We are trying to make small preserves of the land."

He also tells me about his own background. A former Montreal wine journalist, he had his first taste of winemaking in 1985, when his brother gave him a Beaujolais home kit for Christmas. "That's when I became more interested in making wine than in describing it," he explains. Thomas became a successful amateur winemaker, winning competitions. However, it was only when he and his wife, Mary, took a honeymoon trip to Burgundy four years later that he decided to make wine professionally. As honeymoons are wont to do, the trip revealed the depth of his true passion.

Thomas realized he needed to strengthen his winemaking education; his degree from Concordia University was in communication studies. So he enrolled in Burgundy's prestigious school of oenology and obtained the agricultural diploma in viticulture and oenology, becoming only the second Canadian to do so. While studying, Thomas apprenticed at two Burgundian wineries, where he met Pascal Marchand, the first Canadian to have studied at the school and his future boss. (The Quebec bench strength should come as no surprise: the province has a strong wine culture and a consumption rate that's 50 percent higher than Ontario's.)

After graduation, his classmate Luisa Ponzi helped him get a job with her father, Dick, considered one of Oregon's pioneer winemakers. Thomas worked for two years at Ponzi Vineyards in Oregon, then returned to Burgundy in 1995 as head winemaker at the two-hundred-year-old Château Génot-Boulanger in Meursault. He returned to Oregon as chief winemaker at Lemelson Vineyards for four years. During this "wine gypsy" period, he was gradually honing his skills as a specialist in chardonnay and pinot noir.

In 2003, Pascal Marchand, then an executive director of Le Clos Jordanne for Boisset, Vincor's joint-venture partner, convinced Thomas to join the winery. The Burgundian-based Boisset owns famous pinot producers such as Bouchard Aîné et Fils, Jaffelin, and Mommessin. Jean-Charles Boisset, the second generation to run the company, grew up near the Clos de Vougeot, the famous Burgundian vineyard. Boisset has created a global portfolio of wineries through joint ventures and other types of mergers. (In 2009, he married Gina Gallo, heir to the Californian wine dynasty.)

Thomas was drawn to Le Clos Jordanne's strong Burgundian culture of winemaking. Still, it was his native terroir that brought him back to Canada. "I didn't come home out of a dumb sense of national pride; I came because the potential flavors excited me."

He thinks back to those first days at his new winery. "When I arrived, there were no vines, no winery, just little sticks in the ground. I wondered if I'd made a mistake," he admits. "But the contours of the Clos were so beautiful that I just put my head down, took a deep breath, and went to work. I made the first vintage in one-ton plastic bins on the Jackson-Triggs loading dock."

With 130 acres planted, Thomas sought to identify the local flavor in each of the winery's four vineyards and express it in the finished wine—a highly site-specific Burgundian method. He tackled his project with a Jesuitical zeal that took an intellectual's approach to hard labor. He tested and selected the best Burgundian grapes to suit each vineyard, combining them with local natural yeasts. He tended and hand-pruned each vine as painstakingly as a medieval monk illuminating a manuscript.

Nothing Thomas did was revolutionary. It was just the first time someone in Niagara combined all of the classical and modern techniques—tightly spacing the vines; pruning, harvesting, and sorting by hand; keeping the yields low; fermenting in long, unhurried stretches; gravity-flow handling the juice—with the business and viticultural know-how of a Burgundian wine powerhouse.

The winery's most prestigious vineyard is called Le Clos Jordanne. The best grapes from its western side go into the winery's flagship wine, Le Grand Clos. The rest of the grapes from the eastern side are bottled as the Clos Jordanne Single Vineyard. The remaining three vineyards—Claystone Terrace, La Petite, and Talon Ridge—each have a single vineyard bottling from which only the best, most distinctive vineyard pinot noir grapes are used. The rest of the grapes from these three vineyards are blended into the Village Reserve wine. All of the vineyards except La Petite have both chardonnay and pinot noir grapes.

Le Clos Jordanne Vineyard is perched on a natural plateau of limestone soils and rich sediments on the escarpment. The Claystone Terrace Vineyard has heavier, darker clay soils that retain more moisture. This makes its wines more robust and masculine, with fleshy black-fruit flavors wound tightly around a core of minerality, acidity, and tannin. Talon Ridge Vineyard—at seventy-four acres, the largest of the vineyards—is located at the top of the escarpment rather than at its base. It has a southerly orientation, so it's influenced less by Lake Ontario's warming effect and more by the natural sunshine of the slope. With its cooler temperatures and stonier soils, the vineyard's wines are lighter and fruitier than the others. La Petite Vineyard is the smallest and most easterly. The combination of warmer temperatures and sandier soil with better drainage results in leaner but highly perfumed wines.

"No two vineyards are alike here," Thomas says, as we get out at Talon Ridge. "The glaciers pushed the limestone to the Canadian Shield in a heterogeneous way. But they all have a heady mix of glacial till that imbues the wines with outrageous perfume and a strong sense of place."

As we walk through the vineyard, I can just make out the sprawl of Toronto, hovering on the horizon across Lake Ontario like a moveable city pinned down by the CN Tower. Looking around, I see that the vineyard is draped in lacey white nets, as though dressed for a fall wedding. (It cost $300,000 to install them on 130 acres.) As the nets flutter in the breeze, the vines seem to be walking in a procession up the gentle incline of the hill. However, their feet are firmly planted in the limestone below us. Pinot noir, chardonnay, and riesling vines all love rock loaded with calcium, which manifests itself as nervy acidity in the wine.

"The idea is to liberate the trace elements in the soil," Thomas says, going down on one knee to dig a little around the base of a vine. "That means understanding the mineralization cycle in the earth so that when we plow the wild-grass cover crops back under, we make their nitrogen available to the vine roots."

As you might guess, Le Clos Jordanne grows its grapes organically. "With that approach, we're looking for *le juste milieu*—the happy medium," Thomas says. "We want to help the vines just enough to do their thing. Organic treatments sit on top of the soil, whereas synthetic chemicals penetrate the vines and get into their 'blood-stream.' Those chemicals standardize the vineyard."

Niagara's growing season, though short, is still one to two weeks longer than Burgundy's and starts later in the season due to the heat-sink effect of Lake Ontario in the fall. This gives the wines great fruit depth, with exuberance of pure pinot and chardonnay expression. To further focus their flavors, Thomas keeps yields down to just two tons per acre. That concentration shows in his wines, which have classic proportions and textural polish.

When I ask Thomas about the Judgment of Montreal tasting, he says, "It came out of the blue for us. We didn't even know our char-donnay was entered into the tasting." Even more surprising was the fact that the 2005 vintage was only the second for Claystone Terrace. Most Burgundian vintners wait until the vines are ten years old before making their finest wines from them. The lineup of sixteen white wines included Burgundian heavyweights such as the 2005 Hubert Lamy Clos du Meix, which placed second, and the 2006 Joseph Drouhin Clos des Mouches. Among the sixteen red wines tasted, the 2004 Château Mouton Rothschild from Bordeaux placed first.

The judges weren't permitted to talk among themselves as they tasted, in case they influenced one another's assessment. "The tasting room was like a monastery," said Marc Chapleau, the Quebec mag-azine editor who organized the competition. The judges had to guess the origins of each wine, and most assumed that Le Clos Jordanne was French.

The announcement of the winners was followed by the usual accusations of judging bias, a rigged competition, and statistically meaningless results. Of course, blind tastings can be overread or misinterpreted. One wine can be at its peak drinkability while another is going through a dumb stage, aromas and flavors muted or not yet developed. Some wines require years of aging before they taste good, while others are terrific right after bottling. The wines selected for the tasting may not represent the best from the region. As well, certain characteristics, such as big oak, alcohol, and fruit flavor, can make a wine stand out in a tasting, even though it may not be the one you want to drink with dinner. But even with all of these faults, consumers still love a side-by-side comparison, whether it's of pinot noir, Pepsi versus Coke, or Tide and the "other leading brand." We feel they reveal some sort of naked truth.

That may be why so many articles about Canadian wine still start with Inniskillin's icewine several decades ago, and why insider sour grapes didn't dampen the enthusiastic headlines or the cultural impact of encouraging wine drinkers to give Canadian wines a try. I can't help wondering, though, why it's even still news when a Canadian wine wins in competition. After all, New World wines from Argentina, Australia, New Zealand, and California have been besting the French for years where it matters most: in the market.

Thomas is a rising-tide-lifts-all-boats kind of guy and turns the victory into a win for all Ontario wines. "Any number of wines could have been in our place: Flat Rock, Tawse, Lailey, Inniskillin, Hidden Bench," he declares. "It just so happened it was our wine the organizers put into the tasting. It's gratifying, of course, but we need the Céline Dion–Shania Twain phenomenon in the wine world."

I think he's right; Canada needs cult wines that are famous outside of Canada. We think of Italy's Sassicaia, France's Château Margaux, and Pétrus, Australia's Penfolds Grange. They're the $10,000 haute couture dresses on the runway. Few of us can afford them, but we still try to buy a piece of their mystique with overpriced perfume, scarves, and handbags. Le Clos Jordanne is positioned to do just that with pinot noir.

After Thomas shows me the other vineyards, we return to the winery. The fresh wood of the barrels smells like caramel and pine. Thomas has arranged them to mirror the geography of the vineyards: those from southernmost Talon Ridge Vineyard are closest to the door, followed by the others by vineyard subparcel across the cellar floor. "So much of life is intent and visualization," he explains, drawing a sample of the Village Reserve pinot from a cask with a pipette and pouring it into my glass. This wine wraps the finesse of Burgundy around the power of the New World. The black cherry and cedar forest aromas unfurl, rising and sliding out of the glass, like one silky garment after another tossed into the air.

"Don't use too much oak but do use Burgundian wood," Thomas says, knocking on one of the barrels. "It has a tighter grain, so there's less interference from the vanilla and butterscotch notes that it can impart. Oak should oxygenate the wines slowly." He likes to blend barrels that are one, two, and three years old for a nuanced effect. "It's the averaging of the whole that matters.

"I love racy wines that ally finesse, perfume, and power—the kind that frustrate you as a winemaker and excite you as a drinker," he tells me. "In Burgundy, that's Chambolle, Vosne-Romanée, Volnay, Chassagne, Santenay, and Nuits-Saint-Georges. They're the sort of wines you love to distraction: you love them with your mind first, then your senses. I want wines that I still smell after the meal is over and the glass is empty."

I'm still sniffing at my glass even though I've long since emptied it. (I didn't "forget" to spit; I meant to drink it all.) Thomas refills my glass with some La Petite Vineyard pinot. Hundreds of fruit flies swarm around, taking kamikaze dives into my glass. I don't blame them; the wine has a plush, generous body, with a sheen of polished cherries. The small, shimmering pool of ruby in my glass is bewitching.

"The truth of the land is starting to emerge," Thomas says thoughtfully, as we sip. "We will make Ontario sing out of the glass."

The Claystone Terrace pinot is a butch wine that's powerful and masculine up front, followed by a floral finish that runs wild with macerated black cherries. A vein of violets and truffles rippling through it gives me gooseflesh. Nothing could top that, except maybe Le Grand Clos. Its towering structure and massively concentrated black fruit, dark spices, and deep minerality open the core of the wine like a sunlit glade in the middle of a forest. As I taste it, the winery noises fade away and I am alone with this wine.

"Niagara is blessed and damned by being so close to Toronto and Buffalo," Thomas says, bringing me back from my vinous reverie to commercial realities. "Having those large urban markets right on our doorstep has kept us from lifting our eyes to the world stage. We have remained provincial and unfocused in our grape choices." He believes that the region's wineries need to pull together to market their products and to decide on the flagship reds and whites—pinot noir and chardonnay, in his opinion.

How can the Vintner's Quality Alliance (VQA) support this varietal focus, I wonder. Certainly, this quality designation tells consumers which wines are made from Canadian grapes. However, a number of winemakers I spoke to believe that such appellation systems, with their regulations and fees, have no place in developing wine regions; they stifle experimental vineyards, technological innovation, marketing creativity, outside investment, and industry growth. Such systems, they believe, are better suited to mature wine regions (such as Champagne and Chianti), where it's important to protect established names, wine styles, and viticultural techniques. Their main goal is to prevent anyone else from using the names (and brand equity) for commercial gain. That's why the Champagne region of France has fought vigorously and successfully to prevent other sparkling wines from calling themselves Champagne or even having "made in the Champagne method" on the label.

I can't help wondering, then: is Canada an emerging region or an established one? I think it teeters on the edge. Wine grapes have been grown here since 1811. Children born the year of Inniskillin's big win are now of legal drinking age. A vibrant industry can't just be based on a niche wine like icewine. It makes a great gift and a special treat, but it's not what people put on the dinner table every night. A strong wine industry needs to produce good dry whites and reds—both premium wines, such as pinot noir and chardonnay, and more modestly priced workhorses, like vidal, cabernet franc, baco noir, and gamay.

The challenge for Niagara, and for Canada, is to establish an identity that is broader but still regional. Yet I'm not worried. There's a gorgeousness to these wines that will eventually draw people to them. And just as the little town of Niagara-on-the-Lake nestles quietly, almost hidden, near the noise and crowds of Niagara Falls, these wonderful regional wines are waiting here for anyone willing to travel the back roads of the wine world.

Field Notes from a
Wine Cheapskate

INSIDER TIPS

- While $25 to $40 a bottle may not seem like an inexpensive wine, value is relative. Pinot noir is expensive to grow and make.

Niagara pinots are a bargain compared to those in Burgundy, which easily top $50 a bottle as a starting price.

• When a region is stereotyped for one kind of wine—in Niagara's case, icewine—look for what else it does well, such as pinot noir and riesling. These are the best supporting actors, which often offer stellar performances in the glass.

• Organically grown grapes don't guarantee you a better or more healthful wine, but it does mean that the producer is paying close attention to the vine health and the winemaking process. That increases your odds of getting a better quality wine.

WINERIES VISITED

Featherstone Estate Winery: www.featherstonewinery.ca
Le Clos Jordanne: www.leclosjordanne.com
Malivoire Winery: www.malivoirewineco.com

BEST VALUE WINES

Featherstone Winery Black Sheep Riesling
Featherstone Winery Cabernet Franc
Featherstone Winery Pinot Noir
Le Clos Jordanne Claystone Terrace Chardonnay
Le Clos Jordanne Claystone Terrace Pinot Noir
Le Clos Jordanne Village Reserve Pinot Noir*
Malivoire Courtney Gamay
Malivoire Estate Pinot Noir

*My first pick for my own Tuesday dinner.

TOP VALUE PRODUCERS

Cave Spring Cellars
Château des Charmes
Creekside Estate
Fielding Estate
Flat Rock
Henry of Pelham/
  Sibling Rivalry
Hillebrand Trius
Inniskillin
Jackson-Triggs/Open
Kacaba Vineyards
Konzelmann Estate
  Winery

Legends Estates
Mike Weir Wine
Niagara College
  Teaching Winery
Peller Estates
Rief Estate
Rosewood Estates
Southbrook Vineyards
Tawse ·
Thirteenth Street Winery
Union Wines
Vineland Estates
Wayne Gretzky Estate

TUESDAY DINNER FOR A WINE CHEAPSKATE

You'll find Martin Malivoire's recipes for a delicious fall meal at www.nataliemaclean.com/food.

Marinated Quail or Chicken Thighs

Foil Potatoes

Pumpkin Soup

*Baked Upper Canada Comfort Cream with
Grilled Peaches and Icewine Reduction*

TERRIFIC PAIRINGS

Pinot noir is a wine of great sensuality, silky texture, and seductive aromas, such as black cherries, raspberries, violets, sassafras, mushrooms, truffles, and fresh earth. It pairs with a wide variety of dishes because it is flavorful but not heavy in alcohol, oak, or tannin. My favorite pairings include:

Beef bourguignon
Cheese: goat, Brie,
    Camembert, Swiss,
    Gouda, Gruyère
Chicken with pancetta
    and herbs
Chicken, turkey, goose:
    roasted
Coq au vin
Cornish hen, squab, quail
Curries: mild
Duck in port reduction
    or cranberries
Halibut: grilled
    with rosemary

Matzo balls
Mushroom risotto
Osso buco
Pasta with herbed tomato sauce
Pizza: vegetarian, cheese,
    mushroom, Margherita
Planked salmon
Pork chops or tenderloin
Prime rib or rare roast beef
Tuna: grilled or seared with
    pepper crust
Veal: breaded cutlets
Vegetables: grilled

RESOURCES

For information about Niagara wines and pinot noir:

Niagara's Wine Visionaries by Linda Bramble
Icewine: The Complete Story by John Schreiner

A Pocket Guide to Ontario Wines, Wineries, Vineyards, and Vines
by Konrad Ejbich
Ontario Wine Society: www.ontariowinesociety.com
Wine Country Ontario: www.winesofontario.org
Vintners Quality Alliance Ontario: www.vqaontario.com
Ontario Travel: www.ontariotravel.net
World of Pinot Noir: www.worldofpinotnoir.com

RELATED READING

The following books, while seemingly unrelated to the main subject matter of this chapter, provided some enjoyable reading before, during, and after my travels:

A Fool and Forty Acres: Conjuring a Vineyard Three Thousand Miles from Burgundy by Geoff Heinricks
The Heartbreak Grape: A Journey in Search of the Perfect Pinot Noir by Marq de Villiers
Silence of the Lambs by Thomas Harris

FOUR

WEDNESDAY

The Cape Crusaders of Africa

I CAN'T BELIEVE how many teeth this shark has. Two rows of pearly knife tips rim the top and bottom of his gaping maw. I can't see well enough to count them, though, since I'm several feet below the surface of the choppy Atlantic, off the coast of South Africa. The twenty-foot great white shark now circling me will replace his three hundred teeth every three months—over a lifetime that can span more than a hundred years.

Even when his dorsal fin slices through the water, his attacks are a terrifying surprise to seals, dolphins, porpoises, and other prey—a category in which I now find myself. As he comes in for his final attack, I lean forward to get a better look—I am always distracted by trivia. Luckily, I remember to pull my fingers inside the steel bars of my cage just before he slams into them. I almost feel sorry for the shark; he seems bewildered by the tamper-proof meat packaging. After a few seconds, he swims away to look for an easier meal. In these waters, it's eat lunch or be lunch.

Of course, thinking about lunch makes me wonder which South African wine would pair best with a juicy shark steak? This is the urgent question I put to Bevan Johnson, winemaker at Newton Johnson Winery, as he hauls me back into the boat after our bait-and-switch expedition.

"I'm not really sure," Bevan says as we dry off. "I haven't tasted a shark before, but then again, a shark hasn't tasted me, either, so I guess we're even."

Bevan, thirty-seven, with tousled blond hair and a love of surfing, could be mistaken for a Californian—except for his South African accent, which sounds like a cross between British and Australian. As we drive down the Hemel en Aarde Valley in his jeep, I look up at the avalanche of white clouds sliding slowly down the mountains. Rows of emerald vineyards stretch out to the ocean on this glorious March morning. It surprises me just how lovely the Cape wine region is. (Then again, most wine regions are scenic. This is why I don't write about plumbing fixtures and go on world tours of damp basements and smoggy factories.)

This is the only wine region in the world influenced by two oceans: the icy Atlantic and the warmer Indian Ocean, which meet at the continent's most southern tip, the Cape of Good Hope. Although South Africa's wine region is just thirty-five degrees south of the equator, at the same latitude as southern Australia, its climate is more Mediterranean than tropical, much like Italy. That's because the Atlantic ushers in cool air from Antarctica to counteract the African heat.

The Cape is the smallest of the world's nine floral kingdoms, with an area of only fifty-five thousand square miles. Despite this, it's also the most diverse, with more than ten thousand species of plants— more than the entire Northern Hemisphere. Seventy percent of plants here can't be found anywhere else on the planet. The indigenous shrubbery, called *fynbos* ("fine bush" in Afrikaans), is a collection of low-lying plant species that are critical to South Africa's ecosystem. The countryside is stitched in their jeweled colors: yellow and white orchids, red disa, fuchsia king protea, and orange pincushions.

You may be wondering what flowers have to do with wine. They're all part of the same complex interaction of weather, rock, and soil. The Cape has more than fifty soil types, ranging from granite and loam to sandstone and shale; they're the most ancient soils in the world, some as much as a million years old. No wonder, then, that a region that produces such a diversity of plants also produces such an incredible variety of wine styles.

This is my first trip to South Africa. For years, I confused the country of South Africa with the whole continent of Africa, based entirely on watching *Wild Kingdom* as a kid. See cheetah, see gazelle, see cheetah chase gazelle, see gazelle dash left, see cheetah almost get gazelle, cut to commercial. For more culturally aware individuals, South Africa may bring to mind Nelson Mandela, lions, apartheid, Archbishop Desmond Tutu, diamonds, slavery, cinnamon sands, famine, Charlize Theron, cardboard shantytowns, and Jane Goodall. Wine, however, usually isn't on the list.

I'd never associated Africa with wine myself until one evening as I sat sipping on a lime-fresh Mulderbosch sauvignon blanc by the crackling fire under a navy sky of starry pinpoints. Low growls came from rustling bushes nearby, but they didn't concern me. Okay, so maybe it was a wood-burning oven under glitter-glued ceiling with the piped-in soundtrack from *The Lion King*. I suppose it was only natural that my first taste of good South African wine would be at Disney World's African-themed restaurant Jiko (Swahili for "cooking place"), where they also specialize in prepackaged culture.

Did I mention that I'm a woman who enjoys the great indoors? I am not even a camping person, let alone a safari person. Those down-filled vests from L.L. Bean still hang in my closet with the price tags on them. Would I like to portage with a canoe and backpack through the wilderness, you ask? How about I'll meet you at the rustic Holiday Inn, where I'll be playing the loon CD and enjoying the minibar. However, the electrifying icy heart of the Mulderbosch sauvignon blanc was wildly different from anything I had tasted from South Africa—it made me curious (and thirsty) to learn more.

Winemaking in this region is nothing new. Five hundred years ago, European sailors would follow the coast of Africa south to the Cape, then turn northeast across the open Pacific to India to buy spices. Back then, instead of Good Hope, the Spanish named the headland *Cabo Tormentoso*—Cape of Storms. Still, it became a port of call for ships to restock supplies, especially fresh citrus fruit. The British ate limes to prevent scurvy, earning themselves the nickname "limeys." The Dutch, however, preferred wine, which is also loaded with antioxidants.

In 1655, Jan van Riebeeck, a doctor employed by the Dutch East India Company, planted "palliative vines." Four years later, he wrote in his diary: "Today, praise be to God, wine was made for the first time from Cape grapes." (A neighbor was less enthusiastic, noting in his own journal that the wine was only good for "irritating the bowels.")

The first governor, Simon van der Stel, gave his name to the settlement of Stellenbosch (Stel's Bush), today a charming university town in the heart of South Africa's wine country. The evening sun casts a reddish halo around the gabled rooflines of Cape Dutch manor homes and their sprawling verandas, which have the *Gone-with-the-Wind* grace of the Old South.

Simon van der Stel planted vines on his Groot Constantia estate, about forty-five miles from Stellenbosch. In 1688, the Dutch colony swelled with the arrival of the Huguenots, French Protestants fleeing Louis XIV's religious persecution. With the French expertise to guide production, the quality of the wines improved dramatically. They made Constantia's magnificent muscat wines, which at that time cost more than Bordeaux's famed Château d'Yquem. They achieved a concentrated sweetness by twisting the stems of the grape bunches on the vines just before they were fully ripened. This stopped the flow of sap to the fruit and resulted in grapes that were shriveled and raisined with concentrated sugars and flavors. Pickers dubbed them *oumensgesiggies*, or "old people's faces."

This dessert elixir was exported back to Europe, where it became wildly popular. Frederick the Great, Baudelaire, Longfellow, Charles Dickens, and Jane Austen were all among its fans. Napoleon demanded a steady supply for his exile on St. Helena. Thomas Jefferson shipped many cases to his Virginia home. German Chancellor Otto von Bismarck preferred it to his own Rhine rieslings. King Louis Philippe of France bought an entire vintage. Constantia eventually fell out of favor with European courts, replaced by more reasonably priced Hungarian tokaji. Recently, however, the Constantia estate has been revived and is again producing dessert wines of magnificent concentration and popularity.

The South African wine industry developed slowly for the next two hundred years and then suffered the same 1886 blight as the rest of Europe: the vine-killing root louse phylloxera. Growers replanted grapes that were more robust and high yielding, such as cinsault. They produced low-quality wine and were used mostly for distilled brandy. That industry flourished under apartheid, the government system of racial segregation, which also drew economic sanctions from major trading partners in the 1980s. As a result, South Africa's wine was poor or nonexistent for several decades—long enough for a generation of drinkers (like me) to be largely unaware of it.

Happily, more open international markets with the end of apartheid has fostered a winemaking revolution in South Africa. Today a new winery opens here every nineteen days. The industry employs more than three hundred thousand people and produces a billion bottles a year worth more than $3 billion, making it the seventh-largest producer in the world. Some of the largest and most inexpensive wine brands in the liquor store are from South Africa: Two Oceans, Sebeka, Nederburg, Simonsig, Fish Hoek, and Obikwa.

Of all the country's agricultural businesses, wine is the fastest growing and most profitable—despite searing droughts, fierce cyclones, bloody revolutions, and failing infrastructure. As the British writer Auberon Waugh observed, "The world is divided into the reckless, the brave, the amiable—and the rest. The wine community of South Africa is on the A-list. Even in this exasperating, least tamed (but most beautiful) of countries, it renders almost everything easier, funnier, profounder."

This brings me back to the adventurous Bevan Johnson, who's sitting beside me on the terrace at his winery. As we look out at the rolling gray Atlantic, we sip his syrah—liquid black plums roll down a velvet carpet of violets. It strikes me as a perfect transition wine to enjoy on a Wednesday between the lighter riesling and pinot noir early in the week and the more robust wines to come on the weekend. Rosemary and lavender perfume the salty breeze that blows off the water. I'm filled with a quiet happiness. I've found another pocket of like-minded obsessive personalities.

THE NEXT MORNING I drive up the green slopes of Paarl Mountain north of Cape Town to visit Charles Back, a winemaker who loves to butt heads with French authorities. He's named some of his wines Goats do Roam and Goat-Roti—puns on France's famous wine regions, Côtes-du-Rhône and Côte Rôtie. But there's a lot more to Charles Back than a flair for tweaking French sensibilities.

He produces some of South Africa's most coveted premium wines under the labels of Fairview and the Spice Route Company. He also founded one of the most successful black empowerment labels, Fairvalley. Charles was an early practitioner of many of the principles now formalized in the government-funded policy of Black Economic Empowerment. This aims to bring more black employees into management and winemaking roles, as well as improve labor practices, skills development, and employment security.

The Wine Industry Transformation Charter works within this framework and has the ambitious goal for blacks and women to own and manage more of the country's wineries by buying and redistributing land. However, grape farming requires highly specialized agricultural, technological, and marketing skills, which take years to acquire. It's also a capital-intensive business, with low profit margins—not an industry that attracts anyone who isn't already passionate about making wine. As a result, simply turning land over to new black owners doesn't work. Skills transfer partnerships, like Charles Back's at Fairvalley, are crucial.

Even Charles's Goat line of wines is no joke: he exports 65 percent of them to forty countries, and they account for 25 percent of South Africa's independently owned wine exports. Goats do Roam is the bestselling South African label in North America. In front of the Fairview winery is a twenty-five-foot-tall stone tower. Its most famous resident looks down at us from an open window at the top—an old billy goat with long gray whiskers. I learn later that he's a retired member of a herd of a thousand or so hoofers from whose milk Fairview produces a hundred tons of cheese every month. Charles's father, Cyril Back, started the herd back in the 1980s. Charles's grandfather, a self-taught winemaker who emigrated from Lithuania, bought this estate.

Charles approaches me while I'm still looking up at the tower. I jump a little, startled by this compact man with curly white hair and a bushy white mustache. His mischievous eyes seem to scan the area for something to climb up or nibble on.

"Natalie, I see you've met the bearded elder," he says warmly. "The first resident escaped and headed straight for the vineyards. As we chased him, we noticed he was eating only the Rhône grapes: shiraz, mourvèdre, grenache. So we made a blend based on what he nibbled," he explains, smiling, as we walk into the winery.

Inside, I notice the gourmet food shop to the left that sells his wines, cheeses, artisanal breads, and other comestibles. The whimsical names play here, too, such as Paarlesan, a Parmesan-style cheese. On the back of the package, a goat nibbles its way across the top of the bar code that looks like wispy grass.

"For some reason, the French get all twitchy when they see their place names on other wine labels," Charles says, as we walk through the busy tasting room, lit by twinkling lights on goat-horn chandeliers. Drinkers cluster around three tasting bars; the room is abuzz with French, German, Dutch, Japanese, and other languages. (I love the spittoons: gray milking pails.)

Charles's puns are a cheeky riposte to stiff French tradition. There's also Goat Door, a chardonnay wink at Burgundy's Côte d'Or, and the Goatfather, a blend of Italian barbera and sangiovese. My favorite label is from a cabernet blend: it has a rather blasé-looking female goat in front of a French château. The name: Bored Doe.

"The wines originally took off because of the critter-label craze, even though we weren't trying to be part of that," he recalls. "The anti-French sentiment in America over the Iraq war also helped, as some consumers saw these wines as a playful alternative.

"Eventually, I had to separate two lines because Fairview is serious and the goats are frivolous," he explains. "I didn't want to be known only as the guy who makes Goat wines."

Charles reminds me of Randall Grahm, the owner of Bonny Doon Vineyards in California, who also has an irresistible love of wordplay and Rhône wines. Randall's red wine named Le Cigare Volant is a mocking tribute to a Rhône town's ordinance passed in 1954 at the peak of the Cold War forbidding flying saucers—or "flying cigars," as the French call them—from landing in vineyards. His label in the traditional French sepia tones shows a cigar hovering over a vineyard.

Randall and Charles both embroider humor in unexpected places to deftly deflate wine snobbery. However, as Charles points out, the product still has to be good. "People bought the wines as a joke, but then came back for more. The first sale is based on the label; the second sale is based on what's in the bottle."

It certainly helps that the wines are value-priced under $13. Pricing wine is always tricky: too expensive and you exclude most of the market and get eaten by the competition. Too cheap and you suffer the fate of Hungarian, Chilean, and other wines that enter a market with rock-bottom prices and then never get out of that vinous ghetto.

As consumers, most of us like deals, but we don't like the word *cheap*, given its association with *trashy* and *worthless*. The notions of "inexpensive" and "inferior" are deeply entwined in our shopping culture, but it's a false assumption that price always equates with quality. A cheap wine isn't always a bad one, just as an expensive wine isn't always a great one. That's why my quest for good wine value is also a journey into good taste and authenticity. Those qualities aren't found exclusively in pricey wines.

"The consumer perception is that we have cheap labor and low costs in South Africa, and therefore we can produce cheap wines," Charles explains. "But that's not true. With the new post-apartheid laws to avoid further exploitation, labor is expensive. Land costs more per acre here than in the Languedoc. We need to charge more for our wines to stay competitive internationally. Cheap is strictly about price; value is about expectations and over-delivering on them."

Evidently consumers agree that the Goat wines delivered on their promises. The line grew so quickly that Charles created a new company for it and built two new winemaking facilities. His brilliant marketing is backed by solidly made wines. I find the reds, in particular, exceptionally well-made for the money: full-bodied with ripe black fruit flavors, eminently gulpable. If I were a French vintner, I'd lie awake at night worrying about these wines—not for their names but for their quality.

When France threatened to sue for trademark infringement, Charles took a busload of his farm workers to the French consulate in Cape Town. They sang traditional black struggle songs and presented the French attaché with a vacuum-sealed package of goat droppings for his garden.

"I have no idea how CNN heard about it, but they showed up with a camera crew," Charles says, grinning. "We got more from the publicity than we paid in legal fees. Unfortunately, the French backed off, and the story faded. I'd appreciate whatever you could do to stir up the controversy again."

I suggest he launch a new brand called Get Your Goat, with a label featuring French wine legislators and strategically placed ram's horns. He smiles and says, "Well, that would require some hands-on market research. Want to milk a goat?"

"Ah . . ." I hesitate, sensing a test. "You'll show me how to do it?"

"Oh no," he says, laughing. "My days of milking goats are *udderly* over. Let me call my chief goatherder," he says, flipping open his cell phone.

"Yes, she wants the full farm experience," he says into the phone. Then he calls his chief goat-to guy, Chris Bryant, the winery's webmaster, who meets us in the tasting room. Charles tells him: "Take pictures—and be sure to post them everywhere: the blog, Twitter, Facebook. Take this thing international."

We walk to the pasture, where small white kids frolic, kicking up their hooves behind them like children pleased with new sneakers. Others poke their curious pink noses between the slats of the wooden fence. In front of the barn, I meet Donald Mouton, whose last name really is the French word for *sheep*. He has a kind, weathered face and holds the leash of a large white nanny goat that stands docilely beside him, her udder swollen with milk.

"Oh, she's lovely!" I say. "What do you call her?"

"Um, we don't give them names, ma'am, because eventually they . . . have to move on to greener pastures," Donald explains. To cover the awkward moment, he demonstrates how to grasp the teat and pull it down. Milk squirts into the pail. It looks easy enough. He stands and gestures toward the goat, which seems to be looking at me with mild amusement.

I squat down beside the goat, leaning my cheek against her warm belly for balance. Donald, Chris, and a group of strapping lads in grass-stained overalls gather around to watch. I grab one of the teats and pull. Nothing. I try again. Nothing. My cheeks start to burn.

"Start higher up on the teat," Donald advises.

I do, and it works: a long stream of milk sprays at me and then into the pail. I feel Rebecca-of-Sunnybrook-Farm pleased. After I half-fill the bucket, Donald pours some of the milk into a plastic cup and offers it to me. I'm squeamish at first but then drink it. The milk is warm and summer-meadow fresh. I'm curious to see if I'll be able to taste the essence of this milk in the Fairview cheeses back at the winery.

When we're finished, Chris and I walk back to the winery. Charles meets us and asks with a devilish smirk, "What's that smell?"

As Chris leaves to write his blog post, Charles and I go into the Goatshed, the winery's restaurant. It's a busy place, alive with chatter, clinking glasses, laughter, and more milk pails. A young server brings us several bottles of wine and a plate of cheeses.

"Thanks, Victoria," he says, and she smiles warmly back at him. He knows every employee by name, and they respond as though they'd like to share a glass of wine (or beer) with him after hours.

"This restaurant alone has created twenty-nine jobs for people from here—we didn't bring in anyone," he says. "It's all about the right training. We have all the resources we need to do everything for ourselves." He seems to be referring more broadly to the South African wine industry and perhaps even to the country itself.

We taste his Roydon Camembert, with its earthy barnyard flavors, which is beautifully complemented by his Fairview Riesling, an off-dry white with notes of field flowers and white peach. I ask why he makes both cheese and wine.

"Cheese gratifies my impatience: if I have an idea for a new recipe, I make it, and three weeks later, it's ready," he says. "Wine is longer term, but it satisfies a deeper need."

Cheese, Charles explains, ripens and deepens in flavor from the outside in toward the center. His Pont-l'Évêque, an Alsatian-style cheese, has a washed rind that's been bathed in salted water and wine. This breaks down the curd and helps make it part of the cheese, rather than just the skin, intensifying the cheese flavor. Its wild pungency tastes civilized with his Fairview Viognier.

The wine is also surprisingly good with his Blue Tower cheese, which has more holes than a typical blue cheese. This allows the mold more room to grow, so the result is a stronger flavor. I had thought such a strong cheese would overwhelm such a delicate wine, but the wine's floral notes and perky acidity are up to the task.

His Fairview Chenin Blanc is terrific with Le Berle Blanc cheese, which has been aged on straw mats for three weeks to intensify its flavors. Chenin blanc, also known as steen, is the most widely planted grape in South Africa, accounting for a quarter of all vineyards. Sadly, much of it is still used for those cheap brandies and wines that come in two styles: paint-stripper strong or dishwater light. This marvelous wine is far removed from those liquid abominations. It's made from the oldest bush vines, whose grapes produce wines of extraordinary concentration and crisp citrus flavors that rival the best chenins from France's Loire Valley.

Almost three-quarters of South African grapes are white, another hangover from the brandy days. That needs to change, Charles believes. The country needs to focus on red wines, though not the best-known ones, such as cabernet sauvignon and merlot.

"With our climate, we should be looking to the Rhône or Spain or Portugal, not Bordeaux," he says. "When it comes to Bordeaux varieties, we have delusions of grandeur. Instead, we should take risks: plant new red grapes to see what works."

The man knows what he's talking about. Charles was the first in the country to plant varieties like mourvèdre, tannat, petite sirah, tempranillo, and souza, a Portuguese grape. His specialty, though, is shiraz. Plantings of that grape have increased sevenfold since 1990 and now comprise 7 percent of South Africa's vineyards. Shiraz may be best known as an Australian wine, but South Africa actually gave Australia its first vine cuttings.

Charles opens a bottle of shiraz, a smoky black-fruited wonder, from his Spice Route estate on the blustery Atlantic coast. He cofounded that winery in 1997 with three partners whom he's since bought out. The winery, housed in an old tobacco-drying barn, now produces ten thousand cases a year of Rhône varietal wines, which regularly achieve scores of 90 and above from critics.

We try another Spice Route wine, Chakalaka, which takes its name from the traditional, spicy South African relish. Made from low-yielding bush vines, it's imbued with vanilla smoke and fleshy plums with a midnight depth of crushed blackberries and cloves. It's delicious with the steaming plate of grilled springbok that Victoria sets in front of me. The dark meat of this gazellelike creature is tender and savory. The country's popular rugby team, the Springboks, won the 1995 World Cup match against New Zealand, made famous in the movie *Invictus*, starring Matt Damon and Morgan Freeman.

The springbok dish reminds me to ask about baboons, which I've heard make a dinner special of wine grapes. I had already noticed a few crafty baboons sitting by the road waiting for any edibles to fall off trucks. Charles tells me that marauding baboon troupes occasionally raid a vineyard, grabbing bunches of grapes and running back up the mountain. Efforts to deter them haven't worked, from erecting fences to scattering lion dung. Most vintners just write off the 10 percent loss each year to nature.

Wildlife aside, Charles believes in working with the people who are native to this land. In 1997, he donated sixteen acres of land adjacent to Fairview to sixty-three black employees and their families, who created the wine label Fairvalley. The government built the workers' homes. Charles helped with skills training and lent space in his winery to make the wine.

"You can't just throw money at these projects," he explains. "Affirmative action can't come at the expense of profitability because it's not sustainable. Labor laws are strict, land purchase is difficult, and falsely raising people's expectations is worse than doing nothing at all. Just transferring land is not going to change lives; you must transfer skills.

"True empowerment also can't be a marketing gimmick to gain consumer sympathy—politics in wine leaves a bad aftertaste. We have a good story here, and the legitimacy of that story is important—we have to be able to show the goods in terms of both the workers' lives and the quality of the wine."

To prove his point, he pours a glass of Fairvalley sauvignon blanc. It has the vibrant lime freshness of New Zealand, without the grassiness, and the lanolin-soaked richness of the Loire Valley. It sweeps across my mind like a spring rainstorm, carrying aromas of fresh-awakened earth and wild alpine flowers.

Charles's cousin, Michael Back, who owns Backsberg Winery, also worked with a group of black employees to create the Freedom Road label named after Mandela's biography, *Long Walk to Freedom*. Profits from the sale of the wine go to building the workers' homes. Still, less than 1 percent of the country's wineries are currently owned by blacks, despite the best efforts of businessmen like Charles and Michael. What inspired them to lend a hand?

"We always had two or three runaway or orphaned children living with my family when I was growing up, so my parents set a good example," he says. "But Fairvalley is not a charity. Charity is short-term and isn't based on economic value. This is a business proposition with a social dimension. I've been farming since 1978, and I know how much this land means to me. And all of these people worked the land with me, but none of them owned a piece of it."

It seems to me that few other winemaking regions have such historic moral obligations. Charles agrees. "Success, not legislation, is the greatest lever for change here," he asserts. "Other wineries see that you can do it and still make money. Something as simple as selling a good bottle of wine can change many lives. Three hundred workers make it, and they all have families—that's two thousand people."

Today, Fairvalley produces 150,000 cases of wine and exports to both the United States and the U.K. The original workers' homes are being converted into cottages for tourists to finance building new homes and winemaking facilities.

"Our industry has been playing catch-up for ten years," Charles muses. "Apartheid isolated us entirely from modern techniques of grape growing, winemaking, and marketing. We were denied outside capital investment for years, and so we were left in a time warp. We thought we could just pick up where we left off, but now we're paying the price. We could only watch as Chile, Australia, and California flooded the international market with decent, inexpensive wines."

Academics at Stellenbosch University devised the structure of apartheid (separateness)—the legal racial segregation of whites and blacks—which the National Party government introduced as law in 1948 and which lasted until 1994. In the late 1980s, twenty-three nations, including Canada, the United States, and the U.K., imposed economic sanctions against South Africa to protest apartheid, stopping all commercial trade with the country. This was just as the wine boom in North America was beginning: the CBS television show

60 Minutes announced the health benefits of red wine, and North Americans turned from hard liquors to wines and started ordering them by the grape.

Those forty years of isolation also took their toll internally. Most of South Africa's wine industry was controlled by the government-backed KWV (Kooperatiewe Wijnbouwers Vereeniging), the cooperative wine growers association that dictated prices, yields, production quotas, and varieties. It was geared to producing large volumes of cheap grapes for brandy distillation. Winemakers weren't permitted to travel abroad to get experience in other regions. The quarantine system made it impossible to import good vine stock. Chardonnay, for example, was illegal.

Then, in 1990, President Frederik Willem de Klerk began negotiations to end apartheid and freed black activist Nelson Mandela, who had spent twenty-seven years in prison. In 1994, Mandela's African National Congress (ANC) won the first democratic elections in which blacks were able to vote. Observers compared the end of apartheid to the fall of the Berlin Wall. They celebrated the planned revitalization of the country's wine industry—though at the time, they toasted the new democracy with truly terrible wine.

"Back then, we were exporting wines that were so bad we didn't even drink them ourselves," Charles observes. "That didn't help our image. After the Mandela effect faded, our wines had to compete on taste."

The real strides have come in the last decade; millions of people who moved away during apartheid have returned home, bringing with them an influx of talent. The average age of winemakers in the country has decreased by ten years, and this new generation has a more global perspective and training. Even the basic infrastructure now supports the industry. Under apartheid, only 30 percent of townships had electricity and running water; now, 80 percent do. The next step is for South African wine to reinvent itself, as Argentinean and Chilean wines have done. Early growth—replacing cheap bad wine with cheap good wine—is easy. The real challenge is sustaining that momentum as competition increases and as your wines move up-market in quality and price.

"One of the few good aspects of our isolation is that it kept us from developing a homogeneous international style," Charles says. "We're neither Australia nor France. We're the oldest New World country and the newest Old World country. So we can focus on making wines that are a different interpretation of what others are doing—wines that are uniquely South African."

THE STORIES OF Fairvalley and Freedom Road make me curious about other black brands in the country, such as Thandi, Tukulu, New Beginnings, Winds of Change, M'hudi, and Seven Sisters. A recent book titled *Ithemba* ("hope" in Nguni, the language of a pastoral South African clan) profiles more than thirty black vintners. It's partly an inspirational business story and partly an exploration of the industry's socioeconomic and racial transformation since the end of apartheid. It's filled with words like "righting historical wrongs" and "social upliftment" that hint at how deep and old the rifts are and how much work still remains to be done.

On the book's cover is a photograph of a beautiful woman in her late thirties who could be Halle Berry's sister. Carmen Stevens's head is cocked to one side, her lips curved in a just-watch-me smile. She's described as South Africa's first female winemaker "of color," a term that includes not just blacks but many other races in the country that Mandela described as a "rainbow nation."

This morning I'm meeting Carmen at her winery, Amani Vineyards, on the southern slope of Kanonkop, near Stellenbosch. Off to the west, I can see Table Mountain, its long, flat top draped with a tablecloth of white mist. It towers over the Capelands, a constant presence. Last night a fiery sunset drenched its granite dominance in Technicolor reds and oranges.

Amani is the Swahili word for "peace"; a metal medallion is affixed by hand to every bottle the winery produces. The winery is the physical expression of its name: the vineyard rows look as though they've been trimmed with fingernail clippers. Canna lilies frame the doorway. South African artwork—tribal masks, spears, and colorful paintings—adorns the walls inside the tasting room. On the floor is a large zebra rug. That's why I'm surprised to be greeted by a broadly smiling barrel-chested white man in his fifties.

"Howdy, you must be Natalie," he says with a deep southern U.S. drawl and an unhinging handshake. "I'm Rusty Myers. I own the place . . . Carmen will be right with ya."

We sit at an oak table by the tasting bar, and Rusty fills me in on his own history. He and his wife, Lynde, moved from Oklahoma to South Africa in 2002 to join Lynde's father, Jim, who had bought the farm the year before as a quick turnaround investment. Rusty had been a financial adviser and Lynde an ultrasound diagnostician, so they brought with them a passion for wine but no experience in making it. They decided to stay in South Africa and have since taken over the ownership of the winery. Rusty met Carmen in 2004 while she was working at another winery.

"I didn't hire her because I wanted her picture on my brochure; I hired her because she was good. Damn good. There she is now," he says, looking up.

Carmen stands at the doorway to the tasting room, haloed by the brilliant afternoon sun. She looks like a winemaking saint—with hellfire in her eyes. She's not what I expected at five-foot-one and maybe a hundred pounds. Then again, Carmen Stevens has spent her life not being what anyone expected.

"My mother worked at a clothing factory for sixteen hours a day to support her three young children," Carmen explains when I ask how she became interested in wine. "She didn't have time to help us with our homework, and I had trouble reading. But one day I found one of her romance novels on her bedside table. The book was set in a winery, and I was fascinated with the young heroine who tasted wines in a dark, mysterious cellar. I read all the books in the series and made up my mind to work in the wine industry."

After finishing high school, Carmen worked as a waitress to save money for the country's top oenology program at Stellenbosch University. She was told she required several courses in agriculture as prerequisites. She completed these, then applied again. This time she was flatly denied entrance. It was the early 1990s, and the entire student body of the university was white.

So she applied to Elsenburg College, another respected viticultural school in Stellenbosch. She was refused twice before finally gaining entrance in 1993, one year before Mandela's election.

"I was twenty-two when I stepped into a wine cellar for the first time, at Elsenburg," Carmen says, her eyes shining with the memory. "It was just like the novels described it, right down to those underground smells of oak and earth hanging in the air. I knew this was what I must do!

"There were only five women that year, the first time they also let women into the program. A lot of the guys thought we wouldn't make it," she recalls.

Her story resonates with me. When I started writing about wine, one of the most widely published wine critics in the country, a man of considerable experience, advised me to "treat it as a weekend hobby, sweetheart." I found that extremely motivational—to prove him wrong.

After all that initial rejection, Carmen was understandably nervous when she finished at Elsenburg. "I thought I was going to drown, I was so scared," she confesses. "I never expected to be welcomed into the industry."

However, luck was with her, or rather, her newly acquired skills and determination. She wanted to get international experience first and worked in California at Simi Winery with Paul Hobbs. She respected him most for how closely he watched his vines: "He'd say, 'This grape must come in at three o'clock tomorrow.' He knew that was the right time for that grape to be picked. That's the way I want to make wine."

In 1998, Carmen returned home to take a job as an assistant winemaker at Stellenbosch Farmers Winery, South Africa's largest wine producer. (It's since been renamed Distell.) The company created Tukulu, a joint venture with a group of black liquor retailers.

"The first year I made wine here, I spent hours at the tank just watching it," she says, laughing. "I was so captivated that I'd even come at night just to have another look. It was the most exciting thing I'd ever done."

When I ask Carmen about her favorite part of the process, she seems equally keen on it all. "I love the personal contact I have with the vines, and I love the link between eating the grapes and drinking the wine," she enthuses. "I taste every day; it's incredible how the wine changes in just a few hours. There's a secret code of communication when you taste someone else's wine. You may never meet them, yet you feel you know them through every bottle they make."

At Tukulu, Carmen worked with Paul Pontallier, the director of Bordeaux's first growth Château Margaux, who had been hired as a consultant. He taught her the master art of blending, the heart of all great wines. "It's one thing to pick up a glass and say 'that's nice' or 'it smells like dark fruit,' but the real trick for a winemaker is to isolate the components that create a great wine. You make your intentions real through blending," she says.

Carmen remembers Pontallier tasting her pinotage, looking up in surprise, and asking, "Did you make this?" She thought she'd done something wrong, but it turned out that he loved it.

She was all the more pleased because she believes that pinotage is the greatest challenge for a winemaker in this country. "You must make the exact right decisions at the exact right time," she explains, pouring us each a glass of it. "Pinotage, like one of its parents, pinot noir, is so fussy at every step in the process. And the longer it stays in wood, the darker it becomes—it'll run to black if you let it."

Carmen's pinotage has a luxurious palate weight, with layers of peppered raspberries, black cherry, licorice, and mocha spice. A smoky, velvet plum heart slowly emerges. We also taste some of her older vintages. As the wine ages, its aromas become less fruity and more like the leather, violets, and cigar box of mature bordeaux.

The story of pinotage is uniquely South African. In 1925, Abraham Perold, the first professor of viticulture at the University of Stellenbosch, crossed Burgundy's pinot noir with what he thought was Rhône Valley hermitage (syrah or shiraz). However, it was really cinsault, a more rustic French grape. He brushed their flowers against each other and the result was four precious seeds. He planted these in the garden of his home on the university's experimental farm.

Pinot noir, known as the heartbreak grape, is notoriously difficult to grow, susceptible to disease and rot. When handled well, it produces wines of great elegance and flavor. Conversely, cinsault is a hardy and prolific producer but usually only results in ordinary, tannic wines. Perold wanted to create a vine that produced flavorful grapes but could survive South Africa's climate and diseases. He evidently wasn't impressed with the results, though: two years later, when he left the university to work for KWV, he didn't take the new vines with him.

After his departure, the university hired a team of workers to clear his overgrown garden. By chance, Charles Niehaus, a young lecturer and former student of Perold, happened to be cycling past just as they were about to rip out Perold's pinotage vines. Niehaus recalled the experimental plantings and asked the workers if he could take them to a nursery. They let him, and he continued tinkering with the new breed.

The first commercial plantings didn't happen until 1943 when the name was changed from Perold's Hermitage x Pinot to the catchier pinotage. Herminot and a few other monikers were also considered. My suggestion for a name based on the tannic monsters that assaulted my mouth with flavors of varnished banana and cold fireplace? Pinosault.

Those early wines were dreadful. At one of the first wine shows I ever attended in 1998, I made the mistake of asking the man pouring the pinotage how a wine could be both jammy and bitter at the same time.

"They can't," the snippy wine booth guy told me. "You just don't understand the style."

Apparently neither did the head of the wine department for Christie's wine auction house, Michael Broadbent. In 1977, he led a group of British Masters of Wine around the Cape. He described pinotage as "hot and horrible," reeking of "rusty nails." The late wine writer David Wolfe described it as the "taste of apartheid."

Pinotage has long been the punching bag of wine critics who

often describe it as smelling like burned rubber. Think smoking skid marks on a hot tarmac. Of course, this imprecision isn't helpful: Were the skids from Michelin or Firestone tires? Steel-belted or radial? Was the tarmac on a small airport or a large commercial one? Nuance is everything in wine.

That description caught the attention of Florian Bauer, a biotechnology professor at Stellenbosch University. He and his research team grappled with the problem of defining the smell and its cause. He tried using gas chromatography to separate the various chemical compounds of pinotage to identify the culprit at a molecular level.

The professor and his research team flew to London to taste sixty South African wines alongside such critics as Jane MacQuitty, formerly the wine columnist for the *London Times* and a vocal critic of pinotage. They nailed nine wines as having the burned-rubber smell. The scientists took the wines back to Stellenbosch for another tasting and singled out two that were the most pungent. Those two wines were used to train tasters to recognize that particular aroma.

Part of the problem, as Bauer admits, is that smell and taste are such subjective experiences. The research was, in his words, "a response to an ill-defined description in a newspaper." Initially, his team was "not even sure what smell we were looking for," he wrote to me in an email. "Each person's perception of taste is different. One man's burned rubber may be another's sun-dried tomatoes. As well, people's descriptions of smells are imprecise. If you don't like a wine, you come up with your own set of terms: dry, medicinal, cat urine."

Back at Stellenbosch, the researchers examined possible causes: rootstock, soils, vintage, storage, and bottling. One popular theory was the leaf-roll virus, which prevents grapes from fully ripening: the virus makes the leaves roll up and die before the grapes can absorb enough nutrients from the sun. In the 1980s, almost every vine in the country was affected, and the Cape's late, hot summer exacerbated the problem. If vintners pick the grapes too early, they're still green and bitter, like a chicory rubber; if they leave them too long, the wine tastes jammy. The only cure for leaf-roll virus was aggressive replanting, which solved the problem for most fine wines that could handle the expense. The virus still flourishes in many bulk wine vineyards.

Still, the team couldn't identify the culprit, and they also found the burned-rubber smell in wines from other countries. The conclusion? Bad winemaking, particularly when fermentation is allowed to run too fast and too hot. Sulfur compounds that come into contact with bacteria can double. The result is a cooked character in the wine that can taste burned and bitter, almost like rubber. Regardless of the cause, South African winemakers were accused of denial and worse: cellar palate—they had become so accustomed to the smell of rubber, they no longer noticed it. Among good quality wines, the rubber smell isn't nearly as prevalent today, though I still find it occasionally.

All that controversy makes pinotage a hard wine to sell: it still comprises less than 3 percent of vines planted in South Africa. Many believe that pinotage is South Africa's viticultural flag, the equivalent of California's zinfandel. But I think that California's best wines are cabernet-based, not zinfandel. Cabernet is a noble variety, with great structure, complexity, and longevity. It's the reason bordeaux is a world benchmark.

In my opinion, pinotage, like zinfandel, can make good wines but not great ones. It works best when blended with cabernet sauvignon, merlot, or syrah—adding a dash of pepper and dark berries. It will always be a niche wine, loved by a small group of people and misunderstood by everyone else.

Among those devoted to pinotage are the judges of the prestigious ABSA Cape Epic competition. In 2000, they selected Carmen's 1999 pinotage as one of the country's top ten wines. She was the first woman to achieve such an honor. More commercial honors followed; the wine became part of the list for first-class Lufthansa passengers. The only downside was some sour-grapes mutterings attributing her success to being a token woman of color. Considering how hard she's had to work, that rumor makes her impatient that her wines don't stand on their own merits.

"Those are the same wrong-headed notions about why a black-made wine sells: because it's made by a black person? No, because it's a bloody good wine!" she says, pounding her fist on the table. "I remember an early advertising campaign with pictures of black people holding wine bottles. Who were these people? They were models! It's so important to show real people for our story to have merit."

That said, she acknowledges that she'll probably be known as South Africa's first woman of color winemaker for a while yet. "But I hope the adjectives eventually go away, and I'm just known as a good winemaker."

Carmen's life sounds like it's been ripped from the pages of a novel: the thrilling story of a young woman who defies odds and follows her heart to international success. The recognition from the competition brought Carmen offers to work at other wineries. Although she was reluctant to leave Tukulu, she accepted the position of head winemaker at Welmoed Winery because she wanted more responsibility at a smaller operation.

Her tough-minded capacity for unflinching hard work and focus also helped her through her divorce several years ago. During the proceedings, she heard about the Master of Wine (MW) program.

The most coveted designation in the industry, it's also the most difficult, requiring five years of intensive study. There are only 288 MWs in the world, and only 84 of them are women. The pass rate is just 10 percent. The odds were again against her, but as she said, "I needed something to take my mind off the divorce, so I applied." She was accepted as a candidate with a full scholarship.

"It opened up my world: the seminars, the travel, meeting people from different countries, tasting their wines. The Australians, in particular, are so generous—they'll tell you all their secrets," she says, laughing. "The program forces you to read more, to understand better, to dig deeper. I have more ideas now about what I want to do. If you stick to one formula, you've lost the plot. The mind is the best winemaking instrument."

We taste her Chardonnay Viognier, a lovely floral wine infused with green apple and apricot notes. There's a Condrieu aspect to it, a hint of ginger and white pepper. Mouthwatering acidity folds all the flavors together and magnifies them. This wine would be perfect with smoke-cured ostrich carpaccio.

"Acidity in wine helps with longevity because it's a preservative," Carmen explains. "But it also helps in your glass right now. After the big rollover of fruit on your palate, you want a clean, dry, refreshing finish. That's where acidity does its job."

Next we sip on her blend of cabernet franc and merlot that's a savory mix of blueberries, coffee, and graphite. The nose is on the move, changing now from blackberries to darker, tarry notes. Cabernet franc gives tannin weight and structure; merlot imparts plushness and fleshiness to the wine. "We give it a touch of oak to bold the palate, but the essence of the grape must remain."

Carmen's rich, concentrated cabernet franc reminds me of the observations of Herman Charles Bosman, one of South Africa's best-known short-story writers: "If you write for the press, why can't it be for a wine press? Your words will then all come out with thick purple sunshine on them. Your words will be like grapes and your thoughts will be like gold, rich with the splendid intoxication of the summer."

Call me shallow, but I agree. I'm just not interested in the technical minutiae of wine. I know that fermentation produces both alcohol and carbon dioxide, but for me, the by-product of wine is contentment.

We walk to the winery cellar, glasses in hand. Carmen tells me some stories from her time at Amani so far. Spotting a stack of barrels in one corner, she says that despite her diminutive size, she's actually "a very physical person. When I started here, I asked two muscular young men to stack some empty barrels. They weren't doing it correctly, so I stacked them myself, twenty-seven barrels in five rows, no machinery. I told them, 'This is how I want you to do it.' They just nodded and stared, but they did it that way every time after that."

As we walk farther along in the cellar, Carmen recalls another story. One of the cellar workers saw Carmen's pay slip on her desk and told all the other employees what she earned. Carmen gathered all the employees together. "I told them, 'Now you all know my salary. Well, my mother was a factory worker, and she earned the same as you do. So make sure your kids go to school, check their homework every night, and someday they can earn what I earn.'

"I believe that we must start with the children; put them in schools, give them at least one good meal a day, select the most talented, send them to university. You ask the children of the workers, 'What do you want to do when you grow up?' They'll all tell you they want to move to the city. They don't want to work on the farm like their parents because they have no idea that they could ever own the farm or be a winemaker."

The legacy of slavery and apartheid isn't just short-sighted career ambitions; it's also generational alcoholism. From 1928 to 1961, labor laws allowed farmers to partially pay their workers with cheap wine. The system known as *dop* (Afrikaans for "drink") only really declined in the 1990s and still continues clandestinely on a smaller scale. As a result, not only is alcoholism endemic among adults, but many children also suffered from the effects of fetal alcohol syndrome. A recent study of a thousand children in the Wellington wine region showed that almost 9 percent of them were affected, up from 5 percent in 1997.

Despite this, South Africa now offers the most guilt-free wine on the market for those who purchase with their conscience. The country is the world's largest producer of Fair Trade wines, made by companies that pay their workers fair wages and meet health and safety standards. As well, there are the black empowerment brands and those that are sustainably farmed, environmentally sensitive, and biodiversity conserving.

As Carmen says good-bye to me, she looks out over the vineyards. "In a previous life, I was a winemaker—and I'm coming back as a winemaker in the next one. In this life, I will own my own winery. It is inevitable because I must pass it on to my daughters."

MEETING ANTHONY HAMILTON Russell, the forty-seven-year-old owner of Hamilton Russell Vineyards, didn't strike me in advance as an unnerving prospect. It's only when the handsome, six-foot-four vintner walks up to me in front of his winery that I realize my mistake.

"Such a pleasure to meet you, Natalie—I've heard so much about you," he says with European elegance and a George Clooney smile.

"Huh, huh, ha-hi," I splutter with North American neuroses and a sardine handshake.

With merciful sensitivity, Anthony pretends not to notice my anxiety as he shows me in to the tasting room, a stone cottage with the vineyard plots of his 420-acre estate painted on the walls. He pours me a glass of his sauvignon blanc, and in the absence of any questions from this intrepid journalist, he launches into a presentation of soils and elevations. I nod vigorously until I regain myself, then wonder about questioning him on something he may have already said. I take a chance and ask him about the history of his family and the property.

Anthony's father, Tim Hamilton Russell, chairman of the South African arm of the advertising agency J. Walter Thompson in the mid-seventies, was an amateur wine enthusiast. In 1976, he planted a few vines in his Johannesburg garden and made a batch of wine in his sauna. He was so pleasantly surprised with the results that he decided to start a winery.

Tim had studied climatology at Oxford University, so he knew how critical climate was. He decided against building in Stellenbosch itself; all the country's wineries were there, so property was very expensive. He also wanted a cooler climate to experiment with pinot noir. In the end, he bought land on the tip of chilly, foggy Walker Bay, an hour southeast of Stellenbosch. His vineyard became the first in the region and the most southerly in South Africa.

Tim's wines were a success, and in 1989 he retired from advertising to devote himself full-time to the winery. Unfortunately, his winemaker and manager were used to an absentee boss and didn't welcome closer supervision. They resigned, and without their support or his executive advertising income, the farm went into a tailspin.

Things were looking grim in 1991 when Anthony, who was then a management consultant at Bain & Company in London, suggested that he come home to help run the winery. Tim agreed, surprised by his son's interest; until then, Anthony's only experience with wine had been, as he laughingly puts it, "drinking down his collection of bordeaux." But Tim thought him quite capable, as Anthony, too, had gone to Oxford, studying geography, and then had completed an MBA from the Wharton School of Business before becoming a consultant.

Indeed, Anthony exudes the confidence of a colonial baron. He brings to mind Cecil John Rhodes, the British industrialist who established a worldwide diamond monopoly when he bought all South Africa's diamond mines in 1880 and formed the De Beers Mining Company. Rhodes believed that "to be born an Englishman, is to win first place in the lottery of life." He established the coveted Rhodes Scholarships to Oxford University for colonial white boys not lucky enough to be born British. (It wasn't until 1977 that women were eligible for the scholarships. Even in 1989 when I and a few other women went for the finalist interviews, it still felt odd—like admitting women was a magnanimous indulgence.)

Like any good consultant, Anthony did his research: an in-depth analysis of the estate's soils. He discovered that clay and shale produced the best wines, so he narrowed the product line, focusing just on chardonnay and pinot noir—the two grapes that thrive in such soils and a cool climate. His efforts paid off; within several years, the winery grew tenfold, and Tim was able to retire from actively running the winery.

"It's a broadminded father who allows his son to take control," Anthony observes, handing me into his battered Jeep. "It's very male, territorial, chest-beating stuff, tied up with a sense of home and domain—it's not easy to give up."

As we drive up the curving gravel road, I see ahead of us the graceful manor house that Anthony built on the hilltop in 1996. He named it Braemar after the name of the original winery. It had been owned by a Scottish woman; the hills reminded her of the heathery moors near Braemar, Scotland. He chose that spot because it was where he would always stop to admire the view when riding his motorbike around the property. "There's an appealing balance between the mountains and the rolling vineyards," he says.

The house is built in a style that Anthony describes as Cape Georgian: simple and symmetrical, precise in scale and proportion. He worked closely with the architect to use local materials, even trying to bake his own roof tiles from clay mined on the farm, but there were too many breakages, so he ended up buying them.

As we get out of the Jeep, I notice three giant turtles on the lawn. Anthony tells me that these fifty-pound Leopard tortoises, more than seventy years old, are ex-pets, whose owners didn't want them anymore and set them loose. They turned up here one day, took a liking to the place, and have never ventured off the lawn in four years. "Ha, I think Sheldon just made a move on Agatha!" Anthony remarks, as one tortoise moves half an inch toward another.

They're not the only animal life around. As the front door opens, an enormous black Great Dane bounds out of the house and comes straight at me—as all dogs instinctively do, knowing that I am both allergic to and petrified of them.

"Horrocks, here, boy," Anthony calls, and the horse-dog skids away from me and gallops over to its owner. Horrocks is named for the large disheveled butler in *Vanity Fair*, which does absolutely nothing to redeem him. He's quickly joined by more household members, both canine and human. Next out of the house scampers a Great Dane puppy named Ophelia (after Hamlet's love interest);

then two golden retrievers, Como and Hendrix (after Perry Como and Jimi Hendrix); and finally, a lovely woman with long dark hair: Olive, Anthony's wife.

In the house, an airy dining room opens directly onto a pillared veranda with large sofas and chairs. Anthony incorporated this Italianate *loggia* to bring together the interior of the home with the rolling green hills it looks out over. The home is ideal for entertaining—and for wishing you could move into it. At the end of the manicured lawn is a grove of olive trees that meets the vineyards. Beyond them, I can see the fishing village of Hermanus, the calm blue expanse of Walker Bay, and the frothy Atlantic.

I still feel nervous, but I realize that writing about wine gives me an excuse to be invited into a beautiful home like this; to ask these successful, glamorous people bold questions; and in a sense, to invade their privacy. Writers are spies, nosing our way into other peoples' lives, making notes in our mental breast pocket to be analyzed in private, then revealed elsewhere. After reading my story about them, a number of winemakers have commented that I sucked in an incredible amount of information while I was with them. Yes. I'm always listening; nothing's off my radar or the record.

The pursuit of beauty runs through almost everything Anthony does. As he puts it, "Making wine isn't a business as much as it's an aesthetic pursuit." Every year, he makes dozens of visual improvements to the estate, from planting avenues of poplar trees to installing garden sculptures. For the last project, he hired a mason from the local funeral home. Every vineyard block is named after women related to the Hamilton Russell family, either directly or by marriage. When Anthony asked the mason to inscribe the four granite headstones with the women's names, "he thought we'd had a terrible number of deaths in the family," he recalls, smiling.

We sit in the dining room, and Anthony pours his 2006 Ash-bourne Sandstone, a crisp blend of sauvignon blanc and chardonnay. The wine is named partly after his great-great-grandfather, Lord Ashbourne, who was Ireland's lord chancellor in the late 1800s, and partly for the sandstone soil in which sauvignon blanc absorbs a mineral-marine depth. The chardonnay in the blend was fermented in clay amphora, which oxygenates the wine like oak barrels do, fattening and rounding its texture. We sip the wine while nibbling on Olive's homemade pine-nut focaccia bread and a Klein River Gruyère cheese. The creamy Gruyère folds into the richness of the chardonnay; the woodsy pine nuts dance with the sauvignon blanc.

"The wine is a sympathetic food partner, wouldn't you say?" Olive asks. I nod, feeling myself a sympathetic partner to the wine. I ask about the paintings on the walls.

"They're all by South African artists—Pierneef, Sekoto, Naude, Van Heerden, Boonzaier, Coetzer," Anthony says. "I started collecting them when I was eighteen, and they've gone up in value so much that I couldn't afford to buy most of them now. I never find that photographs of landscapes are as evocative as a good painting—it expresses so much more than just what's there."

That's his belief about wine, too: it's the distilled essence of place. Anthony talks about the "Hamilton Russellness" of his wines, their somewhereness. "They bear the unmistakable signature of the place. Even from year to year, you recognize them as you would different books by the same author. The story changes, but the style remains— the style is the soul of the land. I'm really more interested in place than in wine."

He's actually interested in a lot of things, and with great relief, the three of us chat about art, books, politics, and anything but wine for the next hour. Anthony loves to chew on an issue, peppering his conversation with witticisms and wide references. He pours us his Hamilton Russell Vineyards Chardonnay; the 1993 vintage was served to Nelson Mandela at a state banquet in Buckingham Palace when he became South Africa's new president.

The chardonnay is a pliant partner with Olive's gnocchi dish, with tender baby shrimp in a mayo-tomato sauce and slivers of avocado marinated in lime juice and lemon-infused olive oil—all topped with lightly toasted almond flakes. The wine's white pear and lime notes cut through the satiny avocado, and the vanilla-smoke finish weaves in with the toasted almonds. Like many chardonnays, this one is aged in oak barrels. Anthony imports the wood from the French forests of Alliers, Vosges, and Tronçais, and lets it air-dry on the estate to infuse it with the icy winds of the Atlantic.

I ask Anthony about the self-medicating sauvignon blanc I'd gulped down at the tasting cottage, having no recollection what it was called. All I remembered was the tree-top foliage freshness and the spine-chill of ice melting on granite. It turns out this wine was from a special project that Anthony started in 2005, on a thousand acres that adjoined the Hamilton Russell estate to the west.

"I wanted to protect the lands and stop more condo development, so I started a new winery focusing just on sauvignon blanc and pinotage. I named it Southern Right in honor of the southern right whales that come into Walker Bay every year to birth their calves. We make a donation to their conservation from every bottle we sell."

Olive brings out a fillet of beef in a creamy mushroom sauce, and some dishes of mushroom risotto, bright green beans, and baby beets. She believes that the best-stocked pantry is mother nature: she's a forager for food on the estate, and a curious cook who searches for new flavors behind a stone or a tree. She found the porcini and oyster mushrooms for the sauce in the pine forest beside the winery. They're oven-dried and mixed with some finely chopped jalapeño peppers for a hint of heat.

The mushroom sauce and risotto are earthy echoes of the pinot noirs that Anthony pours to accompany them. They're from the 2007, 2008, and 2009 vintages, along with the 2005 Ashbourne Pinotage. The slight charred quality of the pan-fried beef is hugged by the wraparound velvet tannin in the wines.

I'd love to drink them all; always a good sign. For me, quality is always in the second half of the bottle, or even the second bottle. It's whether you want to finish the wine or you've become exhausted by too much. Anthony describes those who buy his wines as aesthetes with a global perspective. I'd describe them as lucky. Even though pinot noir, notoriously difficult to make, is the benchmark wine here, he senses a greater challenge.

"I don't want my tombstone to read, 'He made great copies of burgundy,'" he declares. "I want to add something to the world of wine. Our chance to do that in South Africa is pinotage." Like Carmen Stevens, he's passionate about the wine. Anthony's whole reason for being is pinotage: site expressive, age-worthy, benchmark wine to show the world what South Africa can do. He blends in some other red grapes for complexity. The wine telescopes aromas of dark berries and open-fire wood smoke.

"South Africa is a hard country to place on the wine map; we're neither Europe nor the New World," he says. "We need to build more meaning into that middle place rather than trying to be a mini-Australia. Making wine is an expression of place, a gamble with nature, an accident in time. It's not that we're clever winemakers; it's just that we happen to live on an interesting plot of earth."

Earth and time also merged when Anthony did his soil analysis. He discovered that his estate is littered with prehistoric stone tools.

He now has more than a thousand specimens, which he invites me to see in his wood-paneled study. A large cabinet with glass shelves contains the collection: rough-hewn stones of various shapes and sizes. The centerpiece is a pear-shaped Acheulean hand axe made by *Homo erectus* 1.5 million years ago.

"The larger, cruder hand axes are usually older than the smaller, more intricate ones," Anthony explains with the enthusiasm of a gentleman paleontologist. "The tools themselves cannot be dated, but surrounding material in deposits where they're found can be. It astounds me that humans have lived on this very land for 1.5 million years." He takes a spearlike rock out of the cabinet and hands it to me. "When I found this tool in the garden, it looked like it had been dropped there the day before. I'm not a mystic, but these tools make me feel a deep connection to this valley's past."

Last year, he deepened that connection by starting to build a stone chapel beside the family burial plot, in a remote spot on the estate. Around it, he planted olive trees grown from cuttings from the Garden of Gethsemane. "I'm not religious, but I am spiritual," Anthony says. "I was inspired to build the chapel after I saw one of the vineyard workers praying under a tree here."

Looking to the future, he hopes one day to leave the estate to one of his four daughters, as his father did to him. "I wouldn't want the winery to be fragmented or sold in pieces, so I hope that the most interested or capable daughter will take over. I'm not worried—think of all the formidable women running the great wine estates of the world," he says.

Back in the dining room, Olive has set out malva pudding, a traditional Cape dessert: warm sponge cake with apricot jam and a hint of ginger. Over it is poured a melting custard with gooseberries, whose piquant tartness lifts the sweet warmth of the custard and cake. The dessert is a lovely contrast to the Muscat d'Alexandrie from

Aan De Doorns winery—Hamilton Russell doesn't make a dessert wine. With crumbs and empty glasses in front of us, we retire to the veranda tipsy and full.

"Mind if I smoke?" Anthony asks. I abhor cigarettes but love the smell of wafting cigar smoke; it reminds me of a mature bordeaux. From a wooden case he takes out a Cuban cigar, a Hoyo de Monterrey Epicure, and from his back pocket, surprisingly, he pulls out a ten-inch knife to cut the tip. The knife, he tells me, is his favorite from a collection of Mediterranean knives and has traveled with him to nine countries. The steel blade was made in the Italian town of Berti, just north of Florence, and its blonde ox-horn handle was crafted in central Africa.

The cigar lit, he takes long, slow puffs, arms folded, looking out over the hills. He's the benevolent feudal lord and the Hemingway man of action, yet there's also the Anthonyness of him. I am more interested in people than in wine.

"If you're lucky and you work hard, a winery can pay for itself," he says. "But it's everything around the winery—the people, travel, food, conversation—that are the real rewards. I live and work in nature—I don't spend two hours stuck in traffic every day to get to a cement tower." He gazes across the hills of his estate. "South Africa offers the possibility of an extraordinary life to those who are open to it."

Field Notes from a
Wine Cheapskate

INSIDER TIPS

- International trade bans are tough on any country, but it can motivate domestic industries to be more competitive afterward. South African wine has made amazing progress quickly following the end of apartheid.

- Check your perceptions about which regions can make wine. South Africa benefits from the confluence of the oceans as well as the cooling breeze of the Antarctic. Who would have thought that this created ideal conditions for growing wine? Now you know.

- There are so many terrific South African wines on the shelves these days. Start out with the familiar grapes, such as sauvignon blanc, shiraz, or cabernet sauvignon. Then, as you discover the producers you like best, branch out into their chenin blanc and pinotage wines.

WINERIES VISITED

Amani Vineyards: www.amani.co.za
Fairview: www.fairview.co.za
Hamilton Russell Vineyards: www.hamiltonrussellvineyards
.co.za

BEST VALUE WINES

Amani Vineyards Cabernet Franc Merlot
Amani Vineyards Chardonnay Viognier
Fairvalley Sauvignon Blanc
Fairview Chenin Blanc
Fairview Shiraz*
Fairview Viognier
Goats do Roam Pinotage
Goats do Roam Shiraz
Hamilton Russell Vineyards Chardonnay
Hamilton Russell Vineyards Pinot Noir
Newton Johnson Winery Syrah
Southern Right Sauvignon Blanc (Hamilton Russell)
Spice Route Chakalaka

My first pick for my own Wednesday dinner.

TOP VALUE PRODUCERS

Bellingham
Boekenhoutskloof
Bon Cap
Boschendal
Cathedral Cellars
Delheim
Diemersfontein
Drostdy-Hof
Durbanville Hills
Fairvalley
Flagstone Wines

Graham Beck
Ken Forrester
Le Bonheur
Meerlust
Mulderbosch
Nederburg
Obikwa
Porcupine Ridge
Robertson Winery
Rustenberg
Rust en Vrede

Sebeka

Simonsig

Spier

Stark Conde

Two Oceans

The Winery of Good Hope

Wolf Trap

WEDNESDAY DINNER FOR A WINE CHEAPSKATE

You'll find Olive Hamilton Russell's recipes for the dinner we shared with Anthony in their home at www.nataliemaclean.com/food.

Olive's Homemade Focaccia

Fillet of Beef with Mushroom Sauce

Mushroom Risotto

French Beans

Gnocchi-Avocado Ritz Style

Malva Pudding

TERRIFIC PAIRINGS

I find that many of the pairings that work for Australian shiraz also do well with South African shiraz. So in this section, I'll focus instead on pairings for South African's refreshing sauvignon blanc, with its signature aromas of freshly mown grass, lemongrass, gooseberry, green bell pepper, green melon, grapefruit, canned peas, asparagus, lime, nettle, acacia, hawthorn, and herbal notes.

Asian dishes

Avocado dishes,
    guacamole

Ceviche

Cheese: goat, Brie,
    Camembert, Gouda

Chicken and feta tostadas

Coquilles Saint Jacques

Corned beef and cabbage

Curry: green Thai

Lamb: Irish stew

Lasagna: vegetable

Mushrooms: Portobello

Pasta with cream or
pesto sauce

Pizza: Hawaiian, vegetarian

Quiche: spinach and
cheese, asparagus

Salads: green, Cobb, chef

Sauerkraut

Shellfish: crab, lobster, mussels,
oysters, scallops

Shrimp cocktail

Spring rolls

Sushi

Swordfish

Turkey: roast

Vegetables: green, especially
asparagus, peas

RESOURCES

For more information about South African wines and sauvignon blanc:

Africa Uncorked by John Platter
John Platter South African Wine Guide by John Platter
Sour Grapes by Neil Pendock
Wineries of South Africa: www.nataliemaclean.com/wineries
Wines of South Africa: www.wosa.co.za
Wines of South Africa USA: www.wosa.co.za/usa
Wines of South Africa Canada: www.wosa.co.za/canada
South Africa Wine Society: www.southafricanwinesociety.ca
Neil Pendock, wine columnist, South Africa's *Sunday Times*
blog: www.blogs.timeslive.co.za/pendock

RELATED READING

The following books, while seemingly unrelated to the main subject matter of this chapter, provided some enjoyable reading before, during, and after my travels:

Mafeking Road and Other Stories by Herman Charles Bosman
Long Walk to Freedom: The Autobiography of Nelson Mandela by
    Nelson Mandela
Conservationist by Nadine Gordimer
Jaws by Peter Benchley

FIVE

THURSDAY

Vino Under the Volcano

I EXPECTED SOMETHING a little more dramatic: the sizzle of a lava river oozing down the volcano, the rumble of the earth as it split between my feet, the screams of villagers running for their lives. Instead, all I hear are the clicks of tourist cameras as we look up at Mount Etna, its white tip puffing peacefully against the blue sky.

"To have seen Italy without having seen Sicily is not to have seen Italy at all," Goethe wrote. "For Sicily is the clue to everything." That's why I'm here on this island of dazzling sunshine and menacing shadows, with its barely controlled wilderness and passionate personalities. I've heard that the people here have fiery tempers, forming friendships over lunch and falling out by dinner. No one does vendettas like the Sicilians.

I like my wines with a little hellfire in them; volcanic viticulture fascinates me. Making wine from water is so BCE, but making wine from lava—now that fires the imagination. I also believe that just as Sicily is the clue to Italy, today's winemaking unlocks the country's vinous past. The ancient Greeks believed that Sicily was the birthplace of wine. One of their legends describes the journey that Bacchus made from Mount Olympus to the island, carrying a tiny vine in a hollowed-out bird bone. As he traveled, the plant kept growing, so he moved it to a lion's bone and then into a donkey's bone. When he got to Sicily, he planted the vine; and from the grapes it bore, he made the world's first wine. The symbolic message is that a little wine will make you as light as a bird, a little more will make you as brave as a lion, and a lot more will make you as dumb as an ass.

The Greeks called Sicily Oenotria, meaning "land of vines," from the Greek *oinos* for "wine." The Athenians invaded the island in 415 BCE, according to the historian Thucydides in his *History of the Peloponnesian Wars*, determined to spread Hellenic culture and government. Greek city-states such as Siracusa (Syracuse) had been long established on Sicily, along with the cultivation of grapevines. Homer described Sicilian vineyards as "watered by Zeus, yielding wine of strength in which ambrosia and nectar flowed in abundance." Odysseus used that robust local wine to intoxicate the Cyclops, so that he and his crew could escape from the island. The boulders strewn along the coastline are supposedly the ones that the Cyclops hurled after the departing ship.

By 404 BCE, the Spartans and Persians had helped the Sicilians to oust the Athenians, and they in turn were ousted by the Romans, who were eventually kicked out themselves by the locals. The island's strategic position in the middle of the Mediterranean meant that someone was usually invading it. You can see the successive conquering influences in the architecture of the capital city, Palermo: a Greek temple, a Norman church, a Roman theater, a Moorish roofline, Arab flourishes on a balcony and window, a Bourbon archway. Stairs between buildings tilt right and left like a game of snakes and ladders. The markets feel ancient and mysterious, bustling with colorful people and produce but edged with dark, shadowed alleyways. Palermo is an open-air museum: a boisterous blend of narrow streets, piazzas lined with multicolored mosaic tiles, fashionable wine bars and bistros, grand opera houses, and soaring cathedrals.

On this sixteen-thousand-square-mile island, a tiny football a mile off the toe of mainland Italy, there are about three hundred thousand acres under vine, more than in Bordeaux and Chile combined. It produces 185 million gallons a year, more than all of Australia. If Sicily were a country, it would be the fifth-largest wine producer in the world. Producers here refer to the island as a continent of wine for both its production and diversity.

As one of the world's oldest and youngest winemaking regions, Sicily is trying to resolve the conflict between ancient local traditions and modern international style. For years, southern vintners had no incentive to make fine wine for export. Grape prices were so low that producers earned more money making workhorse wines for local consumption and low-end export. Most wine made here was sold by the tanker-load to beef up prestigious but anemic wines in northern Italy and France, where it was often delivered to the estates' back entrances at night.

Sicily also has a cultural divide with the rest of Italy, especially the north, which produces some of the most beautifully designed clothing, cars, and wine in the world. The brand names roll luxuriously off a consumption-loving tongue: Ferragamo, Ferrari, Tignanello. In fact, few countries have such a contrast between an industrious north, with its sleek fashions, fast cars, and 4 percent unemployment; and a languid, lawless south, with its agrarian focus, slower pace, and 20 percent joblessness. There's even a divide between southern Italy and Sicily. The islanders refuse to build a bridge to the mainland just a mile away, even though it would help with commerce and tourism. No wonder Sicilians are often considered the most Italian of Italians: fierce, loyal, stubborn, passionate.

That divide in Italian culture extends to winemaking, which the rest of the world has long perceived as either cheap and cheerful or costly and confusing. Think of those squat, straw-wrapped chianti bottles (candle is optional) that epitomized the sixties and seventies. Now think of the sleek, gold-embossed labels of Super Tuscans, such as Sassicaia and Tignanello, that represented the greed-is-good eighties and nineties. There's never been much of a middle ground for consumers who just want good quality, reasonably priced Italian wines.

However, since the 1980s, the market for low-end wines has been drying up. The only way Sicilian producers could survive was to improve quality. And frankly, there was plenty of room for improvement. Unfortunately even today, Sicily's best-known wine is also its worst-regarded: marsala, a fortified dessert wine. Historically, it was hard to swallow, with its oxidized, burned flavors.

In 1773, when the British merchant John Woodhouse (stranded on Sicily for several days during a storm) tasted the wine at a local tavern, he realized that it would keep on a long sea journey if it were fortified with brandy. Marsala eventually replaced port as the British sailor's drink of choice, Nelson's navy drank it up, and Woodhouse retired a rich and groggily happy man.

Marsala is still unfairly tagged as plonk. This wine has the potential to be a divine after-dinner drink—a fact foreseen perhaps by the Arabs, who originally named the town *Marsa el Allah*, meaning "port of God." It's a mystical watery world between land and sea on the island's western shore, where the setting sun plays off the salt flats, sending shafts of red and purple light up through the clouds. Like sherry, marsala uses the solera method of aging: wine from the current vintage goes into the first barrel and is gradually siphoned from one barrel to another, year after year. Wine from the last barrel is drawn off to be consumed, and that barrel is then topped up with wine from the second oldest. This fractional blending preserves the flavor signature of the wine over years because, in theory, a little wine from the first vintage, and from all others since then, is in every bottle.

However, in the 1940s, marsala fell from grace, no longer suiting the taste of the times. Shoddy winemaking, such as adding egg yolks, almonds, and other unmentionable ingredients, hastened its demise. This syrupy wine was relegated to cooking sauces, no longer considered a digestif like port or brandy. Soon most Sicilian wines were described as *marmalata* because they were so jammy-overripe— hardly surprising when temperatures in Sicily can soar to 115°F during the harvest.

Even though Sicilian winemaking has improved considerably over the past decade, marsala's former image still sticks to it. Poorly made wines are like a crime-ridden neighborhood, tarnishing the reputation of an entire city. However, marsala is worth trying. It's graded according to color, sugar, alcoholic strength, and length of aging. The best types are Vergine (five years aging) and Stravecchio (ten years). Some of the most reputable producers today include Florio, De Bortoli, Martinez, and Lombardo.

One of my favorite Italian authors is Giuseppe Tomasi di Lampedusa, whose brilliant novel *The Leopard* chronicled the decline of the nineteenth-century aristocracy in Sicily. The author could have been describing the local wine industry when he observed: "If things are to stay as they are, then something has to change."

The setting of his book is now a winery called Donnafugata, meaning "fugitive woman." It was named for Queen Maria Carolina of Naples, who fled to the estate when Napoleon's army invaded her city at the end of the eighteenth century. My favorite wine from Donnafugata also has a romantic, windswept name: Mille e Una Notte—a thousand and one nights.

When the market for marsala collapsed in the 1960s, the local government created winemaking cooperatives that bought 80 percent of the harvest, mostly from small farmers. These co-ops still exist; the largest, Settesoli, is now the size of an oil refinery, capable of crushing more than 110 million tons of grapes. The company occupies much of the village of Menfi on the western shore, employs more than twenty thousand people, and owns more than 5 percent of the island's vineyards.

By the late 1980s, the market for bulk wine started to tank as well. Europe had become a wine lake, producing much more than it could drink or distill into spirits such as vermouth or even turn into ethanol for automobiles. Government subsidies dried up, and the big co-ops had to change their strategy. One of the most prescient executives was Diego Planeta, president of Settesoli, who started the drive to improve quality. With the help of oenologist Giacomo Tachis, who had just retired from the respected Super Tuscan winery Sassicaia, Diego planted experimental vineyards with a wide variety of grapes to determine which best suited Sicily's climate and soils.

The winner? Nero d'avola, the black (nero) grape from the town of Avola in eastern Sicily. Apart from small plantings in Calabria, on the toe of the mainland, it's only grown in Sicily today. Nero d'avola produces a wine packed with distinctive flavor, reminding me of the quirky Italian actor Roberto Benigni in *Life Is Beautiful*. This inky wine with a tightwire streak of acidity is as plush and quaffable as merlot, but it also has the darker, peppered-violet character of syrah. It shares the chameleon nature of Tuscany's sangiovese grape, which makes chianti such a round, generous wine, but becomes austere and structured in brunello di montalcino. It's a perfect complement to our Thursday night pasta meals.

Even within Sicily, the style of nero d'avola varies according to climate and soil. It can be spicy and taut like Rhône syrah in the limestone soils near Noto, or fleshy and fruity like Australian shiraz in the clay soils near Menfi. The thin-skinned, late-ripening grape is susceptible to rot, like merlot, and so it thrives in Sicily's hot, dry climate. The island is on the same latitude as Tunis, North Africa, and gets an average of 130 days of sunshine a year. A hot, stinging, sand-laden wind called the scirocco often blows north across the Mediterranean from the Sahara Desert, sometimes reaching hurricane speeds of eighty miles an hour. It ripples the horizon, whips up dust clouds, burns off excess moisture. The few raindrops that fall on Sicily acquire a sandy coating before reaching the earth.

Working a Mediterranean vineyard means tending a scorched garden under an apocalyptic sun. Until the sun sets, that is. Of evenings on the Sicilian coastline, Colombian novelist Gabriel García Márquez wrote that "the sea on windless nights reflects the beams of African lighthouses, while on the bottom of the sea lies a sleeping wine amphora."

When it comes to winemaking, nero d'avola is best when yields are kept low to focus the vine's nutrients in fewer grapes, which produces more concentrated flavors. It likes a slow, temperature-controlled maceration and fermentation to extract more flavor, color, and tannin compounds from the grape skins and seeds. These compounds give it structure, balance, and the ability to age. It also has the ability to blend; nero d'avola is a grape swinger, mating easily with merlot, cabernet sauvignon, syrah, and the local red grape frappato. On its own or blended, it's a wine with a robust love of flavor that's not heavy, making it an excellent house wine: it's charm-on-the-cheap.

Like most Italian wines, nero d'avola has a vibrant acidity that makes it taste fresh and clean. This helps it to pair well with the savory profusion of Sicilian food. The island's rustic cuisine is complemented by the flavors of many cultures: capers, olives, garlic, peppers, mint, fennel, almonds, raisins, citrus, and dried herbs. The

Arabs introduced spices, mint, fennel, saffron, eggplant, almonds, lemons, limes, oranges, raisins, capers, pine nuts, anchovies, pasta, pastries, and couscous (which they adapted to make a dish based on fish rather than lamb). The Greeks made honey, olive oil, and wine; the Romans grew wheat, vines, and beans; the Normans brought salt cod; the Spanish made rich tomato sauces. The food and wine here speak of history, terrain, identity, and people. You can devour Sicily's history on your plate.

The white wine grape that thrived in Diego's Planeta vineyards was insolia, a grape also known as inzolia or ansonica. It's the backbone of marsala, which never helped the grape's reputation. But by keeping yields down and using temperature-controlled fermentation, insolia produces a wine that's a wonderful jumble of white peach, mango, lime zest, and coconut sliver aromas. It reminds me of excellent dry riesling and makes my mouth water to think how well it would go with the island's seafood, especially fresh grilled swordfish with olives, tomatoes, and capers.

Diego was impressed with the results of his vineyard experiments, which included clonal selection, trellising, and irrigation methods. (Sicilian wine regulations forbid irrigation except by an emergency ruling, but there seems to be an emergency every year.) In 1995, he started his own boutique winery, Planeta, on the hillside village of Sambuca di Sicilia. Planeta's flagship nero d'avola, Santa Cecilia, is a heady aroma cloud of blackberries, sage, and dark chocolate. A potent core of dark, fleshy flavors roll over your tongue, finishing with a blast of black raspberries and anise. Dare I liken it to the smoldering, dark bride in *The Godfather*? Slap me twice if I try to weave *The Sopranos* into this chapter.

Still, it was Diego's chardonnay that first gained worldwide attention, receiving rave reviews in the 1990s. Critics compared it to the California cult chardonnay from Kistler, though some criticized it for having too much oak and butter. Like many vines in Sicily, though, his are more than eighty years old and produce grapes with enough depth of flavor to absorb the oak. In fact, some Sicilian chardonnays rival the elegance and length of good burgundy.

Soon other producers followed Diego, entering the world wine market with recognized, brand-name grapes. Some bemoaned the "cabernetization" of their wine industry and the loss of local identity. The international style has such market power today that it can trample eccentricity, the vinous equivalent of big, blond Texan hair and too much makeup that leaves little room for local, unadorned, odd-ball wines. By the late 1990s, Sicilian producers were blending international and local grapes to offer more interesting flavors yet keep the safety of brand-name grapes on the label. Since then, grape and wine prices have risen, fostering the growth of modern boutique wineries.

Even today, only one-quarter of Sicilian wine is bottled on the island, and just 2 percent is labeled DOC (*Denominazione di Origine Controllata*), the quality-control designation that specifies the approved grapes and winemaking methods. Maybe that shouldn't surprise us, since the Italians aren't exactly noted for following authority. Another 8 percent of wine is labeled IGT (*Indicazione Geografica Tipica*), which is like France's *Vin de Pays* (country wine) designation. What Diego would like to see is more family names on the labels to dispel the anonymity of Sicilian wine.

The Planeta family now owns a thousand acres of vineyards in three locations on the island, and the winery produces two hundred thousand cases. Six cousins work in the business; Diego's daughter, Francesca, is in charge of marketing; nephew Alessio is the winemaker; and another nephew, Santi, oversees domestic sales. Family is all-important in Sicily; everyone seems suspicious of everyone to whom they're not related. Did I mention that this is the birthplace of the Cosa Nostra? Palermo's Falcone Borsellino Airport is named after the two anti-mafia judges who were murdered in 1992. I'm afraid that's all I can say.

In 2008, the Planeta family started planting vines on Mount Etna to complete their "rainbow of Sicilian soil colors," as Alessio says. He believes the black volcanic earth produces wines of unparalleled depth and complexity. The soil, a mix of slivered rock, pumice, lava, and ash, has a low acidity that keeps the grapes' natural acidity from getting too high. It has many fissures, so it drains well. Another plus: the root louse phylloxera, which devastated the rest of Europe's old root stock, can't survive on volcanic rock, so many vines here are old and ungrafted or, as they say, *pied frau*, which sounds delightfully footloose and fancy-free.

So I've come to the volcano to taste the wines borne from these fractured rocks and fiery depths. The name Etna comes from the ancient Greek word *aitho*, meaning "I burn." At thirty-three hundred feet above sea level and covering 750 square miles, it's Europe's largest and most active volcano—almost three times larger than Vesuvius, which destroyed the city of Pompeii in 79 BCE. *La Montagna*, as the locals reverently call it, is supposedly the home of Vulcan, the Roman god of fire and smithery. The ancient philosopher Empedocles leapt into the crater in 430 BCE to prove he was immortal. (He wasn't.)

When there's an eruption, locals say *"scassau a muntagna"* ("the mountain has broken"). A 1669 eruption destroyed the hillside village of Catania and most of its twenty thousand inhabitants. Although the volcano has been fairly quiet since then, just a few decades ago, in 1985, Etna sprayed its fiery discourse across the sea for miles around. When it hardened, it left a lunar landscape onshore and daggers of black rock piercing the turquoise sea. The lava came *proprio vicinissima* (really close) to the vineyards. So far, the solidified rivers of black rock have stopped just a few meters above the vines. In such places, the locals erect white statues of the Madonna, her arms held out from side to side, as if to say, "Stop!"

In 2002, a major eruption closed the Palermo airport for two days of ashfall—islanders used umbrellas when they went outside. Etna still sends out smoky reminders of her presence, like a whispered "I'm still here." On this crisp April morning, though, she seems more prim than menacing: a fulsome Victorian lady wearing a snow lace collar above the folds of her black dress.

Leaving the tourist stop, I fold myself back into my five-inch Fiat. It takes about ten hours to drive to the top of the volcano, though I'm not going that far today. Still, with every twist and turn in the road that takes me higher up the mountain, my ears pop and my heart beats faster, as I wonder whether I'll come head-on with a tour bus barreling downward. Out of the corner of my eye, I see vineyards tucked between the medieval villages, chunks of volcanic stone in marvelously strange shapes crouching between the vines.

I'm on my way to meet Giuseppe Benanti, of Vinicola Benanti, a vineyard that's been in his family for eleven generations. I finally arrive, shaken but safe, in front of the stone winery that clings to the hillside like a small gray boat on a rolling ocean of green. The land has belonged to the family since 1734, when King Vittorio Amadeo II granted 320 hectares in the village of Catania to his faithful servant Antonio Benanti. The Benanti family were knights for the king, and he wanted to establish a large and loyal clan in southern Italy.

I learn this family history from Lisa Sapienza, the winery's export sales director, a beautifully coiffed woman with red-polished nails. She also outlines the business goals to merge science and tradition, which usually translates to: *We're using fancy technology to improve profits, but we keep our historical look in the brochures for branding purposes.* She leads me into the oak-paneled hall to meet Giuseppe Benanti, great-

great-grandson of Antonio. He looks just like the successful pharmaceutical executive he is: mid-sixties, silver-framed glasses, Armani suit, quizzical expression. His features resemble those of his ancestors, who seem to be watching us from the gold-framed portraits along the walls.

Giuseppe sits at the head of the oak table to my right, while Lisa sits across from me to translate, since apparently Giuseppe's English is not strong. Giuseppe's father, Lisa explains, taught cataract surgery at the University of Catania, preferring the sterile environment of the operating room to the family business. He didn't want muddy shoes, Lisa explains. He died in 1958, and the vineyards sat dormant for four decades, until Giuseppe decided to revive the winery in 1988.

As Lisa translates, Giuseppe watches me with his head cocked to one side and a faint smile. I nod and smile too much at both of them, unnerved by this conversation, which makes me feel like Alice with the Queen of Hearts and the Cheshire Cat in the tree.

Although he had followed in his father's footsteps, earning a doctorate in chemistry and pharmacy, Giuseppe remembered harvests with his grandfather: the grapes that smelled so sweet, the workers who sang the old songs, the outdoor feasts with everyone gathered around the table. His first challenge was buying back the estate, which had been divided among seventeen cousins. ("The first sixteen were no problem—it was the seventeenth who gave all the trouble.")

Next, he hired local winemaker Salvo Foti, who was working just a few miles down the road, making wine for Mick Hucknall, lead singer of Simply Red. After centuries of assaults from various countries, the latest invaders of the island are celebrities: Hucknall, Madonna, and Gérard Depardieu all own wineries here. Hucknall called his wine Il Cantante, "the singer." Though why he didn't use Simply Red and Simply White is a mystery—and a lost cobranding opportunity.

Unlike Diego Planeta, Giuseppe decided not to plant any international grapes. ("When in Rome, why eat at McDonald's?") Nor did he choose nero d'avola, which doesn't grow well in volcanic soil. Instead, he focused on Etna's two specialty red varieties: nerello mascalese and nerello cappuccio. These grapes are variations of the nerello mother vine, one of the oldest on the planet. They don't grow well anywhere else but thrive on Etna's ashen slopes, producing incredibly complex wines.

Mascalese is planted more widely than cappuccio; it's a slow ripener planted higher up the mountain, so it's often not picked until late October. The grape knows how to hold its acids and tannins, and yields wines with long aging potential. Cappuccio ripens earlier and is picked in September; it's fleshier and rounder, with very little tannin. The two grapes are often blended: mascalese has a cabernet character; cappuccio is considered more merlot-like. Rumor has it that almost a century ago, when Bordeaux suffered a vineyard blight, nerello was sold there as the local wine, and few people noticed the difference.

As Lisa is explaining Giuseppe's 150 trials on fermentation methods, he takes a small camera from his coat pocket and starts taking pictures of me. For the first few shots, I turn to smile at the camera, as if this is, of course, an expected part of an interview for any journalist. But when he starts tilting the camera this way and that, moving closer across the table and then pulling back for different angles, I become fascinated with Lisa's explanation of the fourteen yeasts that were tested.

"Dr. Benanti is a true visionary," Lisa says. I also suspect that he may be a lonely visionary, as the white flashes continue to my right. "He has brought forth the wines that best express the indigenous soil and the indigenous mind. He believes there is a difference between wines merely produced on Etna, and Etna wines made by Etna people."

"Mano Uona Etna," Giuseppe says, setting down the camera.

"Etna Man," Lisa translates. The door opens with the welcome distraction of an assistant carrying several bottles and three glasses.

"*Si, i vini*, they speak for themselves," Giuseppe says with surprisingly good English. "They speak better than we do, so let's taste!"

He pours his Rovittello, a blend of nerello mascalese and nerello cappuccio, from eighty-year-old vines. The wine has aromas of fresh-turned earth, dried tobacco, and blackberries. As the wine matures, the oak notes will recede as the tertiary nuances—aromas that develop from bottle age—emerge, such as leather and violets.

"We are pursuing the ancient fragrances," Giuseppe says as we savor the wine.

Next we try his Serra della Contessa. Drinking it is like plunging headfirst into a vat of fleshy plums. There's a mild tingling in the mouth from the dark spices, then a mouthwatering acidity that washes it away on soft layers of ripe blackberries that roll over each other. This makes you wonder if your first impression of the wine was correct. Naturally, you must take another drink to confirm. Giuseppe and I are confirming many impressions, while Lisa is now absorbed in her BlackBerry email.

"White wines must be young and fresh," Giuseppe says, smiling slyly, "but reds just get better with age."

Although Sicily is better known for its red wines, being more climatically suited to making them, two-thirds of the island's grapes are white. Most were originally selected for their resilience to extreme heat and drought. Obscure varieties such as grillo, grecanico, carricante, catarratto, damaschino, and insolia delivered large yields and were fermented at high temperatures, which resulted in whites that were tired and oxidized.

Today, though, improved techniques, such as night harvesting and temperature-controlled fermentation, prevent premature fermentation and allow the fresh fruit character to come through. Modern

Sicilian whites are crisp, clean, and zesty. Sadly, few of them travel well, so they're often not sold abroad. These lovely local wines are best consumed in Sicily, preferably on a sun-drenched terrace overlooking the dazzling Mediterranean. Sipping them is like staying at a small family-run inn rather than a big chain hotel.

Giuseppe pours me his Benanti Bianco di Caselle, a zesty white made from the carricante grape, with an apricot-lemon core. Tasting these strange and wonderful wines is like discovering an island of gem-colored butterflies when you've been living among moths.

"When I taste the wine, I see the vineyard," Giuseppe says enthusiastically. "You must see the vineyards, come!" As I marvel at how quickly he has become fully bilingual, we leave Lisa at the table, clicking away at her email, and head out into the fresh morning air.

Giuseppe's vines are cultivated using the ancient *alberello* method: low freestanding bushes tied to wooden stakes. The volcanic soil extends down a good thirty-five feet, giving the vines a longer life— many are more than a hundred years old. Vines of this age, Giuseppe believes, are best tended by people of the same age: "They understand each other." Walking through this forest of gnarled stumps makes me feel like a giant stomping through a magical forest where the trees might come alive any moment and wrap their limbs around my legs.

Giuseppe possesses each vine with his eyes. There is a fierce, visceral attachment to the land here; some families have owned their vineyards for generations, even if they've let them grow wild. Family-run operations have usually long since paid off their property and capital costs, so their wine prices don't have to account for these costs. Many of them are more interested in preserving the family name on the label than in making an overpriced "badge wine." There's another reason why wine is so affordable here: it's an intrinsic part of the culture. The diversity of the industry in terms of grapes, styles, prices, and quality is the result of a strong domestic market.

As we walk, Giuseppe plucks a stray leaf here and a dead branch there. "Winegrowers don't like things to come to an end; we are perpetual tinkerers," he tells me. "We know our vines personally and individually. When we prune one, we know exactly where to put our shears without thinking—like a lover when you put your hand on her waist."

His next question takes me by surprise: "Have you ever suffered from cenosilicaphobia?"

Huh?

When I ask him what that means, he shakes his finger at me with a conspiratorial smile: "Ah, only a crafty wine journalist would pretend she didn't know what cenosilicaphobia is. Very disarming, brilliant!"

"No, I can assure you that I'm just an ignorant wine journalist," I say, hugging my embarrassment. "I'm really just a highly functioning liver with a few superfluous organs attached."

Giuseppe laughs dismissively, refusing to believe me—or perhaps refusing to believe that he's spending so much time with someone who hasn't heard of cenosilicaphobia. So I admit reluctantly to having felt it once or twice, but not recently, still wondering what on earth he's referring to. Later when I check online, I discover that it means "fear of an empty glass." *Ceno* comes from the Greek word for "empty" (as in *cenotaph*, an empty tomb), and *silica* is the Roman word for "glass." Occupational hazard for those in the wine biz, I guess.

"Would you like to see my chapel?" Giuseppe asks me next, spider cunning in his eyes. "We are no longer *sconosciuti* (strangers)," he says, wrapping his forearm in mine. It's an offer from a Sicilian vintner I can't refuse. We walk down the cobblestoned path through the vineyards to a small white building, nestled amid silvery olive trees. The late-morning light burnishes the stained-glass windows and the golden pointed spire.

Inside, a twenty-five-foot ceiling invites my eyes upward. Large oil paintings of biblical scenes hang on the walls along with wooden crosses. Giuseppe takes me up to the tiny choir loft that overlooks two pews facing the small alter below. As we lean over the balcony, light streaming in through the windows like a Vermeer painting, he starts singing a Latin hymn. His rich, baritone voice fills the chapel. Then he stops, we smile in the silence, and we walk downstairs.

It is a contemplative end to the visit. As we say good-bye, Giuseppe says something to Lisa in Italian; his English has mysteriously vanished again. He looks away shyly as she translates: "Dr. Benanti says you ask questions with your heart. He hopes there is a good man at your side."

I smile at Giuseppe as we kiss on both cheeks, twice. When I climb back into my Fiat, Lisa walks back into the winery. Giuseppe stands in front of the chapel, waving.

SICILY IS ALSO known as *mezzogiorno*, "the land of the midday sun"—and of the midday nap. This May afternoon is so warm that I decide to take *la pausa* before my next visit. I love that notion of an afternoon pause: it doesn't sound lazy, just meditative. I retreat to my dark hotel room and flop on the cool bedsheets, mesmerized by my ceiling fan as its breeze evaporates the sweat on my arms and legs. Outside, a dog barks, someone laughs, a door slams. Then quiet.

After several hours of drugged sleep, I head out again along a rutted road farther up the mountain. The land on either side still seems wild, reminding me of Lampedusa's observation in *The Leopard*: "'Countryside' implies soil transformed by labor; but the scrub clinging to the slopes was still in the very same state of scented tangle in which it had been found by the Phoenicians, Dorians, and Ionians when they disembarked in Sicily."

I'm on my way to a small trattoria to meet Marco de Grazia for dinner. I spot him at a small table in the corner, a stocky, ebullient man with brown velvet eyes. A former wine importer in the United States, he recently started his own winery. "I had sold the most remarkable wines to dozens of countries for thirty years," he tells me, as he pours me a glass of his rosé open on the table. "But I have never sold a wine that everyone wanted as much as these. It's the power of Etna."

Marco's grandparents lived just southwest of Etna, where his mother, a successful Italian painter, was born. His father, Sebastian de Grazia, was a professor of political philosophy at Rutgers as well as an author; his book *Machiavelli in Hell* won the Pulitzer Prize. They met while Marco's father was on a fellowship in Italy, then moved to the United States, where Marco was born. They returned to Italy when Marco was just eight months old. Marco was also academically gifted, studying at the University of Florence, the Sorbonne, Rutgers, and Berkeley, earning degrees in philosophy and comparative literature.

"I guess the ineffable paradoxes of Etna draw unusual characters to it," he says, pushing back a red beret that gives him a Che Guevara look. "I suppose I must belong in that category as well."

Marco got his first taste of winemaking at sixteen, when he helped his best friend, Sandro, at his family's nearby farm. He recalls the first bottle that they shared one weekend when Sandro's father was away.

"I'll never forget that gentle beauty," he reminisces of that youthful escapade. "We had intended to drink it with a dish of snails—we had captured hundreds of them and kept them in the cellar, feeding them lettuce. But we discovered that they had escaped and were crawling all over the veranda, inching toward a getaway. We just sat on the steps drinking the wine, watching them and laughing."

A server brings us freshly baked bread with warm ricotta cheese.

It melts on my tongue with a tangy bite. I cup my hands around an earthenware bowl, steaming with fresh chunks of glistening pink tuna in a broth of herbs, garlic, and cognac. The evocative flavors of the ancient south waft up from the bowl, thick with flavor and memory. Marco's Feudo di Mezzo Il Quadro delle Rosé, with its aromas of field berries, goes beautifully with them.

Sicilian food, with its honest, rustic flavors, is a cuisine of the senses, with the fragrances of the fresh and local. The waters teem with fish; lemon, orange, and olive trees hang heavy with fruit; and the hillsides ripple with wheat for pasta. This natural bounty is perfumed with the flavors of many cultures.

"Sicily is a layered civilization, so many tribes and nations have contributed to what Etna is today," Marco says, his eyes closed as he breathes out the wine's finish. "Hands from around the world have worked this soil. Invaders come and go, but the land stays. Winemakers come and go, but the vineyard stays."

Despite his evident passion, Marco didn't think of wine as a profession until he was an undergraduate at Berkeley. He wandered into a local wine shop that had a decent selection of Italian wines but told the owner that he could do better. The owner didn't believe him, so Marco invited him to dinner at his apartment. They got sloshed on Marco's stash of wines from Italy, and the merchant offered him a job. Eventually, he became a full-time, independent importer.

Marco describes Etna as the Burgundy of the Mediterranean because its climate and soils also produce wines with an obsessive-compulsive edge. Like Burgundian producers, he doesn't blend grapes. "It's a difference in philosophy: burgundy versus bordeaux, Plato versus Aristotle, the ideal form versus moderation in many things," he muses. "Just as philosophy is the struggle to impose order on thought, winemaking is the struggle to impose order on nature. My goal is to express the classical ideal of wine."

Marco raises his glass. "We drink with the angels," he says as we clink tumblers.

The server sets down a platter of deep-fried calamari and a wooden board covered with *spinchone*, a traditional Sicilian pizza made with diced tomatoes and fresh basil. The calamari's crisp batter gives way to buttery richness in my mouth, and the tomatoes on the pizza dance with the tangy Etna Rosso, Marco's basic red made from nerello mascalese. The early evening light streams down from the high windows in the trattoria, catching the jeweled colors of the food and wine and illuminating our ghostly hands and faces like a Caravaggio painting.

"Sicily has the ancient recipe for producing great wines," Marco says. He pours his Calderara Sottana, also a nerello mascalese but made from the lower terraces in the vineyard, which produce more full-bodied wines. I'm entranced by its edgy eccentricity. It's a wine that teleports you to a place in your mind: I've disappeared into a grove of olive trees.

"The Mediterranean climate concentrates flavor, and an active volcano keeps everyone on their toes." But does he worry about the volcano erupting?

"The volcano gives so much that if, once in a while, it takes something back, no one seems to really mind," Marco observes with a volcanic mentality—that fatalistic happiness shared by those who live with other natural time bombs, like tornados and earthquakes. "Etna will devastate you and then give you everything. The more she betrays me, the more I love her.

"There's a certain edge to making wine when, at any minute, you could be buried under molten lava. Etna is the goddess of fertility, but she's six hundred thousand years old. Anyone can get cranky at that age."

Next we try his Santo Spirito Rosso, radiating the freshness of the mountain air and the power of the Sicilian sun. Its mineral core is wrapped in fleshy berry fruit flavors that pair beautifully with our entrée: a meaty red mullet baked in a pistachio crust. The bushlike pistachio trees are planted all over the island, and their green nuts are used in many local dishes.

"We need to stand out from New World wines flooding the market," Marco observes. "Even more, though, we need to cling to our heritage as we find a new way to do that." I have to agree: Sicilian wines strike me as an intriguing application of new methods on ancient grapes. The result is distinctly Sicilian yet also newer than *nuovo*. A good example is his Guardiola, a towering, tightly woven wine with a stone heart. The layers of blackberries and plums finish with a spicy slap of licorice.

After that, we enjoy a traditional dessert of cannoli: pastry tubes filled with ricotta cheese, candied fruit, and slivers of dark chocolate. It belongs to a category of desserts called *agrodolce*, with their contrasting flavors of sweet and sour. Cannoli supposedly originated in the city Caltanissetta (Kalat Annisa), where sultans locked up their harems in great castles. These women, bored out of their minds, made cannoli to pass the time. Another Arab creation popular in Sicily is granita, an ice dessert infused with the flavors of jasmine and rose petals.

Dinner over, we leave the trattoria as the lengthening light of evening drapes itself across the hills. Marco has suggested that we visit his winery, Tenuta delle Terre Nere (Black Earth Estate), nestled on the northern slopes of Etna, just a few minutes away. We climb into his VW van, which bears the scars of brushing against many vines and an argument or two with some larger branches. When we arrive, I breathe in the heady scents of fuchsia and oleander and wonder if there's an extra room, so I can move in.

"The challenge is to coax from this traditional grape my interpretations of these different patches of land," Marco says as we walk. "If I can do that, people will recognize these wines the way they recognize the sentences of certain writers. This is what we mean by terroir."

His hillside concave amphitheater has some thirty terraced rows, each edged with a low moss-covered black stone wall. Some of his vines are more than 140 years old, their green narrative punctuated by black commas of lava stone. The gnarled gray stumps lining each row look like grumpy old men waiting for the show to start.

"The more transparent I am as a winemaker, the better—I'm the least important link between the vineyard and the bottle." He waves away my protestations about his role in this wine. "My job is just to remove anything that might damage the vines and then stay out of the way." To him, that means gentle tilling of the soil so the roots can breathe, and a gravity flow in the winery so the juice isn't bruised. "I extract what's beautiful and leave the dross behind."

A light evening wind called *et alaria* makes the leaves tremble. I notice that they're planted in such a way that no vine covers another. This keeps the ventilation in the vineyard constant, which prevents mildew and rot. The vineyard style is said to be *a lada all'aria*, "in the air."

"There's a rhythm to this work and a joy in working with the seasons. I remember as a child spending October afternoons picking grapes, lathered in sweat, then plunging into the lake, the cold water shocking us.

"History takes a long time," he says, his smile not quite reaching his eyes. "You're making decisions today based on what you think the wine will be in twenty years. Yet making wine happens just once a year, so it takes a long time to become good at it." In his opinion, winemaking school gives you the technical skill to create correct wines but not exciting wines. "You need a palate that can distinguish good from great. Tough vintages are for the pleasure and interest of great winemakers; they seek and achieve the beautiful year after year."

Marco opens the door to his winery. Despite the late hour, the bottling line is in full swing, and the sound of clashing and clinking bottles rushes out at us. A half dozen employees are working the line, making sure the bottles are in place and taking the filled boxes over to the towering white stacks of cases. It's a gray mechanical whir, with a few human hands darting in and out.

In another area stands a stack of brightly colored boxes adorned with crayon drawings. They're the work of Marco's three-year-old daughter, Elena, after whom the wine is named. She produces a new set every year, so they graphically follow her development. (The profits from this wine go to the local children's hospital in her honor.)

We retire to his kitchen, where we sit at a rough wood table. Bronze pots hang on the walls, in between mesh bags of onions, garlic, and herbs. Marco seasons a nine-pound piece of steak on a wooden plank and slides it into the blazing wood-fired oven. Dried vines crackle and hiss, infusing the meat with a smoky flavor that curls around the kitchen. He's hosting a gathering of local winemakers later tonight.

"In Sicily, few things are what they seem," Marco observes as we drink his La Vigna di Don Peppino, made from pre-phylloxera vines that are 140 years old. There's nothing earthy about this wine: it tastes like clouds. We watch the sun wash the hills in greens and golds as it sets. "But once you come to terms with this most complex of places, learn to respect its profound identity—and work like a dog to express it—it will reward you with wines that rival the finest in the world."

THE NEXT MORNING, I drive farther up the mountain along a narrow, vertiginous lane called Passopisciaro, or "fishmonger's road." It was originally named after a seaman who used to sell his catch here on sunny afternoons. He charmed his female customers, generously offering them his services in addition to the seafood. Eventually, their husbands banded together and killed him.

Most of Andrea Franchetti's wines are labeled Passopisciaro, but his customers are safely scattered around the world. In 2001, having spent ten years in Tuscany making wines that received rave reviews, Andrea decided to buy land here. His nineteenth-century stone winery sits on a rock terrace as though it's barely glued to the ledge. His vineyards stretch their long green fingers around the mountain, trying to hold it.

When I pull up in front of his villa, Andrea Franchetti strides out to meet me. In his mid-fifties, six-foot-six, and looking like a successful Parisian architect, he sports square black glasses, a cashmere sweater tied carelessly around his shoulders, and highly polished Ferragamo loafers. He greets me, encasing my hand in a firm shake, and gets right to the point. (I'd heard he hates small talk.)

"I started making wine on Etna just to have an excuse to live here," he explains, unprompted, as we start an almost straight-up ascent of the mountain. "This is an authoritative land, the Orient of Italy—exotic colors, shapes, seasons, people. I came here not just because it's the best place for making wine but also for what it suggests to my imagination."

Andrea's family tree blooms with eccentric imagination on every branch. In 1530, his ancestor Giuditta Franchetti was burned as a heretic after she took to the streets, screaming and railing against the church. ("She was a polemicist and had a collection of books that the Vatican didn't like.") In 1894, his great-grandfather Giorgio Franchetti bought the famed Ca' d'Oro (the golden house), considered one of the most beautiful palaces on Venice's Grand Canal. The palazzo, with its ornate gothic style and lavish gold finishes, was originally built in 1428 by the Contarini family, which produced eight Venetian doges. Giorgio Franchetti helped to add some dazzling mosaics to the house. When he was finished, he committed suicide, donating the palace and his vast art collection to the city, where it is now displayed in the Museo Franchetti alla Ca' d'Oro.

Giorgio's brother was the composer Alberto Franchetti, who wrote widely acclaimed operas for the Belle Époque, such as *Asrael, Cristoforo Colombo, Germania*, and *Notte di Leggenda*. Alberto's mother, Luisa, had learned to play the piano from Franz Liszt. Andrea calls Alberto's son Raimondo Franchetti "the Italian Lawrence of Arabia," noting that he explored Borneo, Ethiopia, and the Sudan. "He was a quintessential Italian explorer—he crossed the Abruzzo Park at night alone, when it was full of wolves." Raimondo died in 1935, when his small plane crashed in Africa's Great Rift Valley. He later became the inspiration for the dashing adventurer *Corto Maltese* in Italian comic books. Raimondo's son Nanuk was an ichthyologist, mountain climber, speleologist, and friend of Ernest Hemingway—Hemingway often hunted ducks in his marshes.

In the early 1950s, the Franchetti family ran a circus that traveled around Europe. Andrea recalls his father's gypsy soul and his love of dressing in circus clothing. While in the United States, his father met his American mother, heiress to a South Carolina textile fortune. She moved to Rome with her new husband but didn't trust Italian hospitals, so Andrea was born in New York. She returned to Rome, where Andrea grew up. His mother made him sing in the choir of the Sistine Chapel until his voice broke at thirteen.

When he turned seventeen, he jumped on his bicycle and pedaled from Italy to Afghanistan via Brindisi, Istanbul, Tehran, and Kabul. Then he sold his bike in Afghanistan and went home by train. "It was the best trip of my life," he says now. "I was fanatical, frightened, and alone."

When Andrea returned to Rome, he started writing for the Italian magazine *L'Espresso*, made two avant-garde films, and acted as an extra in several movies. When he got restless again, in 1982, he moved to the United States to become an importer of Italian wine. That, too, failed to hold his interest after four years. In 1986, he moved back to Italy and bought a Tuscan villa. "When I woke up the first morning, I decided to make wine," he says. "I could not go back to city life, even with its exuberance of people coming and going."

As he strides up the mountain and I pant to keep up with him, Andrea sweeps his hand to indicate a broad swath of land. "All this was a tangle of weeds and thorns. I had to use a pickax to clear it away. But it was worth it, just for the light. When I arrived, I was struck by it." He pauses to look around as I start to sink onto one of the low rock walls.

"A sash of light lay along the mountainside, through hidden carpets of broom and wild roses, inviting restoration. The sea reflects shadows and light up to the sky, which throws them down into the vineyard. It's a saturating light that illuminates my vines on every side. Luminosity, yes, but even more: limpidity, a crystalline light that comes from how close we are to the sun," he says, answering the question I haven't asked, and starts back up the mountain.

"I am inspired by the way the light changes about around me throughout the year, with its days of green and red and gold, the white mornings and violet nights. The weather swirls round us. The powerful process of photosynthesis affects both the vines and the owner. The transformation of berries into wine is a shade of nature's essence, hidden, then caught by surprise in the turmoil of fermentation, captured in a thick, red mirror."

While he's talking, I notice the lava stone terraces encircling Etna, following the slope's steep decline. They look as though Vulcan had absentmindedly traced a finger around and around the mountain. The walls were actually built by peasants a thousand years ago, without a bulldozer or drill. I think about how their fingers must have bled.

Today, it's difficult to hire vineyard workers, since climbing the slopes is exhausting. It's a world of clouds and stones. "I had a team of swearing Frenchmen who were accustomed to the light soils of Médoc," he tells me. "Still, they came back, year after year. They accept that you're a foreigner, so you're already crazy."

We're standing at thirty-three-hundred feet, and the deliciously cool air lines my lungs with mint. Andrea's vines are planted at the highest possible elevation on Etna, where the difference between day and night temperatures can vary greatly. This diurnal dip extends the growing season a month or so longer than on the rest of the island. It also creates polished wines of superb depth, acidity, and minerality.

While Giuseppe Benanti and Marco di Grazia are traditionalists, Andrea is a modernist. He plants and blends both international and local varieties, and has little patience for those who scorn this. "The wine itself is more important than the grapes that go into it," he says. "What you taste isn't just an expression of nature, it's also an expression of thought." Like many modernists, he thinks that nature is overrated. "Nature buffets the imagination, prods it to create, but we are the greatest mystery."

Andrea learned how to make wine in Bordeaux and has planted those varieties here: cabernet franc, cabernet sauvignon, merlot, and petit verdot. Those vine cuttings came from old parcels of vineyards that had produced some of the best wines in Graves and Saint-Émilion.

"For the French, making wine is like breathing. They're generous and will tell you everything you need to know. Bordeaux winemakers have selected and discarded for generations and have gathered a number of grapes that are exceptional both by themselves and in their capacity to be blended with others."

Those plants, Andrea explains, had it too easy in Bordeaux: he had to thin 60 percent of their crop late in their first summer when they started to lose their vigor. He believes that small berries are the secret of good red wines: more concentrated flavor and better air flow between bunches so that mold doesn't set in. These small stressed grapes thicken their skins to protect themselves and concentrate on maturing their fruit. It's also best, he believes, to make wine from at least three types of grape, each maturing at a different time. Then, ideally, at least one grape every year will fit its particular cycle to the weather changes of that vintage.

"We interpret this place and create terroir where none existed before," he says. "Etna wines harness the lush fruitiness of the grapes with the acidity of the volcanic soil in an ineffable combination of contrary impulses." This creates a concentrated wine, he says, that is more recognizable and imprints itself in your memory. "Every year that passes increases the wine's identity, its ability to become more itself. That is terroir: a taste that says, 'Ah! *There*.'"

Understanding terroir involves understanding the times we live in, he explains. The vineyard changes with changes in taste. When wines meant to be consumed after the softening of long aging are in vogue, a vineyard is starved, production reduced to a quarter to concentrate the wines.

"Our image of wine is as capricious as our views on architecture, fashion, and automobile design," he continues. "Right now, our idea of viticulture is the restoration of nature. That image is stressed. Once we considered ourselves titans ruling over the earth, exaggerating our interventions. So now it's time for us to be humble and follow nature."

However, he does listen to nature to time the harvest, the most important and difficult part of what he does. "People get too damn poetic about harvest time. You work your ass off all year long, and then you can lose it all in an hour. It's wet and cold and discouraging.

What's romantic about that?" he says, his voice growing hard and enameled.

"Viticulture may be the Hollywood of farming, but it's lost its way and is too caught up in the glamour. We are farmers. Every year, you think you've lived through it, but you haven't; you suffer horribly. You should *never* talk to me during harvest," he says, tightening his eyes on someone in the past who made that mistake.

Got it.

Once harvest is over, he assembles the wines that have emerged from more than fifty fermentations. Slowly a style forms, he says, from discarding and choosing and mixing. His resulting wine receives the full I-don't-need-to-earn-a-profit treatment that comes from starting a winery with family wealth: barrels made from the finest French forests and rigorous declassification of any less-than-perfect wine into a second label. His top wine is left on its lees for a year to develop in a crescendo of flavor.

At last we sit down on the rock wall, and Andrea reaches into a tuft of wild grasses behind it and pulls out several bottles and a couple of glasses. The first one he opens is his petit verdot. As he pours me a glass, he observes, "A vein of tar sneaks into the taste of all the wines of this area; we must take care not to lose it." As I sip, I'm not getting the tar, but I do taste that lovely Italianate bitter-fresh, dark-savory flavor of chiseled darkness, with two opposing forces holding tension down through its center. I feel as though I'm invading the private history of the grapes in this wine.

As we drink, he continues. "I don't want to make fruity wine; I'd rather eat fresh fruit. I want to make an earthy wine because I want to taste this place. Vines have such a long vegetative cycle that they really show the territory in their fruit. The ground under our feet was once the ancient ocean floor. The crushed fossils of prehistoric creatures are in the sediment of this wine."

I nod in agreement, my mind more on the warm Mediterranean light moving across the slopes. I think of D. H. Lawrence's observation of Etna: "Anyone who has once known this land can never be quite free from the nostalgia for it." Then I think of the volcano again. Does Andrea worry about it?

"Not at all. We are gladiator winemakers here: all or nothing," he says, smiling as he pours me his cabernet franc. "The danger gives your work a knife-edge focus. This is an insane way to make wine." This dark-berried wine is insanely good. It seeps through my pores and along my veins until I'm running warm and flush with its flavor.

"You need to discover what is too much, to cross that line and then come back. The mountain draws stubborn people to it. It gives us something to struggle against—ourselves."

Looking around, I spot a few blackened patches of earth to our right. Andrea tells me that the local shepherds burn the grass because tasty and nutritious plants sprout up afterward that are good for their flocks. Unfortunately, several times these uncontrolled fires reached his vines. The twisted dark stumps look like dead hands reaching out of their graves.

"Oh, that's such a shame," I say, consoling myself with more wine.

"Everything dies, Natalie," Andrea says, his eyes settling on me. "There's something joyfully self-destructive about Etna. Nature throws an element of desperation at you, and you respond. You can't change nature, only your response to it. The value of life is defined by death. Here we live on top of a symbol of death—and enjoy life more because of it."

Field Notes from a
Wine Cheapskate

INSIDER TIPS

- Ultra-fashionable wine regions often get all the attention for any particular country, as do Italy's Tuscany and Piedmont and France's Bordeaux and Burgundy. Look for the lesser-known regions for your best value bottle, like Sicily in Italy and southern France's Languedoc-Rousillon.

- Some of the most ancient wine-producing regions are now the "newest" ones in that they've revitalized their techniques and styles. The advantage is that they have a deep knowledge of their soils and grapes, and often, family-run operations aren't paying high capital costs, since these have been paid off long ago.

- Regional food and wine matches often make sense, since the food and wine "grew up" together in the same soils and climatic conditions. It's not a rigid rule but a great starting point when you're looking for pairings.

WINERIES VISITED

Passopisciaro: www.passopisciaro.com
Tenuta delle Terre Nere: www.marcdegrazia.com
Vinicola Benanti: www.vinicolabenanti.it

BEST VALUE WINES

Planeta Insolia
Planeta Nero d'Avola
Tenuta delle Terre Nere Etna Rosso*
Vinicola Benanti Bianco di Caselle
Vinicola Benanti Rovittello

My first pick for my own Thursday dinner.

TOP VALUE PRODUCERS

Ajello Majus
Canaletto
Cantine Colosi
Cantine Francesco Minini
Caruso & Minini
Cusumano
Donna di Coppe/
    Nativo/Picciotto
Donnafugata
Duca Di Castelmonte/
    Cent'are/Cavallina
Fazio/Torre Dei Venti

Feudo Arancio
Feudo Montoni
Firriato
Girelli/Lamura
Lagaria
Morgante
Pellegrino
Planeta
Podere Castorani Picciò
Rizzuto
Spadina

THURSDAY DINNER FOR A WINE CHEAPSKATE

You'll find delicious Sicilian recipes that are similar to the meal Marco and I shared at www.nataliemaclean.com/food.

Fresh Tagliolini with Cuttlefish Sauce and Olives

Deep-Fried Prawns and Squid

Red Mullet in Pistachio Crust and Oregano Sauce

Redfish and Broken Spaghetti Soup

Cassata of Ricotta Cheese

TERRIFIC PAIRINGS

Beef roast or stew
Cheese: bianco sardo, cheddar, smoked, Swiss
Chicken: herb-rubbed roasted
Pasta alla norma or tomato sauce
Pizza: ambrosia, meat lovers, neopolitan
Red mullet
Sausage
Shepherd's pie

RESOURCES

For more information about Sicilian wines and nero d'avola:

Journey Among the Great Wines of Sicily by Andrea Zanfi
Wines of Sicily by Kate Singleton
Palmento: A Sicilian Wine Odyssey by Robert Camuto
Association of Sicilian Wines: www.assovinisicilia.it
Made in Italy: www.italtrade.com

RELATED READING

The following books, while seemingly unrelated to the main subject matter of this chapter, provided some enjoyable reading before, during, and after my travels:

The Leopard by Giuseppe Tomasi di Lampedusa
Machiavelli in Hell by Sebastian de Grazia
The Godfather by Mario Puzo

FRIDAY

A Smoldering Liquid Tango

MY HORSE REFUSES to budge. Her name, Briosa, probably translates to "one who despises gringo wine writers." As I look up at the snow-capped Andes, I feel very Ralph Lauren—even without *bombachos*, the traditional Argentine riding trousers. I breathe in the crystalline mountain air to the bottom of my lungs.

The region of Mendoza, 650 miles southwest of Buenos Aires, has a big-sky, Wild West feeling. In fact, I'm hankering to mosey over to a campfire and whittle me a stick. But I decide to clutch the reins more tightly as Briosa turns her silky black head to snuffle at me. After a seven-minute standoff, 967 pounds of horseflesh grudgingly starts clopping behind her bemused trainer, Carlos Fernando, riding in front of me.

As we move through the vineyard rows, the few words that Carlos and I exchange are absorbed in the mountain quiet. The suede-smooth folds of the foothills beg to be touched.

I'm visiting the aptly named Cheval des Andes (Horse of the

Andes) winery, a joint venture between Bordeaux's Château Cheval Blanc and the Argentine estate Terrazas de los Andes. Cheval des Andes makes spectacular malbec–cabernet sauvignon blends—and owns a polo team. The thirtysomething winemaker Nicolas Audebert is an avid player on the team. As he tells me later, "We make wine in Argentina like we play polo: passionately."

Polo is one of many national obsessions here, along with Evita, tango, and soccer—recall Diego Maradona's "hand of God" goal that beat England in the 1986 World Cup quarterfinals. Some of us remember the country's 1982 Falklands War with Britain, described by Argentine writer Jorge Luis Borges as "two bald men fighting over a comb."

The country's capital, Buenos Aires, is often called the Paris of South America. I spent a few days there before heading out to wine country, and was surprised at its beauty and cosmopolitan feel as I walked the streets, carrying the short stories of Jorge Luis Borges, who was born there in 1899. In his miniature fictions, he captured the intensity of feeling and color in this bustling city of twelve million people and forty-seven barrios, or neighborhoods: the smart cafés and designer boutiques, the flea markets and brothels, the Belle Époque architecture and the black granite vault of Evita's tomb, the taxis who treat driving as blood sport, the chatter of people and parrots, the expansive tree-lined avenues and the darkened cobblestone alleyways. Buenos Aires doesn't close: light and people spill out of tango bars at four a.m., just as the cafés start making fresh brioche for early risers.

However, I had only a vague notion of this South American country that's five times the size of Spain. It spans more than a million square miles, from the subtropical jungles and parrots in the north, near the equatorial Tropic of Capricorn, to the Antarctic ice fields and penguins of Patagonia in the south. In the east lie the expansive cattle-grazing grass fields of the pampas; in the west, the country rises to the crescendo peaks of the Andes.

I knew even less about the country's wines, often lumping them together with next-door neighbor Chile's vino. Both countries hug the Andes—the mountain range that runs down the spine of South America, with valleys and plains thrown to either side, as though Bacchus had cleaned out his topography drawer. Both have evolved from dictatorships to democracies. Both are Spanish-speaking with Latino flair.

Both countries also produce wines that are incredibly well-priced for the quality. The reason is that they share some natural advantages: a warm climate that produces consistently ripe grapes, so there's less crop loss, as well as cheap land and labor costs. This translates into comparable wines that are often less than a quarter of the price of those from Napa, Tuscany, and Bordeaux.

While Chile and Argentina are terrific bargains, stylistically, the wines are quite different. Chile, situated to the west of the mountains beside the Pacific Ocean, has a cooler, more humid climate than Argentina on the eastern side. The Andes block the cooling Pacific breezes and trap rain clouds on their snowy peaks, making Argentina's climate dry and hot.

What kinds of wines does such a climate produce? Traditionally, not very good ones. When I first tasted Argentine wine twelve years ago, I spat it out immediately. (This would have been fine had I not been in a restaurant.) The wine tasted of scorched prunes speared on lacquered toothpicks. Face-sucking tannins squeezed it into a tight, rusty package. However, in the last five years, I've discovered that Argentina has started producing wines of ravishing vivacity. They're perfect for Friday night barbecues at the end of a long week, when you want something hearty but don't have the energy to cook a big meal. So I'm here to find out how they coax such fresh, vibrant wine from this hostile land at such ridiculously low prices.

Meanwhile, as we return to the polo clubhouse at Cheval des Andes, the tingling menace I felt from Briosa is fading. (I later learn that her name means "high-spirited.") She seems to have settled into a companionable tolerance. As I slide off her with one foot still stuck in a stirrup, she rolls her eyes—fondly, I think.

NEXT MORNING, I abandon equine transport for the motorized kind and drive to the Bodega Catena Zapata winery, one of the country's largest wine producers. Catena is also the wine that changed my opinion of Argentine wine: I remember drinking it one night at a friend's house and guessing that it was Australian shiraz. My body hummed with contentment as I let myself down into its berry decadence. I was pleasantly surprised to find out what it was and started buying more malbec.

Now, as I follow the long gravel road, a space-age stone temple rises from the vines, framed against the silver peaks of the Andes. This extravagant architectural statement is the concrete gesture of one man's desire to revolutionize his country's wine industry. As owner Nicolás Catena later explains, "We could not build a French château or an Italian palazzo here. We had to tell the world that we are doing something different in Argentina."

The artistic inspiration for the building came from the ancient Mayan civilization, despite the fact that Mayans never ventured beyond Central America. However, they were great architects, fascinated with mathematical symmetry and the sacred geometry of pyramids. This winery is built according to the same philosophy: every angle at exactly the same inclination toward the sun. Although it looks like a temple of molecular displacement, the beige stone gives it an earthy warmth.

Inside the sixteen-foot doors of burnished copper, I meet Catena's export manager, Jorge Crotta, who takes me on a tour of the tank room and cellar, while giving me the winery's background. It now produces about 3.6 million bottles of wine a year, exporting 85 percent of it. Seventy percent of the wines are red, with malbec accounting for 55 percent of production. The wines include Alamos, Catena, Catena Alta, and the flagship, Catena Zapata, as well as a joint venture with Bordeaux's Château Lafite-Rothschild called Caro.

Afterward, he leads me up to the top level of the winery, to a quiet study filled with books and big leather chairs. Sunlight streams in through large open windows that look to the Andes. I'm to be granted a rare audience with Dr. Nicolás Catena. As I wait, my stomach flip-flops. I recall thinking how what a coup it would be to interview Argentina's most brilliant and insightful winemaker. Now I'm wondering how I can carry on a conversation with a man whose IQ is in a range that I'll never see, except maybe on the bathroom scale. I'm not prepared to defend any thesis to this professor.

A few minutes later, the door opens and a silver-haired, bespectacled man enters. He looks every inch the distinguished scholar in a navy corduroy jacket and crisp white shirt. This takes me right back to one-on-one tutorials at Oxford University; I can feel the sweat between my fingers and down my back. His blue eyes radiate from a tanned, weathered face as he greets me in a soft Spanish-accented voice, "Please, call me Nicolás." As he pours me a glass of his brooding, blackberry-rich Catena Malbec, he tells me about his life as an academic and a vintner.

Nicolás Catena has lived among the grapevines for all of his seven decades. He was even born in the vineyard, since his mother didn't make it to the hospital in time for the birth of the last of her five sons. At age six, he was already walking the family horses out to their pasture several hours before school in the mornings, and then bringing them back home again at the end of the day.

That robust work ethic has been in the Catena family for generations. In 1898, his grandfather Nicola left a small village in Sicily for Argentina. He started planting vines in 1902 and raised a family. His eldest son, Domingo, married Angelica Zapata, a daughter of a large landowner, increasing the family's holdings. By 1973, the winery had become the country's largest producer of cheap wines, pumping out 240 million bottles a year.

Nicolás, the son of Domingo and Angelica, was a brilliant boy and finished high school at fifteen. At the request of his father, he delayed university to work in the vineyard. After several years, he continued his education, eventually earning a PhD in agricultural economics from Argentina's University of Cuyo and then a master's degree in economics from Columbia University. But sadly, in 1963, his mother and grandfather were killed in a car crash. Nicolás returned home to help his father run the winery, postponing a doctorate at the University of Chicago.

"I worked side by side with my father. I was too young and too arrogant then to learn anything—but at least I knew I was arrogant," he says, smiling.

Eventually, when the winery stabilized, young Nicolás longed to go back to academia, despite his love for the family business and making wine. "The pull of the intellectual life has always been as strong as the entrepreneurial for me. I have tried all my life to resolve that. Perhaps this is why I've always felt like two people."

In 1982, he accepted a post as visiting professor of agricultural economics at the University of California at Berkeley. The academic environment was stimulating: his colleagues won six Nobel prizes while he was there. He also enjoyed discussing wine matters with professors in the viticultural program. One weekend, he and his wife, Elaina, drove up to Napa Valley and toured the Robert Mondavi winery. Much later, he learned that his grandfather and Mondavi's father had lived only fifteen miles apart in Sicily, though they never knew each other.

Nicolás admired both the quality of the wines and the energy of the Mondavi people. "I remember the shock of the freshness and the fruit in the wine, its balance and complexity," he says, tilting his head slowly to one side and then the other, as though considering the visit from different angles. "I thought, there's no reason we can't do this in Mendoza. That visit opened my eyes to the fact that a New World country could compete with Europe."

After that, Nicolás and Elaina spent most weekends visiting Californian wineries. When they returned to Argentina in 1992, he took over the winery and sold all the family's vineyards except for the original Bodega Esmeralda, planted by his grandfather. He invested in advanced computer and robot technology as well as stainless-steel tanks and French oak barrels. He also convinced Paul Hobbs, a respected Sonoma winemaker, to work with him during the harvest. Since Argentina lies south of the equator, the grapes are picked from January to April, conveniently off-season for Hobbs.

Nicolás planted chardonnay and cabernet sauvignon, believing (like many others) that these two grapes alone defined wine quality internationally. "I made the same mistake as the Californians: I tried to imitate France in order to beat them," he admits quietly.

It was his father who convinced him to consider malbec, which the senior Catena believed to be the country's patriotic grape, making it in the popular oxidized style that Nicolás calls the "sherry approach to winemaking." Malbec got no respect in fine-wine circles, the stunt double of brute strength but no subtlety. Its only role was to beef up the color, alcohol, and tannin in more aristocratic cabernet blends.

"I loved my father very much, so in order to please him, I started a little project on malbec," he recalls.

That "little project" lasted fifteen years and involved planting 145 malbec "clones"—the same grape but from different parent vines—to see which would do best in different sites. ("Wine caters to obsessive personalities; it makes you worse," Nicolás observes with a sigh.) He knew that until the late 1800s, when phylloxera destroyed most European vineyards, malbec had been one of the most planted grapes in Bordeaux, whereas today, it's less than 10 percent of vineyards there.

Malbec still thrives in the warm region of southwest France called Cahors, which makes a tannic, deeply colored, palate-whacking "black wine." This may be why the name malbec is believed to be derived from the French *mal bouche*—"bad mouth," referring to this rustic style. Thankfully, Argentine malbec is a much friendlier, cuddlier creature than the inky monsters of Cahors. (I recall drinking Cahors for the first time and thinking that I could use it to restain the front deck.)

Ever the scientist, Nicolás narrowed down all those clones to the five best, a process he says married his bookish and business interests. "As a theoretical economist, I'm trained to develop a hypothesis and then to use a methodical approach to prove or disprove it," he explains, taking off his glasses and rubbing his eyes.

He was aided in this quest by a friend, Bordeaux winemaker Jacques Lurton, who also has wineries in both Chile and Argentina. Lurton convinced Nicolás to plant at higher altitudes, which further improved the grape quality. ("Jacques has a genius for climate.") In gratitude, Nicolás had a thousand pounds of prime Argentina grass-fed beef delivered to Lurton in Bordeaux.

Like many artists, Nicolás is fascinated with light: its luminosity, its diffusion, its interplay among the vine leaves. "It's all about funneling that extraordinary intensity of sunlight here into the wine."

His scientific mind is also engaged with light, studying its effect on the health benefits of red wine. Intense sunlight doesn't mean hotter temperatures, just more intense rays. The intense ultraviolet light at higher elevations speeds photosynthesis, making it more efficient, so the plants are healthier.

It also causes the grape skins to thicken in an attempt to protect themselves from the increased radiation. This accelerates the development of natural compounds, such as polyphenols, flavonoids, and anthocyanins, which give wine its color, tannin, and flavor. These compounds, or phenolics, in grapes grown at over fifteen hundred feet are three times higher than in grapes grown at sea level.

The phenolics help to inhibit the development of endothelin-1, the nasty enzyme that blocks arteries and contributes to heart disease. Since only red grape skins are fermented with the grape juice, these benefits are mostly in red wines. (I love it when I can rationalize my alcoholic intake with medicinal benefits. And at my rate of consumption, I should live forever—or at least be well preserved [completely pickled] by the time I make my exit.)

The result is wine of extraordinary elegance, with a rare combination when young: solid structure and silky texture. Argentine wine isn't just bottled sunshine; it's the liquid expression of solar energy. When I drink malbec, I feel voluptuous and expansive—that's probably why I'm also often wearing my buffet pants with the elasticized waistline. I like to indulge my thirst and my hunger to just this side of plump.

The Catena Alta Malbec Cabernet we're drinking smolders in the glass. Its sultry edge is more enticing than the sweet, soupy international style of many brand-name grapes. Nicolás believes that drinkers are shifting away from the herbal flavors of cabernet and turning more toward wines like malbec (and syrah, tempranillo, and grenache) that have fleshy dark red fruit and violet flavors. Blending malbec and cabernet grapes is still traditional. "These blends give us

French elegance and Latin passion," as Nicolás explains. However, he no longer believes that malbec needs cabernet sauvignon—or any other grape—to make great wine.

Nicolás is aided in his research by his daughter, Laura, who also has both a scientific mind and a bent for commerce. While she was pursuing her medical degrees at Harvard and Stanford universities, her father gave her a credit card.

"I told her that she could spend as much as she wanted, but it had to be on wine," Nicolás says, a playful glint in his eyes.

Laura now divides her time between San Francisco—where she, her husband, and their three young children live, and where she works as an emergency room doctor—and Argentina, where she's export director for the winery. She's conducting fifteen hundred experiments on different variables that contribute to wine quality, such as vine exposure to the sun, pruning at different times of the year, irrigation methods, and fermentation temperatures. Every season, she applies the successful methods to next year's vintage and adds more variables.

Laura and her father believe that there is no one optimum moment in the vineyard, as other producers do; rather, there are many captured in the glass by harvesting the grapes as many as eight different times. Their view is that one harvest with one vinification (fermentation) is a one-dimensional wine, which is why they have more than three thousand separate vinifications. That may sound iconoclastic, but as Nicolás observes, "We can innovate because the consumer has no history for us; we are creating that now. The French have a five-hundred-year lead on us, but every year, we jump a decade in learning."

Argentina may be new in consumer memory, but it has a long history of winemaking. It's another country that doesn't fit neatly into either the Old World or the New World categories, but is more Middle Earth. In 1541, Spanish conquistadors in search of silver (the

Latin "argentum," after which the country is named) planted tempranillo grapes here to make wine for religious services (and for thirsty invaders).

For three centuries, that rough local wine was the only kind produced here until the nineteenth century, following Argentina's independence from Spain, when a flood of immigrants began to arrive from Spain, Italy, and France. Most were farmers, and they brought with them treasured vine cuttings from the old country: Spanish tempranillo and torrontés, Italian barbera and sangiovese, and French cabernet sauvignon, viognier, and malbec.

However, things started to go downhill for the wine industry throughout the twentieth century, thanks to a variety of basket-case economic and political policies. But it was President Juan Perón who really sent wine consumption into decline when he imposed high domestic taxes in the 1950s. (Someone had to pay for his lavish lifestyle with Evita.)

The 1982 Falklands War with Britain also didn't help the economy or exports. Then there was hyperinflation that exceeded 3,000 percent a month, which discouraged foreign investment. Vintners made up for the lost revenue by producing high volumes of poor-quality wines that smelled like bananas rotting in an attic.

Meanwhile, neighboring Chile's economy was much more stable, and the country was already producing more wine than it could consume, so it was focused on export in the 1980s. Chile took advantage of this to position itself at the very low end of the market— bottles of wine under $10. (Ironically, Chile has struggled ever since to get up out of that category.) Argentina started to focus on exports in the 1990s, when government subsidies dried up for volume production and there were economic incentives to rip out inferior vines.

How did all this affect Nicolás Catena? In 1991, he shipped his first vintage to the United States and faced the dilemma of how to price his wines. At that time, the most expensive Argentine wines sold in the United States cost $4, and those from Chile cost $6. Nicolás made the gutsy move to price his chardonnay above the vinous ghetto at $13 and his cabernet sauvignon at $15. Fellow producers told him he was crazy, but word of the wine's quality spread, and he sold the entire vintage's production in two months. Still, it took another five years before the North American market fully accepted the Catena wines as part of that price segment.

I ask him which wines are the best in the world today. However, the professor dodges the question with a theoretical explanation. "If you accept that the dynamics of the market economy reflect the value judgments of its participants, then the best wine is the most expensive one."

And do critics influence which wines the market deems best?

"Critics increase market efficiency, but the consumer ultimately decides which is the best wine—and who is the best critic," he says, smiling at me. "I am market driven; I make wines that please people. If people did not like my wines, I would change them," he says.

Nicolás tells me he believes that wine allows people to show their affective side. "I cannot prove this theory, of course," he says earnestly, raising a finger. "But I have seen it many times. When you bring out a bottle of wine, something in your emotional, sensing nature is revealed. This is why people often drink wine with those they are fond of."

As it happens, I am terribly fond of this Catena Zapata Malbec. It floods my senses with a wanton perfume of violets and black plums. There's an unabashed Latin fire in the glass, with a lick of French polish.

"We're still scaling the Andes for cooler sites, taking vines to the very limit of cultivation," Nicolás says, his eyes moving up the mountains in front of us. "We are not producing our finest wines yet. That challenge is always ahead of us—we are always pursuing it."

*   *   *

THE NEXT DAY, I drive to meet Michael Halstrick of Bodega Norton, the country's sixth largest winery and exporter. Once I had changed my perception of Argentine wine, Norton was one of the first malbecs that I bought by the caseload. (I have a hard time with moderation in anything.) I even decided to serve it at a fancy dinner party one night, long before Argentina was thought to be a good producer. I can get away with this because everyone thinks that as a wine writer I will only serve them the best and most expensive wines. As usual, a Greek chorus chanted in my head, "Don't do it! Don't do it!" But I persisted and poured the wine into a decanter. My guests loved it, and I enjoyed having them guess at the wine's origins. They couldn't figure it out.

The sun burns a white hole in the sky. Flaming yellow and orange Alamos trees stand sentinel along the road, windbreaks for the vineyards behind them. Beyond the vines, creamy scrolls of sand stretch out into the blue distance. As I fly past, my mind keeps returning to my economics discussion with Nicolás Catena. How, I wonder, can a country like Argentina, with such great natural wealth, squander it so easily? But then, I'm always fascinated by beautifully flawed countries—and people. They have a thousand stories to tell.

Nicolás also gave me an idea of the extent of foreign investment in Argentina. Almost 50 percent of Argentine wine exports come from foreign-owned companies that have strong sales channels in other countries. Only two of the top ten exporters, Catena and Zuccardi, are owned by Argentines.

The devaluation of the peso not only made local wines inexpensive abroad but also attracted investors to the domestic industry. Making wine here is a tenth of the cost that it is in Europe, since the land, labor, and vineyard maintenance are all much less expensive. The

Argentine climate is also consistently warmer than Europe's, reducing crop losses, with sufficient warmth to ripen the grapes every year.

As a result, in the last ten years, foreign companies have invested more than $10 billion in the Argentine wine industry. In addition to the joint ventures I already mentioned between Château Cheval Blanc and Terrazas de los Andes (Cheval des Andes) and Nicolás's Catena Zapata and Château Lafite-Rothschild (Caro), other foreign-owned wineries include Bianchi (Seagram's, Canada), Navarro Correas (Diageo, Italy), Vina Patagonia (Concha y Toro, Chile), and Finca Flichmann (Sogrape, Portugal).

As well as bringing in cash from abroad, these companies also import winemaking expertise and technology. They train local vintners, often with the help of "flying winemakers"—international consultants who advise wineries in many countries. The most famous of these is the Bordeaux-based Michel Rolland, who owns the winery Val de Flores as well as part of the joint venture Clos de los Siete, both in Mendoza. He also consults for several other Argentine wineries. Foreign companies have also created a cadre of "flying interns," a new generation of young winemakers who choose to double their work experience by working in the Southern Hemisphere during the "reverse harvest."

One of the first foreigners to buy an Argentine winery was Gernot Langes-Swarovski, the Austrian crystal magnate, who purchased Bodega Norton in 1989. The winery was founded in 1895 by Sir Edmund Palmer Norton, a British engineer who came to Argentina to work for the Buenos Aires Railroad Company. In 1991, Swarovski's son, Michael Halstrick, took over as president.

I meet Michael, who's in his mid-forties, in the barrel room of Norton winery while I am on yet another obligatory tour with another export manager. Michael's broad smile and booming voice match his six-foot-six frame. Although he's made lots of changes at the winery, he still honors its traditions. For the last 105 years, local residents have gathered at the winery every Thursday afternoon to fill their bottles and demijohns with wine at cost. However, it was the opportunities for innovation in this country that drew him here.

"Unlike Europe, Argentina is a place where not everything has been done," Michael says with a clipped Austrian accent, as we walk through the shadowy cellar. His candor is a refreshing change from the euthanizing euphemisms in desperately perky wine press releases. "I came here because I wanted to create my own story."

His biggest challenge is to sell both his own brand and Argentina itself. Norton, which produces about eighteen million bottles a year, is one of the country's leading exporters. But for the past ten years, Argentina's wines haven't been able to gain a stronger foothold in foreign markets. The country is the world's fifth-largest wine producer today by volume, behind only France, Italy, Spain, and the United States, but it accounts for only 1 percent of global exports. Granted, it's hard to crack Europe's traditional 75 percent share of the $7 billion export market. But even Chile does better than Argentina, exporting twice as much, even though it produces a quarter of Argentina's output.

Yet many North Americans are gripped with a passion for Latin music, dance, cooking, and wine. So why isn't Argentine wine flying off liquor store shelves? Michael believes that the problem is image, or lack of one.

"Consumers drink a place in their minds when they drink wine," he theorizes. "When they drink Australia, they think of the Outback. When they drink California, they think of the beaches. But when they drink Argentina, they don't have a clear picture."

To combat the problem, the label on his Norton Lo Tengo wine features one of Argentina's most iconic images: a couple doing the tango. The label is actually a hologram that makes the dancers dip up and down as you change your viewing angle. You can always tell where the bottle is in the wine store: just look for the group of shoppers standing in front of it, tilting their heads one way, then the other.

Tango was born in the dockyards of Buenos Aires. As burly men waited for prostitutes, they danced with each other in a lusty expression of loneliness. The sad insistent notes of the accordion underscored their desire.

Eventually, women joined the dance, which became known as the vertical expression of a horizontal desire—about as close as two bodies can get with their clothes still on. The dance was further popularized in bars and nightclubs during the 1920s, especially by Carlos Gardel, the "King of Tango," with his buttery baritone voice. Hundreds of his recordings have been made into tango numbers. Today, tango is hotter than ever: there are Broadway-style shows, small crowded clubs called *milongas*, and even a twenty-four-hour tango cable channel, Solo Tango, devoted to national stars and competitions.

While I was still in Buenos Aires, I took in a tango show at a local club. I trained as a dancer for twenty years, so I respond with my body to most things. But watching tango made even the small muscles between my shoulder blades tighten with the dancer's arching back; my inner thighs shivered with memory when she straddled his leg with hers. Men and women pressed their foreheads together as they pushed against each other to get closer.

Domination, submission; rejection, passion; alienation, possession. Tango is as close as feet can get to talking to each other: a pointed toe placed there, another toe touching the floor beside it. Kinetic poetry.

Yes. No. Oh, yes!

"Journalists and the wine trade know Argentina, but most consumers don't," Michael says, snapping me out of my reverie. "In the past, most of our sales were accidental—a customer wandered into the Chilean section of the liquor store and mistakenly grabbed a bottle from Argentina. We're the Europe of South America, the last undiscovered jewel in the wine world, but we need to convince consumers of that."

We walk up to his tasting room beside the vineyard, where there are eight long-stemmed glasses of red wine on a long oak table. Shafts of sunlight pierce their violet-mulberry layers as the wine smolders in the glass, seducing my eyes.

"I fell in love with the color of the grapes first," Michael says as he hands me a glass of Norton Malbec. "The deep, saturated, bluish color that mirrors the depth of their fruit flavor."

He explains that the intensity of both color and flavor are produced by the climatic calibration of altitude and latitude. Argentine vineyards run down the spine of the Andes, spanning more than fifteen degrees of latitude, as far as the Champagne region of France is from northern Africa. In altitude, they range from twelve hundred to ten thousand feet above sea level. That's higher than the European Alps and almost a third of the way up Everest.

Of all the factors that influence Argentina's wine style, altitude has the most profound effect. For every three hundred feet higher up the mountainside vines are planted, they experience half a degree drop in temperature. This produces a different style of wine and often caters to a different grape.

Altitude also widens the difference between day and night temperatures by as much as twenty degrees. During the day, the vine absorbs sunlight through its leaves and converts it into carbohydrates, basic plant food. This is carried through the stems to its reserve organs, the grapes.

During the night, photosynthesis stops, and the plant consumes some of its stored carbohydrates. But at lower temperatures, less is consumed. This means the grapes keep more nutrients to enhance their color, flavor, and tannin structure. This long, slow ripening yields incredibly mature fruit flavors in the finished wine.

Higher-altitude wines tend to have darker floral aromas, such as roses and violets, while those produced at sea level have lighter floral notes, such as daisies and field flowers. As well, oxygen concentration is halved at higher levels, which reduces oxidation and intensifies the flavors. That's why we're short of breath and food takes twice as long to cook at higher elevations.

The benefits of altitude are such that among some producers, there's the inevitable "my vineyard is higher than your vineyard" braggadocio. Of course, at a certain point, more altitude (or length) becomes ridiculous, and it becomes too cold for the grapes to ripen.

Although Mendoza is the same distance from the equator as Napa (thirty-three degrees), the climate is much hotter and drier. The year averages 350 days of sunshine, with very little Pacific humidity making it past the Andes. Only dry winds roll down the mountains into Argentina. The most famous of these is called the Zonda, after the Greek god of wind. It can blow a hundred miles an hour and raise the temperature by twenty degrees in a couple of hours. This forces the grapes to produce thicker, protective skins, deepening the concentration of flavor.

Chilean vineyards, on the ocean side of the mountains, are planted according to how the Pacific breezes affect the vines as they glide inland and up through the river valleys. The country constantly battles humidity-related diseases, such as odium, mildew, mold, and botrytis. But Argentina's desert air almost eliminates such problems, so fungicides, herbicides, and pesticides are rarely needed. This makes organic and biodynamic farming much easier. In fact, most Argentine vineyards are organic in all but name. However, Michael, like many other Argentine producers, shies away from the organic marketing angle.

"Organic, inorganic; I don't believe in promoting that," he says. "All our wines are made naturally, so making that distinction doesn't help sales—and it hurts the ones we don't label as organic."

He pours me a glass of his Norton Malbec Barrel Select, a lovely weave of fruit and oak. It flows like a river of satin over my mouth, with vividly ripe black cherries and a smoky, mocha-infused finish.

The downside of a dry, desert climate is the challenge of finding enough water to keep the vines alive in a region that gets just eight inches of rain a year. (The great châteaux of Bordeaux get thirty-two inches, and even the dry-farmed vineyard of Australia's famed Henschke Hill of Grace gets twenty-four.) Argentina must depend on the torrents of crisp, clean meltwater that run down from the snowy peaks of the Andes and gurgle along a lacework of narrow canals that hug the vineyards and roads. The ditches were originally dug by Huarpe Indians a thousand years ago to irrigate their crops and cool their villages. The scarcity of this water limits how much land can be cultivated: only 3 percent of Mendoza has vineyards. Vineyard land without irrigation costs about $10,000 an acre; with irrigation, about $40,000.

The scarcity of water can be good for the vines. If they have enough to drink, the plants get lazy and their roots stay near the surface, drinking in only the water and nutrients at the top layers of soil. But if they're exposed to a little water stress, they're forced to push their roots much farther down into the soil to quench their thirst, allowing the roots to absorb the diverse nutrients of the lower soil layers, which deepens the grape flavors and expresses the terroir.

"The only thing we add is a little water," Michael says, winking, which sounds as though he's making instant soup. But the wines are anything but watery: they have the dark luxury of damson plums and peppered black raspberries. "We want the vines to be just a little grumpy."

Another reason to manage irrigation closely: during extrahot weather, the fruit sugars rise too quickly, before the grape's other elements—tannins, flavor, and color pigments—ripen. Wine made from such grapes is out of balance, with high alcohol, baked-fruit flavors, and a flat structure. But decreasing water to the vines slows that rapid rise in sugars, allowing the other elements to catch up. The result is wine with greater balance, maturity, and complexity.

Another advantage to canal irrigation is that it prevents the spread of the dreaded phylloxera, the aphids that eat vine roots and destroy entire vineyards. Although phylloxera does exist in Argentina, it doesn't cause damage because the pest's underground tunnels get washed away when the irrigation canals are flooded. As well, the flying variety of phylloxera is kept at bay by natural barriers: the sandy soils, the arid climate, and the Andes themselves.

Without the threat of phylloxera, the original Bordeaux vine cuttings of malbec have thrived here in splendid isolation for 150 years. Malbec is a stubbornly independent grape that prefers its own rootstock; it doesn't do well when grafted with other vines. The old vines produce tiny concentrated berries that yield wines of gorgeous concentration and deep spiced-berry flavors.

Although Malbec is the best-known grape here, there are more than a hundred varieties planted, many of them obscure and no longer grown in other regions. The weird and the wonderful thrive in this museum of lost grapes: primitivo, bonarda, corvina, mourvèdre, and especially torrontés—Argentina's most distinguished white wine. Michael pours me a glass of Norton Torrontés as we wrap up the tasting.

In the past, the warm climate made producing fresh whites difficult. However, modern controlled-temperature fermentation and storage changed that for many white wines, and none more so than torrontés, a crisp, aromatic tumble of daisies, lychees, and white peaches. The wine has been described as "the new viognier." Viognier's home is France, especially in the northern Rhône Valley regions of Condrieu and Château-Grillet, where it is the only white grape used and produces magnificently floral, voluptuous, and expensive wines.

To me, the Norton Torrontés seems closer aromatically to Alsatian gewürztraminer or muscat of Alexandria. It's a peach-fest of pungently floral aromas that makes you expect sweetness, but it's as bone-dry as chablis, with a crisp, feisty finish. It will thrill anyone looking for a value-priced condrieu, since it has the same mouth-filling, voluptuous texture as that rare Rhône Valley white.

The epicenter of torrontés is 850 miles north of Mendoza, in the Salta region near the Bolivian border. The light-skinned fruit was originally thought to be related to the Spanish grape of the same name. However, Carole Meredith, professor emerita of the University of California at Davis, has proved it to be a cross between the muscat grape of Alexandria and a local grape called criolla chica. Torrontés supposedly arrived in Argentina in the hatbox of a Jesuit priest.

Torrontés has since gone international, gaining a cultish following in Thailand, where its Turkish delight–tangerine essence suits the cuisine so well. It also pairs wonderfully with many spicy dishes and curries; works well with salads, seafood, shellfish, and vegetarian dishes; and makes a terrific aperitif. Torrontés is best consumed young, within a year or two of the vintage.

As we sip quietly on the wine, Michael leans back in his chair. "There are wines for thinking and wines for drinking," he says. "A very expensive wine makes only a few people happy. We want to make a lot of people happy."

THE SUN-BATHED UCO Valley, fifty miles southwest of the city of Mendoza, is bounded by the Cerrillos hills to the north and the San

Rafael Valley to the south. The challenge with visiting wineries here is that there are almost no road signs, so that pockmarked gravel path you just drove past was probably the one you should have taken. I discover this several times while trying to find Familia Zuccardi (Zuccardi Family Wines) before I finally pull up to a sleek building of glass and granite.

In 1973, Don Alberto Zuccardi, whose father had emigrated from Sicily, invented a deep-bore process to extract pure Andean meltwater from deep underground reservoirs to irrigate various crops. To prove that his invention could work, he bought land and planted vineyards here. His neighbors laughed, telling him that making wine in this dust-bowl region was impossible. Today, the family owns nearly fifteen hundred acres of vineyards, and the Uco Valley is the fastest-growing wine region in Mendoza. Don Alberto's irrigation company has since sold many systems to his neighbors.

I'm meeting Don Alberto's son José Alberto, who now runs the winery. Like his father, he studied engineering, but he also completed a degree in oenology. When he took over the company in 1985, he switched to organic farming and hand-harvesting to improve the quality of the wines. Today, the company produces fifteen million bottles a year, including some of the most successful brands in North America: Zuccardi Q, Fuzion, and Santa Julia, named after José's daughter, Julia, who runs their restaurant.

Although the company is large, it's also very much a family operation. His eldest son, Sebastian, is assistant winemaker; his second son, Miguel, makes the olive oils sold in the winery gift shop; and even Don Alberto, now in his late eighties, doesn't seem to realize that he's supposed to be retired. He still putters around the vineyards, plucking dead leaves off any vines within reach and gardening on the winery grounds.

José, an avuncular man in a gray cardigan, greets me as though

I'm a daughter returning after a long journey. "Welcome, welcome Natalie," he says, holding both my arms. "Shall we walk through the vineyard?"

Zuccardi's vines grow to six feet tall before spreading their tendrils horizontally across latticed wires overhead. This "parral" system of trellising forms a protective canopy roof for the grapes from the blistering sun. There is something *Secret Garden*–like about these leafy corridors, with bunches of grapes dangling overhead like purple chandeliers.

Many producers abandoned this method decades ago because they felt that it encouraged the vines to produce too many grapes of too little flavor. They preferred the European method of Guyot training, with vines planted more closely together and the cane of the vine only a few feet off the ground.

José disagrees. "Parral allows us to get more sunlight into the wine without the grapes getting sunburned," he says, as we stroll down one of the airy green hallways. "Grapes that are too exposed to the sun get scorched and give raisined flavors to the wine. For me, the age and care of the vines are more important than the trellising method."

Below us is dry, rocky soil—a geologist's wonderland. As the Andes rise, the stones get larger in size as measured by their "granulometry" (a word that I am dying to drop into casual conversation when I get home). This mother rock fractures into smaller pieces as it rolls down the mountainside or is swept down by meltwater. Loose-textured soil has much better drainage than sand or clay and contains fewer nutrients. Tough-love dirt makes vines work harder for their sustenance.

As we walk, I notice a number of large copper barrels hidden among the vines. These, José tells me, are essentially giant space heaters. Even though parral-trellised grapes are higher off the ground and thus more protected, frost still poses a threat. Every fall, there are a few nights when he must ring the bells to alert "the frost squad." A hundred or so farmhands, friends, and neighbors run to the vine-yards in the darkness to light fires in these cauldrons. This generates just enough heat to prevent damage to the vines. José turns these evenings into festive occasions by roasting marshmallows and serving warm drinks.

The night also brings forward the wild, evident only the next morning from the dusty prints of rattlesnakes and pumas between the vineyard rows. But those creatures pose less of a threat to the vines than do the squawky green parrots in the daytime. Perched along a hydro line or rooftop, they give a beady-eyed expert's appraisal of the grapes' ripeness. A dawn raid could strip a hundred-acre vine-yard in a few hours. Fortunately, the vines are protected by the vast hail nets that cover them.

Hail nets? It seems odd that in such an arid region, hail is a prob-lem. In fact, Argentina suffers from the world's most violent hail-storms. Stones as big as golf balls can dent cars, kill grazing cows, and strip the leaves and fruit off vines in minutes. They can even damage the wood of the vine stalk, endangering next year's crop. José estimates that despite the netting (which costs about $8,000 per acre), he still loses 10 percent of the crop every year to hail.

Some larger producers also monitor hailstorm clouds with satel-lite technology and when they amass to dangerous levels, send up a plane to seed the clouds with silver nitrate. This forces them to pre-cipitate their moisture as small, harmless pellets. The technique doesn't always work, though; sometimes the clouds are too large and high to be dissipated. Hail, frost, heat, draught: cue all the biblical afflictions. Who forgot to throw in flood, plague, and locusts?

We head back to the winery to see the "experimentation room." José opens two large barn doors to reveal a chamber gleaming with more than fifty small tanks and vats of various sizes. Lining the walls are panels of multicolored buttons, switches, and gauges.

"This is to make life more interesting. Wine constantly changes, so if you work with wine, you need to keep changing, too," he says enthusiastically, leaning in toward me to make his point. As a North American Scot, I have an emu's sense of personal space, so I tilt backward a little from the waist for every inch he moves closer in this cross-cultural conversational tango.

A tireless tester of winemaking techniques, José has tried micro-oxygenation, roto-fermenters, mechanical fermentation aids, and many other methods. He was the first producer to market a modern style of tempranillo in Argentina, and now he's experimenting with thirty-five varieties. His passion for the grapes is as sensual as it is intellectual. As we pass a large basket of pressed grapes, he grabs a bunch and extends his hand for me to smell the hedonistic perfume of crushed berries. Violently purple-black juice seeps between his fingers and drips to the ground.

As we continue around the winery, José greets every employee by name and *como estas?* Of the more than four hundred people who work here, most are locals who have been living in the vineyards since the vines were planted. Unlike many wineries, here they're employed year-round, not just for the harvest. José also believes in education: if new employees haven't completed high school, they attend school in the evenings at his expense.

"Terroir is as much about people as soil," he observes. "Making wine isn't just farming with fancy adjectives; it's about the deep connection between people and vines."

As the sun softens with evening, José invites me to join him for an *asado*, the traditional Argentine cookout. Most families in this beef-loving country have a barbecue in their backyard. Gauchos, the country's nomadic cowboys, started the tradition. Wherever they camped for the night on the great open grasslands of the pampas, they'd build a campfire and grill the least cooperative member of the herd for dinner.

At his home behind the winery, José lights the old knotty vines on the open grill. No wimpy charcoal briquettes or propane tanks here; the fuel is the old gray canes of the vines. And don't even think about chicken or tofu; beef is at the heart of Argentine cooking. *Parrillas* (steak houses) are to Argentina what cafés are to France, dotting the street corners of Buenos Aires and most small towns.

When families have an asado, they count on a couple of pounds of meat each. In this country of thirty-eight million people, there are two cattle for every person. (Fine with me as long as there's also a case of wine for everyone.) These cattle, which feed on the fertile grasslands, have juicier and more richly marbled meat than their corn-fed North American cousins. They don't have to walk far to feed. The younger the cattle and the less exercise it gets, the less muscle and fiber it develops and the more tender the meat.

The quality of Argentine beef has been recognized for centuries. When Charles Darwin stopped in for a visit two hundred years ago, he wrote in his diary that "the meat is as superior to common beef as venison is to mutton." Favored cuts include *lomo* (sirloin), *asada de tira* (short ribs), *vacio* (flank steak), and *bife de chorizo* (filet mignon). Steaks as thick as telephone directories are served with a sprig of parsley—a risible gesture toward vegetables.

A century ago, Argentine beef held 40 percent of the global export market. Today, it struggles to find a place on the foreign dinner table in an age that deems beef less healthful than white meat and seafood. Surely, Argentina must be a vegetarian's vision of hell: wherever you go, flame-broiled meat.

José and I sit at a small table under a shady trellis of vines while we wait for the burning wood to turn into coals hot enough for grilling. He hands me a glass of Santa Julia Malbec, with its heady scents of woodland berries and raspberry jam spread on warm bread.

"People don't care who makes Coca-Cola, but they *are* curious about who makes wine," he says. "They want to know the story behind it, the people, where it comes from, and how it's different from other wines."

Despite this, several years ago, José's Fuzion Malbec had the kind of product launch that Coke and Pepsi dream of. In just one year, it had sold five hundred thousand cases, the fastest ever sales spike in North America. A number of factors contributed to the wine's success: it was priced under $10, had a name that was easy to pronounce, and had an elegant label with lots of white space, which consumer tests show makes a wine look pricier. Most important, the wine tasted twice as expensive as it cost. Wine critics, always on the hunt for an undiscovered gem, gave it lots of free publicity. Fuzion sold so well that it didn't just take market share from similar wines; it brought new consumers into the wine market.

"There's no recipe for making wine," José tells me. This comment reminds me of the question from artist Rajinder Singh, whose work adorns the winery: "What is the numerical equivalent of lovely?"

"You can't make wine just to make money," he says earnestly, touching my arm gently. "Wine is personal; you need passion."

José certainly doesn't lack for passion. In 2005, at the age of fifty-one, he and his son Sebastian climbed nearby Aconcagua, the highest peak in the Andes—and in the Western Hemisphere—at 22,851 feet.

"I live five hundred feet from the mountain, I wake up to it every day, my vines live in its shadow," he muses. "How could I not be curious enough to get closer to it?

"To climb a mountain is to know another dimension of time and space. It is 170 million years old and four thousand times larger than you are. You realize just how small and fleeting your life is. Better do what you can with the time you have!"

The smell from the burning wood wafts into our glasses. It's time to put the glistening slabs of meat onto the grill. José turns them gently in his hands and pats them with rock salt, as if to reassure them. Fine-grained salt would be absorbed completely into the meat, making it too salty. The Argentines also don't drown their beef in sugary barbecue sauces; salt is all the seasoning they use because it brings out the flavor without smothering the tender meat.

Once the juices start oozing, the meat on the grill is turned just once. In contrast to the quick searing of North American barbecues, asado is a slow cooking method that takes at least an hour, with several sets grilled in succession. The social event usually lasts an entire evening. Our filets hiss and sizzle, sending a smoky signal up to my reptilian brain that triggers ancestral memories of carnivorous feasts.

Finally, the meat is ready. José sets a large plate of steaming beef in front of me. I bite into a filet, as soft as freshly baked bread, and it falls apart in my mouth. I don't even have to chew; I just rub the meat against the roof of my mouth. Its sweet, slightly nutty flavor ripples across my tongue, its juices mingling with the figgy-rich notes of the malbec.

Slicing into my third piece, I realize that malbec was made for beef: the dark berry flavors pierce and soak the savory strands of meat. And the extra antioxidants make this defibrillation red the perfect foil for meat. Malbec is a knife-and-fork wine that not only suits anything grilled but also pairs well with tangy dishes, such as pasta in tomato sauce, pepperoni pizza, hard cheeses, and lamb with rosemary and thyme.

Malbec is a wonderfully in-between wine, more supple than cabernet sauvignon, more robust than merlot. Its velvet bite dances with the heat of Latin dishes, such as the ones José sets out before us now: tender pork with a spicy chimichurri sauce (a mix of spices such as oregano, garlic, parsley, paprika, pepper, and thyme in fresh balsamic vinegar); piping hot *chorizo* blood sausages; and warm empanadas, half-moon, scalloped-edged pastries filled with savory meat, onions, and cheese. These were baked in the igloo-shaped adobe oven beside the grill, another traditional feature of Argentine backyards.

As the evening deepens, the cool, limpid air of the mountain peaks slides in around us, and the trees and grass start to darken. José brings out a traditional dessert made by his eighty-three-year-old mother: slices of queen's jelly and the local Mantecosco cheese. It goes beautifully with his Malamado, a late-harvest blend of torrontés and viognier perfumed with ripe apricots and honeysuckle.

"No one retires in this company," he says, smiling and shrugging. "For us, work is a way to live; there is no separation between them. My father taught me that freedom is the equation between what you produce and what you need. If you don't need too much, you will always be free."

That's music to my cheapskate ears. But I think about how far away I am from my husband, my son, my life. It's a happy sadness I get when I travel on my own. Yet it's only when I'm away from my creature comforts that I'm more alert, more vulnerable, more prone to emotional cloudbursts. That's when I'm using more of my senses and synapses to write a good story.

Right now I'm flush with this emptiness as I lean back in my chair and take another drink of the malbec. The day's thoughts and worries and conversations fade into evening quiet. The sun drenches the mountains in sliding pinks and reds and then finally disappears behind their black-haloed peaks.

Field Notes from a
Wine Cheapskate

INSIDER TIPS

- Take a chance on lesser-known grapes. Varieties like malbec just don't have the brand awareness and cachet of cabernet sauvignon and merlot. Therefore, producers must compete more aggressively on price. In this book, you'll discover lots of grapes that you may not have heard of before.

- Go for regions where the currency gives you an advantage. Canadian and American dollars are much stronger than Argentina's pesos, so that builds in another discount on the import cost.

- Look for late bloomers: regions that entered the North American wine market after a number of other countries had already established themselves. These newcomers have to prove themselves, in terms of both price and quality.

WINERIES VISITED

Bodega Catena Zapata: www.catenawines.com
Bodega Norton: www.norton.com.ar
Cheval des Andes: www.chevaldesandes.com
Zuccardi Family Wines: www.familiazuccardi.com

BEST VALUE WINES

Alamos Malbec (Catena)
Alamos Torrontés (Catena)
Catena Zapata Malbec Cabernet
Fuzion Malbec Shiraz (Zuccardi)
Norton Malbec
Norton Torrontés
Santa Julia Malbec (Zuccardi)*
Zuccardi Malbec Series A

*My first pick for my own Friday dinner.

TOP VALUE PRODUCERS

Alamos
Alta Vista
Argento
Benmarco
Chakana
Conquista
Crios De Susana Balbo
Dominio Del Plata
Doña Paula
Finca El Origen
Finca Flichman
Fuzion
Gascón
Graffigna
Kaiken
La Posta

Luigi Bosca
O. Fournier
Masi Tupungato
Michel Torino
Navarro Correas
Piattelli
Punto Final
Santa Julia
Terrazas de los Andes
Tilia
Trapiche
Trivento
Urban Eco
Vinecol
Viña Cobos

FRIDAY DINNER FOR A WINE CHEAPSKATE

You'll find José Alberto Zuccardi's recipes for the asado that we shared at www.nataliemaclean.com/food.

José Alberto's Best Barbecued Beef

Zuccardi Family Chimichurri Sauce

Warm Fuzion Empanadas

Emma's Queen Jelly

TERRIFIC PAIRINGS

The malbec grape produces wines that stylistically fall between cabernet sauvignon and merlot, with more plummy richness and roundness than cabernet but firmer tannins and structure than merlot. Signature aromas include plums, blackberries, black cherries, spices, earth, and wood smoke. Here are some of my favorite malbec pairings:

Barbecued beef ribs
Barbecued pork spareribs
Beef cooked in red wine
Beef stroganoff
Bison steak
Bittersweet chocolate
Braised lamb shanks
Brisket
Casseroles and stews
Cheddar cheese

Hamburgers, meat loaf
Herb-roasted lamb
Herb-rubbed roast chicken
Meat lovers' or pepperoni pizza
Peppercorn steak
Prime rib
Rack of lamb with rosemary
Rib roast with a coffee and
  pepper rub
Roast game

Spaghetti and meat balls	Steak fajitas
Steak and kidney pie	Venison

RESOURCES

For more information on Argentine wines and malbec:

*Vino Argentino: An Insider's Guide to the Wines and Wine
Country of Argentina* by Laura Catena
The Wines of Argentina, Chile, and Latin America by
Christopher Fielden
Wine Routes of Argentina by Alan Young
Wines of Argentina: www.winesofargentina.org/en
The Real Argentina: www.therealargentina.com
French Malbec: www.french-malbec.com
South World Wine Society: www.southworldwine.com/
contactus.html

RELATED READING

The following books, while seemingly unrelated to the main subject
matter of this chapter, provided some enjoyable reading before, during, and after my travels:

Borges Collected Fictions by Jorge Luis Borges
Evita: The Real Life of Eva Perón by Nicholas Fraser and Marysa
Navarro

SEVEN

SATURDAY

A Storm of Pleasure in Every Port

IF YOU REALLY want to know port, you can't loll about in the comfort of Oporto. You must go upriver to the wild heart of the Douro Valley of northern Portugal. Forget driving, though: the twisting mountain roads take forever. The best way is this ancient train, which left the coastal city an hour ago and is now wheezing its way past sheer granite walls. Over the millennia, the Douro River has carved a gorge that cuts some two thousand feet into the rock. As we follow the river deeper into the valley, I feel very Joseph Conrad on this May morning.

Black vultures circle in the sky above this remote, rugged landscape; more than a thousand square miles of cliffs dare anything to survive on them. The vines barely clinging to the rocky soil look as though they're threatening to jump. Others are abandoned, both men and plants having given up in exhaustion years ago. Nature teaches humility. Don't visit the Douro if you're lonely; it'll make you desolate. But for those who find some part of themselves in silence, it's perfect.

Boom! I hear an explosion in the distance, then another. It sounds like the invading forces are only a mile out. However, this is the echo of modernity on the Douro: they use dynamite to build new vineyard terraces into the rock face. Farming these steep slopes is expensive: it can cost up to $75,000 to develop one acre for Darwinianly low yields. Several wineries now use laser-guided bulldozers that calculate the angles of the slope precisely. However, a bulldozer still occasionally topples down the precipice into the water.

True port is only made here, in this valley, which stretches about eighty miles west from the central mountains of Spain down to the Atlantic Ocean. The climate is perfect for these grapes: the Serra do Marão mountains block the cool, moist air from the Atlantic, creating hot, arid growing conditions. The sun's intensity infuses port grapes with the extra ripening they need to sustain their flavor for decades. Port grapes love to bake in this ovenlike heat that can soar to 115°F. If they could, they'd probably slather on the suntan oil and roll over.

Although port isn't Europe's oldest wine style, the Douro is the world's oldest wine appellation: it was demarcated in 1756. For almost two hundred years, longboats with square sails and oars called *barcos rabelos* carried port down the Douro to Vila Nova de Gaia, at the mouth of the Atlantic. Trains and trucks have since replaced the boats—as well as the oarsmen who drank the port as they rowed and then topped up the barrels with river water.

The narrow cobblestone streets of Vila Nova de Gaia are lined with the historic port houses, which sit atop more than a hundred thousand barrels sleeping in their cellars. Some won't be moved for another fifty years. The wine is brought here to be aged beside the ocean because it's more humid than in the Douro, so there's less evaporation. Still, the aromas of caramelized alcohol and spiced oak waft out of the doorways, luring visitors into these alcoholic candy shops.

This charming town sits across the river from Oporto, the country's largest city after Lisbon and the one after which port is named. Oporto derived its name from the Latin word *portus*, or "haven." Legally, the wine can only be called port after it ships out of Oporto and leaves Portugal.

Now I have to confess that I've always enjoyed port a little more than I should—it brings me to my bliss point more quickly than any other wine. The high alcohol, at about 19 percent, helps, but its charm is more than that: the tangerine tints in the glass, the toffee richness on the tongue, the fireside warmth it creates inside you. You drink port to come alive in a time and a geography unknown to you.

I love those early October evenings when a chill in the air outside is countered by the warm contentment of a good meal inside. The dishes have been cleared; the rosy conversation becomes quieter with comfortable silences. You cradle a glass bowl of amber liquid in your palm. All that's missing is an Irish setter sleeping at your feet.

My favorite after-dinner consolation is to sink into a leather chair with a big book and a small glass of port—or, more often, a small book and a big glass of port. I also love finding references to port in literature. In George Meredith's eighteenth-century novel *The Egoist*, a professor tries to expose his daughter's fiancé as a fraud by tempting him with hundred-year-old port. As they descend into his cellar, he discusses what makes it different from other wines, such as Rhône Valley hermitage, German riesling (hock), and burgundy:

> Port is deep-sea deep. It is organic in conception, like a classic tragedy. An ancient Hermitage has the light of the antique. Neither of Hermitage nor of Hock can you say that it is the blood

of those long years, retaining the strength of youth with the wisdom of age. To Port for that! Port is our noblest legacy! I cherish the fancy that Port speaks the sentences of wisdom, Burgundy sings the inspired ode. Or put it that Port is the Homeric hexameter, Burgundy the Pindaric dithyramb. Pindar astounds. But his elder brings us the more sustaining cup. One is a fountain of prodigious ascent. One is the unsounded purple sea of marching billows.

It's a lovely ode to port, but she married the guy anyway. Another favorite passage comes from George Saintsbury's eighteenth-century *Notes on a Cellar-Book*:

> He drank it as a port should be drunk—a trial of the bouquet; a slow sip; a rather larger and slightly less slow one, and so on, but never a gulp; and during the drinking his face exchanged its usual bluff and almost brusque aspect for the peculiar blandness— which good wine gives to worthy countenances. And when he set the glass down he said, softly but cordially, "That won't do any harm."

It's such a seductive wine that the writer Samuel Johnson struggled to keep his daily ration to just four pints. And after one day in Portugal, I'm admiring the man's restraint. So it pains me to think that many people mistake port for a liqueur or a spirit because of its high alcohol and sweetness. In fact, it's a fortified wine like sherry. It starts off like regular wine, and then is made stronger with brandy. That's why I often enjoy it on a Saturday evening, when I don't have to get up early the next day.

Port also shares the dilemma of champagne: both terms are often used generically—though wrongly—for all fortified or sparkling wine, respectively. True, other countries do make port-style wines that offer good value, but they don't have the complexity and depth of flavor of true port. Like the Champenois, the Portuguese are trying to protect the name *port* as a trademark. In response, clever vintners in other regions have devised alternative names, such as starboard, export, or trop, which is *port* spelled backward—not exactly great marketing when it means "too much" in French.

However, this background can't help me with my current task, wickedly devised by George Thomas David Sandeman, the seventh-generation of the House of Sandeman, founded in 1790. A trim fifty-eight-year-old in a bespoke suit, George is the latest in a long line of master port blenders in his family firm. Despite his aristocratic bearing, he is quite a bon vivant, who almost bounces on the spot with enthusiasm as he talks. He's set a challenge for me: match his sample wine by blending the contents of three unmarked beakers of port, in the right proportions, by only smelling and tasting them.

Is this even possible, I wonder. Over the centuries, the Sandemans have perfected the art of blending dozens of wines from thirty or more vintages for their renowned tawny ports. The house style is one of elegance, finesse, power, and balance. Creating it takes years of daily practice to master: George tastes samples from his barrels every day so he can track the wines' maturity. If I tried to do that, they'd find me lying between barrels in the first week.

"How long did it take you to get an instinctive feel for blending?" I ask him.

"Oh, about twelve years," he says cheerfully. "But I'm sure you'll get it this afternoon." Beside him, his young assistant, Maria, muffles a laugh.

George hands me a white lab coat, an empty wine glass, a measuring cup, and a sample of the port that he's blended, with an encouraging nod. "The very first wine you make as a producer is the easiest," he explains. "It's every wine after that that's difficult because you're trying to keep the house style consistent. You have to remove all vintage variability and the differences in the aging capacity of each wine. There's very little room for error; consumers expect to taste the same style each year."

I feel my old nemesis, exam anxiety, rise in my gut, imaging the likely outcomes of this exercise. To calm myself, I mentally run through what I know about the Sandemans and about making port in general. I've heard that George's great-great-grandfather discovered the missing magic ingredient of port. He added a quarter barrel of brandy to a barrel of rough red wine before all the sugar in the grapes had been converted to alcohol. Since the brandy's high alcohol (77 percent) killed the remaining yeast cells, it stopped fermentation, resulting in a sweet wine with about 19 percent alcohol. Aging the result for twenty to thirty years ensured that the spirit was well integrated into the wine and that there was no burning sensation from the alcohol when consumed. This fortified wine also kept well during the long journey to foreign markets.

When it comes to aging, there are two broad categories of port: those aged in oak barrels and those aged in bottles. Wood-aged ports include white, ruby, tawny, and colheita; bottle-aged ports include vintage, late bottle vintage, and crusted. The result is two very different styles, which I think of as molten toffee versus primordial fruit. Those of the former style are aged in barrels, where their fruitiness makes a lovely trade with the barrel's toffee richness. Almost all wood-aged ports are blends of different vineyard parcels and vintages. The latter style comes from bottle aging, which preserves its core fruit character.

As I "evaluate" the blending for these samples, George watches me with merry but shrewd eyes. When I sip them, I taste a signature flavor that runs through them, yet they're also quite different from one another. How the hell am I going to do this? Where do I begin? I pour myself another comforting sample and gulp it down, then I whip out my notepad with a serious flourish and write down, "Buy Kleenex and toilet paper."

"You want to select your base wine first," George suggests. "That's your entrée wine; the other two will be condiments. Careful with your selection, though: you don't want to make the house style impossible to match next year."

Encouraged (and unnerved), I choose the second sample, my favorite, from the spectacular 2007 vintage. It has a generous nose that delivers rich aromas of almond and caramel, with just a hint of clementine, which adds a zing and lift to its toffeed heart.

"So should I make the blend mostly from the base wine and add only a dash of the other two?" I ask.

"Try it and see what happens," George says. "Remember that even a percent or two matters when your blend makes a hundred thousand cases."

Well, that really takes the pressure off. Not. I decide to try 70 percent of the 2007, then 20 percent of the 2006, and 10 percent of the 2008. I measure the proportions in a test tube, swirl the wines in a beaker to mix them, then I pour a sample of my new "blend" into all of our glasses. It tastes terrific, but nothing like George's sample, which is subtle and nuanced. The power and fruitiness of the 2007 has made my attempt far too exuberant.

George consoles me: it's an easy trap to fall into, he says, but an important one to avoid. Relying too heavily on one fine vintage would leave the business stranded in future years, when the vintage isn't as good.

I start over, swaying gently on my feet, as more port splashes on my lab coat. By this time, I've consumed more port than I've blended, so measuring the quantities is getting tricky. My effort to be scientifically thorough seems to be coming at the cost of basic precision. This time, quite uncharacteristically, I choose restraint. I stay my hand on the 2007, using only 20 percent of it, along with 30 percent of the 2008 and 50 percent of the 2006 as the base wine.

I swirl and pour into our glasses, and we all taste it. At this point, I imagine George exclaiming, "This is good—as a topping for ice cream! You fraud, get out!"

Instead, George asks Maria, "Should we tell her?"

Tell me what, I wonder. That I'm a complete idiot? I had thought my sample smelled a little closer to George's this time, but I bite my tongue rather than blather my neuroses.

"You've got it," George says, grinning.

"I've got what?" I ask, thinking anosmia or a cold sore on my upper lip.

"This is our house blend," he says. Maria is no longer smirking.

"No!"

"Yes."

Wow, I can't believe that I've stumbled onto the vinous equivalent of the Caramilk secret.

George smiles at me and takes my glass. "Good work," he says. "Let's go to the lounge."

I'm all for that; after all this tasting, I need a stiff drink. On the way downstairs, we pass a small museum with a collection of weird and wonderfully shaped port bottles from the sixteenth and seventeenth centuries. In those days, before brand names, labels, and advertising, it was the name of the buyer that was inscribed on the seal before shipping. Sandeman was an innovator in this regard, too, the first to create its own trademark in 1805, using an iron brand to stamp its barrels before shipping.

Sandeman was also among the first wine companies to advertise its wines. In 1928, George's great-grandfather Walter Sandeman bought the rights to "The Don," by the Scottish artist George Massiot Brown. The iconic drawing, a silhouetted man wearing a broad-brimmed Spanish hat and a Portuguese cloak, became the world's first wine logo.

Today, the Don is one of the three most recognized booze brands in the world, along with Johnny Walker and Captain Morgan. To me, he looks like a cross between Columbian coffee guy Juan Valdez and that 1950s radio drama *The Shadow.* The Sandeman tour guides wear the same outfit, giving the cellars here a mysterious cloak-and-dagger feel.

"For years, the Don was a flat figure, a cardboard cutout," George explains. "A few years ago, we gave him a makeover: we incorporated movement to his cape, added more three-dimensional shading, and even gave him feet for the first time. We had long meetings about his shoes, which started off looking like Hell's Angels boots, then eventually they morphed into something that was more in character and continues the mystery," he says.

"Some people scoff at brands as banal, but having a well-established brand is a tremendous responsibility to your customers who come back to you year after year, trusting that you'll deliver the experience that they expect."

As we sink into big lounge chairs, I'm reminded of the fine tradition of passing a decanter of port around the table. I've heard that it started with British sailors on those long sea voyages between Portugal and the homeland. Sitting after dinner in the officer's mess, the senior officer passed the decanter to the person on his left, or clockwise from "port to port." I ask George whether this etiquette is still practiced today in modern homes.

"The decanter still circles clockwise, symbolizing the passing of time," George explains. Tradition and manners require the decanter to keep moving from hand to hand, which is why some military decanters had rounded bottoms: they could never be set down. However, if the decanter gets held up anywhere on the table, it's considered bad manners to ask for it directly. The correct form is this:

"Do you know the bishop of Norwich?"

"No, I don't—why?"

"Well, the bishop is a good fellow, but he never passes the port, either."

Cue the forced laughter over the etiquette gaffe, and the decanter starts moving again. Serious drinkers kept the decanter moving around the table all night, and they challenged each other with "no heel-taps"—to finish the dregs so that a second bottle could be opened.

"There's also a practical reason to pass the port to your left," George adds. "Most people are right-handed, so it's easier to serve themselves when the decanter comes from that side."

One of the earliest references to decanting is in *The Iliad*, when Homer describes Hephaestus as pouring wine for the gods "from right to left." More recently, the ritual may come from the ancient Celtic superstition that all circular motions should be in the lucky direction, as they did in carrying a coffin around the grave three times before lowering it.

This reminds me of my favorite Scottish dance, the Highland reel, which I practiced several hours a day for eighteen years as a competitive dancer. (I also have a soft spot for it because it was the event in which I came fifth in the world championships in Scotland.) From left to right, four dancers weave in and out in a figure eight—essentially two connected circles. Like many Celtic symbols, this unending figure eight represented eternity.

Regardless of its origins, I love the tradition because the decanter becomes a little lighter as it passes from hand to hand, like our cares when shared with friends. However, it's the future of port rather than its glorious past that George wants to discuss. He believes that port can update its image by being the key ingredient in mixed cocktails. Wait a minute, port mixed cocktails? Isn't that as sacrilegious as putting ice into a single-malt scotch?

"Consumers are looking for low-alcohol, high-flavor cocktails," George says. "Port delivers that far better than spirits like gin, vodka, and rum. Those who go to bars and clubs are drinking fewer spirit-based cocktails so that they can drive home safely." As well, he points out, cocktails move port away from its old-fashioned ascots-and-monocles image. Mixed drinks adapt port to any season or social situation—on the deck in the summer, for example.

To prove his point, several of those mysteriously cloaked staffers whisk in trays of cocktails. Despite my reservations, I must admit I love his Porto Fizz, a jazzy mix of ruby port and champagne over ice, served in a wine glass and garnished with a slice of orange. The champagne diminishes the port's sweetness and gives the drink an effervescent zip.

Of the various types of port, ruby is the least expensive. It's made from the lowest-quality grapes and is aged only four to six years. The result is a young, fruity, vibrant wine that's ruby in color but lacks the complex depths and aging potential of vintage port. The cold temperatures of Portugal's winter help to precipitate the sediment from the young wine, naturally clarifying it. Then the wine is said to be "fallen bright," a lovely phrase that reminds me of a diamond dusting of snow across this rugged landscape.

George's sangria is equal parts ruby port and fresh orange juice in a long glass. Topping up with Sprite is optional, and I opt not to, of course, to keep the purity and concentration of the cocktail. After all, I still have my professional reputation to uphold, even if I can't stand up.

The crowning cocktail is the Sandeman Royale, a blend of tawny port and Chivas Regal whisky in a cocktail glass. It has a hypnotic fiery orange glow. When I ask about the name, George tells me he christened it after seeing the James Bond movie *Casino Royale*. It's a fitting name for the cocktail—and a fitting close to a day of being shaken, then stirred.

THE NEXT MORNING, I venture farther upriver on the train to meet Rupert Symington, of Symington Family Estates. Fourteen generations of Symingtons have been in the port business since 1652. Today, the family owns more than twenty-five-hundred acres of vineyards and twenty-six quintas (wineries), which produce more than 30 percent of all premium port. The Symingtons are the royal family of port.

The largest and oldest port producers all have British names: Sandeman, Churchill, Croft, and Taylor's, as well as Symington and their brands Graham, Dow, Warre, Cockburn, and Smith Wood-house. Port may be made in Portugal, but it's a British invention—born of taste, error, and political intrigue. This has always fascinated me because I'm an anglophile, from my Jane Austen bonnet to my Charles Dickens spats. So I dug into several hundred years of history, which I'll summarize in a couple of paragraphs to explain the British connection.

In 1152, Eleanor of Aquitaine, a noblewoman in Bordeaux, whose marriage to Louis VII had recently been annulled, married the Duke of Normandy, Henry Plantagenet, who later became Henry II, making her the queen of England. (For the full story, see *The Lion in Winter*, with Peter O'Toole and Katharine Hepburn.) The Bordelais angled for preferential tax treatment for their wines in the English market. Like most lobbyists before and since, they got what they wanted after a lot of wining and dining. Henry wanted to be king of both countries.

The tax subsidies lasted about three hundred years, until England and France fell out again and went to war. In 1678, William of Orange imposed high taxes on French wine. The death and destruction of war was one thing, but losing their supply of their beloved claret from Bordeaux was really taking things too far. Portugal came to the rescue. In 1703, England signed the Methuen Treaty with Portugal to keep its seaports friendly to the British during the war. In exchange, Portugal won lower import tariffs on all of its products, including wine. British merchants started importing more of the lower-priced port and became the largest shippers of the wine.

As my train pulls into the sleepy, sun-drenched town of Pinhão, I can see Quinta do Bomfim, the most prestigious of Dow's quinta, perched next to the station on the riverbank. Rupert Symington comes out to meet me with a warm greeting. He reminds me of the Duke of Edinburgh, with his impeccable diction and consummate manners. The trim fifty-seven-year-old has two decades of corporate mergers and acquisitions under his Burberry belt, as well as five years as a stockbroker in London and graduate studies at INSEAD, France's most famous business school. He'd be the perfect model for the British Airways annual report photo, showing first-class passengers enjoying a glass of port.

The Quinta House, built by George Warre, of Warre's port, in 1890, is in the style of a Ceylonese tea planter's bungalow. Its walls are lined with sepia photographs of the hardy men and women who first settled this (formerly malarial) valley. Rupert escorts me to the back veranda, where he pours steaming coffee into Wedgwood cups. Like most Symington men, Rupert went to school locally until the age of thirteen, when he was shipped off to boarding school in Yorkshire, England—one known for making men out of boys. Before going on to Oxford for mathematics, he worked at several Australian wineries for a year.

"Running a family business is like managing your own household: it's about keeping harmony with other members, knowing what you can afford, and making ends meet," Rupert says, leaning back on his wicker chair, his steel blue eyes gazing out on the river.

He's referring to the fact that six family members run the business. Rupert's cousin Charles is the vineyard manager and master blender. Dominic oversees North and South American sales with Rupert; Paul manages U.K. sales; Johnny does the same for European sales; and Clare arranges auction sales.

Personally, I can't imagine working with my cousins and siblings all day. But then again, I'm an only child, so I can't imagine living with any siblings at all. So how do six Symingtons manage to work together, let alone keep the business thriving? The old adage about three generations of a family business is make it, spend it, break it.

"We actually like each other, so that helps," Rupert says, smiling. "We've always had consensus on major issues, and we've never taken a vote. We all have the same interest in making good wine. We're all working for our children and our children's children. After all, our reputation today depends on what my father did thirty years ago.

"Negotiants, like our family, were always just shippers of port, not growers and makers of it," he explains. "That's changed with our generation. Now we have much more control over the quality of the product, from start to finish."

Rupert believes that port is best managed by families, since the knowledge of how to make it is passed down from one generation to the next. As well, the long production cycle of ports—tawnies, for example, can be aged for up to forty years—ties up cash flow, making it unappealing to shareholders who want a return next year, not next generation. Producers are legally bound to carry huge inventories; their stock at the beginning of the year must be three times what it sold the previous year. This law, designed to prevent producers from flooding the market with young wine and driving prices down, also means tying up huge inventories and cash. This fact may be why several international conglomerates, such as Seagram's, Diageo, and Pernod Ricard/Allied Domecq, have divested their port interests in the last five years.

"It's a business for the tortoise, not the hare," Rupert says. "A family firm means that you never lock up the shop at five p.m. and go home. The business is also your home; in your mind, you never leave it.

He takes me down to the dock, where we jump into his speedboat. Out on the Douro, the water is sapphire blue, a liquid mirror of the sky. Rupert kicks up the speed and leans into the wind at the steering wheel as I tighten my grip on the edge of the boat. The summer heat has clamped down over the land like a steam-cooker lid: wavy transparent fireballs roll across the rocky hills. Words like *languid*, *torpor*, and *parched* hang in my mind until they wilt. The feral beauty of the scrub on the sun-baked slopes makes me want to lift language from the landscape, but the words melt and dissolve in the jet stream behind us.

Upriver, we slow down to watch some water tortoises warming themselves on rocks at the river's edge. Rupert laughs at the sight of them and tells me a story about his grandfather, an enthusiastic naturalist. He asked his assistant to collect one or two tortoises for him to study. After a week, he asked if the tortoises were ready. The answer: "Sorry, sir, we've only managed to collect 99 so far, but I'm sure we can get you 102."

For most of its history, the river dried up in the summer. Teams of oxen would pull the long *rabelos* boats over the riverbed of rocks for eighty miles down to Vila Nova de Gaia. To control this problem, several dams and locks were built in the 1950s. Now Rupert pulls the boat up to the towering Valeira dam: a 157-foot wall of steel. Someone far above must have spotted us; the wall starts to slowly creak open, like the portcullis of a medieval castle.

We glide into the dam like a water bug in a giant bathtub that can hold fifty-eight million gallons of water. As the wall shuts behind us, we're enclosed in silence and shadow. Then water starts to gush over the wall in front of us. We rise with the water to the equivalent of a ten-story building. Rupert ties the boat to a buoy and tells me about some inebriated tourists who once made the mistake of tying their yacht to the ladder on the wall. As they swigged their port and sang out of tune, the nose of the boat slowly started to point downward as the ladder submerged under the water. By the time they realized what was happening, they had to jump off the now-capsized boat.

After going through the dam, we continue upriver for about twenty minutes, then dock at another Dow property, Quinta da Senhora da Ribeira. I expect this flower-trimmed, white-washed winery to house the traditional *lagars*: the rectangular stone basins that are filled with grapes at harvest. Most are about three feet deep, so that the grapes sit thigh-high for the workers to crush them by foot. (Though a few cunning vintners built their lagars a little deeper so that women had to hitch their skirts up a little higher.)

A dozen men and women would stand side by side in the vat, linking their arms over one another's shoulders. Then they'd slowly march in unison down the length of the sixteen-foot basin to the sound of an accordion and to someone who called the beat. This lasted for three hours and was called the *corte* (cut). The last hour, called *liberdade* (freedom), was marginally more fun, as the treaders are free to dance, flirt, and sing folks songs.

Treading grapes (the Portuguese and French call it *pigeages* for "feet") is the best and gentlest way to extract as much color and flavor as possible from them. The human toe, instep, and heel are extremely effective tools for crushing grape flesh without breaking the seeds, which release bitter tannins. Wine drinkers worried about contaminants like athlete's foot can relax; the process of fermentation cleanses any unmentionables.

I try to imagine myself participating in a grape stomp, the feeling of slippery, squishy grape flesh against my own skin, cold where the fruit has just entered the vat and warm where it's fermenting. I smell the perfumed purple juice splashing my thighs under a hiked-up peasant dress and up across my arms and cheeks. It reminds me of *A Walk in the Clouds*, and the only scene in that ridiculous movie with Keanu Reeves that had any wine merit.

Perhaps grape stomping is how young people met each other in the Douro in the absence of Match.com. However, it sounds like too much work even for love—and I hate being sticky. Labor shortages and costs are also factors for their diminished use.

However, everything here is modern. Like the old-fashioned longboats, stomping grapes is another tradition no longer economically viable. Rupert explains the economics as we enter the winery. "It takes sixty people three hours to tread the grapes in one lagar," he says. "That gives us 1,200 cases, or 14,400 bottles. At 20 euros per person, that's 1,200 euros for just one vat. At this quinta, we crush twenty-five vats for the whole harvest; it could easily cost as much as 30,000 euros, or $40,000." He has a scary mind for figures that I find unsettling, so I just squint and nod, as though I'm mentally checking his calculations.

Not only is cost a factor, so too is convincing tired workers—who've just spent all day under this hot sun picking grapes—to come in for another four hours of marching around a vat. So treading grapes is a dying tradition: less than 5 percent of port today is made using this technique. Silicon and steel are replacing flesh and stone.

In 1998, instead of simply adopting a standard automated crusher, the Symingtons invented a robotic treader to simulate the shape and action of the human foot. They measured the motion and pressure exerted by the human foot, its temperature, and the average time a person takes to tread from one end of the vat to the other. The "feet" are large, flat steel paddles attached to a rail above the temperature-controlled tank, moving up and down on the grapes—their timing controlled by a computer program rather than an accordion. Silicon pads are attached to the bottoms of the feet, made of the same material as the rubber bungs that seal wine barrels, so they impart no color or flavor to the grape must—the squishy mass of pulp and juice starting to ferment.

In traditional lagars, it takes about two hours to run off the wine and shovel out the skins after the treading is finished, during which time the wine continues to ferment—meaning it can easily dry out and lose its fruit freshness. As a result, winemakers traditionally emptied the vat a few hours sooner than they preferred, reducing the optimal contact time between skins and juice. The mechanized vat, though, takes only five minutes, allowing for a longer soaking, with greater color and flavor going into the juice from the skins.

"This is the most significant technological advance for producing port in half a century," Rupert explains, showing me the gleaming steel basin and computer panel. The family now operates seventeen robotic lagars, and they are in widespread use in other Douro wineries. "The paddles' precisely calibrated pressure ruptures the grape skins, so they impart their color and flavor to the juice before fermentation starts."

This is more important in making port than in making most wines because copious amounts of tannin, flavor, and color must seep out of the skins and into the juice quickly, since fermentation is stopped halfway through with the addition of brandy. Port juice only has about thirty-six hours in contact with the skins, compared to five or six days for dry red wines.

Those massive tannins in port bond with the color and flavor elements so that the latter doesn't fall out of the wine along with other sediment—insoluble particles that settle to the bottom of the wine bottle over time. If too much color and flavor precipitates out of the wine, you're left with a faded, flavorless, high-alcohol drink. These depth charges of tannin give the wine "grip." Port must have a gathered density of tannin at its core that allows it to hang together for decades, which is why most ports are monstrous to drink before they've matured at twenty to thirty years or more.

Back in the 1600s, these rough young wines were called blackstrap and sold off to undiscriminating drinkers. Even today, tasting young port is like sensory waterboarding: you're almost drowning in high alcohol, extreme sweetness, and exaggerated fruit flavor. It's like gargling with blackberry-flavored vodka. After ten samples, you just want it to stop—and you'll tell whoever's leading the tasting whatever he wants to hear.

Rupert shows me Quinta da Senhora's barrel room, where we taste several ports. We start with the 2008 Vintage Port, a black core of mouthwatering plums, currants, and blackberries wrapped in vanilla smoke. It's still just a baby, so there's a tarry grip running through the middle. Nothing that a couple of decades won't solve.

The 1991 Dow's Vale do Bomfim Vintage Port, up next, seduces me with its cedary tobacco and truffled blackberry depths. It reminds me of the British wine merchant who wrote in 1754 that port should feel like "liquid fire in the stomach, burn like inflamed gunpowder; and have the tint of ink, the sugar of Brazil in sweetness, and the spices of India in aromatic flavor."

To me, this port is a voyage of spicy aromas and images. Acidity, alcohol, and tannin are the three-pronged scaffolding to hold the fruit vibrancy in place. In this age of instant messaging and gratification, it's pleasantly disjointing when someone comments (as Rupert does now) that even the 1927 is still a little young.

In case you're wondering, "vintage port" doesn't literally translate to "old port," even though it does age well. Vintage port is made from a single year rather than from many years, like tawny port. That year is always written on the label. Port and champagne are the only wines whose producers declare a vintage rather than just dating their wines every year. Port producers declare the vintage about eighteen months after harvest, once they assess the quality of the wines aging in the barrels. Usually no more than two or three years per decade are declared for port, and they are the very best years. Dow, for example, has declared a vintage in only twenty-five years of the last century. They're proud to be picky. The result is that vintage port accounts for just 2 percent of all the port made, and as you might expect, it's the most expensive.

In other years, when the weather hasn't been ideal so it's not worthy of declaring a vintage, some winemakers create a single-quinta port from the grapes in their best vineyards that year. Some of the most coveted include Dow's Quinta do Bomfim, Quinta do Noval National, Graham's Malvedos, and Quinta do Vesuvio.

The Douro has hundreds of microclimates, so any winemaker can declare a vintage independent of neighboring estates. However, in the second year after every harvest, the national Port Wine Institute must approve the declaration by tasting samples. When climatic conditions are so good that most producers have a great year, as they did in 2003, the vintage is "universally declared." Some of the best vintages for port over the last eighty years include 1931, 1945, 1950, 1963, 1970, 1977, 1980, 1983, 1985, 1991, 1992, 1994, 1997, 2000, 2003, and 2007.

Of all the age-worthy wines in the world, vintage port is the most talented. That's why so many people choose it when they lay down a case of the birth vintage for a child, grandchild, or the attentive, young trophy wife who stays by their side until their last respirator gasp. Lucky heirs get to collect this stash on their twenty-first birthday (the grandchildren, not the trophy widow, who is presumably a few years older).

Usually, great aging potential in wine means premium prices: think Bordeaux, Burgundy, and Tuscany. Port is the exception, though, being often half the price, or less, of other coveted collectible wines. Why? History. The Portuguese have always priced their wines much lower than other prestigious regions and have yet to climb the price ladder that their longevity might command. Granted, a good bottle of port isn't cheap compared to, say, a Chilean cabernet, but among benchmark wines of the world, it's a bargain.

The one downside to vintage port is inseparable from the way it's made: that sludge at the bottom of the bottle. Unlike other wines, which are filtered, vintage ports can throw a sediment of up to an inch. (I love that phrase, "throw a sediment," as it makes me think that the wine is having a temper tantrum inside the bottle.) The sediment helps the wine to mature and gives it greater depth of flavor over the years. Other ports are filtered, which can decrease their ability to age and strip some of their fresh fruit character.

All ports, like all other wines, should be cellared on their side to keep the cork moist, at 70 percent humidity and about 55°F to 65°F. Older, unlabeled vintage ports have a white mark on one side of the bottle to indicate which way should face up when you lay the bottle down. If not, keep the label faceup. This ensures that the crust of sediment settles on one side, which makes decanting it easier.

Before I open a bottle of vintage port, I stand it upright for one day or two to let the sediment gradually settle at the bottom of the bottle rather than mixing throughout the wine, making it bitter tasting. I remove old corks gently: they can be dry and crumbly. For these corks, I sometimes use port tongs to open the bottle. I heat the tongs until hot, then clamp them around the bottle neck for a couple of minutes just above the shoulder, but below the cork. I remove the tongs and put a cold wet cloth on the same spot. The rapid temperature change makes the glass break cleanly across the neck, sparing me the struggle with the cork itself.

Once the bottle is open, I pour the wine in a slow, continuous motion into a mesh strainer over a decanter or jug. This catches the heaviest crust. When I see the black silt of sediment edging toward the neck of the bottle, I stop pouring and discard the rest—or I put it on my fern. Lighting a candle or standing a flashlight upright under the neck of the bottle helps me see when this trail is getting close to the opening.

If there's still a lot of sediment, I pour the wine from the first decanter into a second, filtering out the smaller debris with a cheesecloth. Even a nylon stocking—preferably unused—works. I just don't use paper coffee filters, as they can add unwanted flavors. I usually end up splashing port on myself whenever I do this. However, I'm comforted by the memory of Julia Child. In one of her 1950s television cooking shows, she drops the chicken she's stuffing on the floor. With her customary panache, she picks it up and tells viewers not to worry: "Only you know what happens in your kitchen!"

Fortunately, all this decanting fuss is necessary only for vintage and crusted ports because they're aged in the bottle and so keep their sediment. All other ports are aged in barrels and then filtered before bottling. As a result, they're ready to drink as soon as you open them and don't need decanting. They also last longer than vintage ports once opened, having already been exposed to air in the barrel and so being more resistant to oxidation. I enjoy tawny ports for up to a month or two after opening them. However, vintage port is best consumed within a day or two. So those decanters of dark vintage port that you see in movies have likely long-since turned to vinegar.

We then taste the 2001 Graham's Late Bottled Vintage, which

oozes decadent black fruit wrapped in pliable smoky leather. Late bottled vintage (LBV) has some of the character of vintage port, but it's more accessible and affordable. LBV blends wine from one vintage that has been aged four to six years in the vat (longer than vintage port) before being bottled. The bottle has two dates on it: the year of the harvest and the year it was bottled. I hold my glass up to the sunlight slanting through the cellar door and watch the amethyst droplets slide slowly down the glass.

I wish I had a Mars bar right now. I wouldn't dare confess this to Rupert, but their chocolate-coated nougat layers are irresistible with LBV port. Another favorite indulgence, Skor, is best paired with tawny port. My hedonistic fantasy is to layer three Skor bars and marinate-melt them in my mouth with a twenty-year-old tawny.

The Dow's Crusted Port has an elemental taste of earth and spice, along with a volcanic warmth that gains momentum as it slides down my throat. (Spit out this wine? You must be kidding.) Crusted port, as the name implies, isn't filtered, so it also throws a sediment that must be decanted. Unlike vintage port, though, this style is a blend of two or three years, aged for two years in the barrel, then bottled and aged for another two to three years. It gives you a mature wine taste without having to wait ten to fifteen years, as you do for vintage port.

As Rupert and I taste, we discuss the market for port. There are two big challenges. First, port, like champagne, suffers from its seasonal and occasional associations. I call it the Christmas-cake dilemma: both wines are pigeonholed with the holidays, and we forget to drink them at other times of the year. In fact, more than 60 percent of port is sold in the six weeks before Christmas. Second, sales have been almost flat for more than a decade. Much of that has to do with the drink's image: tradition isn't exactly the sexiest marketing angle.

"We can't just sell to retired generals and bankers in their clubs," Rupert observes. Port buyers are dying off—or as he puts it more delicately, "The consumer is not being renewed. We need to attract new customers without scaring off the old ones."

Rupert should know; the Symingtons are also the largest producers of Portugal's other fortified wine, madeira, now mostly relegated to sauces. The lesson from madeira and sherry: innovate or die.

"There are more taste barriers for madeira and sherry than port," he explains. "Port is easy to like immediately, with its flavors of toffee, toasted almond, and caramel. To a novice palate, sherry can have a bitter taste, and madeira can taste baked. We need to take a lesson from whisky, especially single-malt scotch. They've marketed successfully to a younger generation and made the drink part of a daily repertoire."

Two of the trendy new Symington ports are Dow's Midnight and Warre's Otima, which have won prizes for their marketing and bottle design. Dow's Midnight has a sleek, elongated form, and Otima looks like a perfume bottle. You might say the redesign is overdue: the shape hasn't changed since 1775, when the Portuguese created the first cylindrical wine bottles that we know today. (The French borrowed the innovation and the concept of vintage dating: their first was the 1787 Château-Lafite from Bordeaux.)

Other producers are also trying to keep up with the current century. Another port family, Taylor's, launched the first pink port under their Croft label several years ago. My instinctive response: could there be a better way to raise the antimarketing hackles of a woman wine writer? I imagined it would taste like a patronizing cotton-candy slap on the palate. The company described it as rosé-style port, which to me sounded as contradictory as Manolo Blahnik sneakers. Then I tried it and, grudgingly, had to admit that it was pretty good. It tasted like the lightest essence of port with wild raspberries, especially when served chilled over ice with a twist of orange. It reminded me of hot summer nights when I'd open the fridge freezer and stand in its cold embrace for a few minutes before hauling out another tub of mint chocolate chip Häagen-Dazs.

Traditionally, women didn't even drink port. After dinner, they'd retire to the drawing room to discuss domestic issues as they sipped on sherry. The men lingered around the dining room table, drank port, puffed cigars, and decided how to run the world. So I was surprised to learn that sales figures refute this cultural image: world-wide, women consume 47 percent of the port sold. In France and Belgium, women actually drink more than men because they enjoy it as an aperitif on the rocks. Chilling reduces the perception of heat, sweetness, and alcoholic strength, making port seem like a pleasant cocktail anytime of the year.

After we've sampled the best of this cellar, Rupert and I jump back in the boat to cross the river to another Symington property, Quinta do Vesuvio. This historic winery is considered one of the finest port producers in the country. It was the first estate to make single-quinta ports and now also produces dry red wines. Perched high on the bank above the river, the winery looks like an Asian dynasty: a white palace with gold-trimmed spires and jeweled tiles that glint in the sun.

As we walk up from the dock, Rupert asks, "Shall we tickle the palate before lunch?" I'm all for a liquid tickle and respond a little too enthusiastically. Up on the quinta's shady veranda, he pours Dow's Fine White Port over ice, with a splash of tonic water and a slice of lemon. White port, the least known of ports, is made from white grapes, then matured for three years in the barrel to give it a light straw color. It may have a slightly lower alcohol level than other ports, at 17 percent.

The drink has a lovely refreshing flavor, somewhere between a light tawny port and a dry fino sherry. Pair it with green olives, spicy prawns, cold crab, fried oysters, steamed clams, smoked fish, or, best of all, a long afternoon nap. It calls to mind summer evenings in a chaise longue under a rustling tree, ice clinking on glass, the coolness of the tumbler in my hand bringing down the day's heat and energy. Rupert and I sink into large cushioned chairs to wait for lunch, eating handfuls of fresh salted almonds grown on the estate. The almonds make me thirsty and the port makes me peckish; it's a pleasantly vicious circle.

After a half hour of idle chat and river gazing, we move over to a linen-crisp table. The quinta's cook brings out a large steaming dish of *bacalhau*, the traditional Portuguese casserole made with fresh salt cod, new potatoes, hard-boiled eggs, onions, garlic, olives, parsley, and paprika. To my surprise, Rupert pours his 2007 Quinta Vesuvio, a dry red wine with flavors of plush blueberry and blackberry. It's another revelation; thanks to the spicy notes in the dish, it actually pairs well with the wine.

These days, most of the surprises in the Douro are coming from dry table wines. More and more producers like Rupert realize that they need to diversify their fortified wine portfolio to attract younger drinkers. To do this, they also have to overcome the unfortunate reputation for table wine that Portugal developed in the 1970s, when vinstrosities like Mateus and Lancers rosés were perpetrated on unsuspecting drinkers.

Table wines have never been Portugal's strength, because the best grapes have always been used for port under a strict classification system known as the *benefício*. The premium vineyards are close to the river, at lower altitudes and warmer temperatures, so they produce the ripest grapes for the powerfully concentrated ports. Grapes for dry wines were grown on less-desirable real estate higher up on hillsides, so they were always the lower-quality leftovers from the harvest.

However, winemakers have recently discovered that the best grapes for dry table wines come from the higher altitudes, allowing for slower maturation without intense sugar levels. So in a happy coincidence, the two styles can complement each other: port grapes at the lower levels, table grapes at the upper levels. The quality of the dry table grapes is improving, and these wines are becoming less of an afterthought.

"The magic of the Douro is in all the different altitudes and exposures that create all the different wine styles," Rupert tells me. "The slopes are mostly schist with intrusions of granite. Schist drains well and captures the sun's warmth reflecting off its shiny facets."

Today, the region produces some eight million cases of port a year and twelve million cases of dry wine. Even so, the only way to economically justify dry red wine production is to assign all the fixed costs of production to port. Like most top Douro reds, the Symington wines are varying blends of the five primary grapes used to make port: touriga franca, touriga nacional, tinta roriz, tinta cão, and tinta barroca.

Touriga franca is the most widely planted grape, accounting for more than 20 percent of vineyards. It infuses blends with aromas of wild violet. Touriga nacional has the most character and acidity but accounts for just 2 percent of the country's grapes, being difficult to grow and requiring stringently low yields. Michel Chapoutier, the famous Rhône Valley producer who also makes wine here, compares touriga nacional to syrah because of its aromas of red plum and savory herbs. Tinta roriz, the Portuguese name for the Spanish grape tempranillo, has notes of spicy cherry; tinta cão gives black cherry and acidity, and tinta barroca adds chocolate and fig notes.

Unlike modern vineyards devoted to single grapes, older Portuguese vineyards are often haphazardly mixed plantings. When vines died, vintners would plant whatever they had on hand to fill the gap. As a result, even today single-variety wines are rare. The challenge is trying to isolate diseases or pests that may afflict one particular variety, as well as trying to manage different ripening speeds in order to choose optimal harvest dates. Tinta barroca ripens first, followed by roriz, touriga nacional, and tinta cão, with touriga francesa always the last by about three to four weeks. This moving window of maturity changes each year.

However, there are some advantages: a mix of grapes in the vineyard strengthens pollination. There's also the curious phenomenon that winemakers have noticed. "Vines are like people," Rupert observes. "The longer they live together, the more alike they become. Eventually, they start to flower and mature at the same time, even if they're from different stocks."

As he pours his 2008 Altano Reserva into my glass, Rupert observes, "The Douro is a lot like the Rhône—a rustic, earthy character but with fresh fruit flavors." The Symingtons have four non–port wine labels: Altano, Quinta de Roriz, Quinta do Vesuvio, and Chryseia, a partnership with Bruno Prats, formerly of Bordeaux's second growth Château Cos d'Estournel. The sweetly spiced cherry and raspberry aromas of the Altano are held in a racy tension by its acidity. It would pair beautifully with other traditional Portuguese dishes, such as sausage stuffed with garlic, venison, partridge in a port reduction sauce, and the local specialty *cabrito*—goat casserole.

Next we try his 2007 Quinta do Vesuvio, alive with vivid black raspberry aromas inflected with peppery spices, with some acidity for freshness. There's also a pent-up power in the wine, like a leopard dozing in a tree, ready in an instant to pounce. We finish with the 2007 Quinta do Vesuvio Vintage Port, a rip-roaring good wine with mounting levels of flavor and pleasure the more you drink. Its black fruit seems bathed in coffee treacle. Rupert and I finish with an espresso, which gives me a much-needed energy boost for my next visit farther downriver with the legendary Dirk Niepoort.

* * *

AFTER MY THREE-HOUR lunch with Rupert, I barely have time to freshen up for the seven-course dinner this evening with Dirk. I had heard much about him before even arriving in Portugal: viticultural philosopher, savvy-sharp marketer, *enfant terrible* of the Douro. He reminds me of what the poet Fernando Pessoa once said: "The Portuguese cannot live within the restraints of a single personality, nation, or faith." (Pessoa was drinking himself silly in a Lisbon bar when he said this, so perhaps he may have just been seeing double.)

Dirk, who now runs the eponymous family business that was established in 1842, is the first generation to actually make wine rather than just ship it. After he graduated with a degree in economics in Switzerland, he worked for the Swiss food company Mövenpick, where two of the company directors gave him "the bug to like wine." He did an internship at Cuvaison winery in Napa Valley and returned home to work in 1987.

While his Dutch ancestors may have worn wooden clogs and circumnavigated the globe, Dirk prefers rubber Crocs as he walks around his kitchen. On this lemony evening, I'm ushered in by his housekeeper, Maria José da Fonseca Mansilha—a small woman in her sixties who looks me up and down with her nose wrinkled, like I'm an eight-day-old sausage. Dirk doesn't seem to notice me; he's busy stirring an array of steaming pots and pans on the stove. The long counter is covered with bowls of green, red, and yellow vegetables; shiitake mushrooms; spices; and two massive slabs of uncooked fish. With his stern expression and runaway curly hair, this culinary Beethoven holds a spatula for a conductor's baton.

Finally, he swims up from his thoughts and notices me. "Ah, you're here; hello," he says. A smile plays at the corners of his mouth as he hands me a bowl of sun-dried tomatoes and a small knife: "First, if you are not comfortable here, this is your fault, not mine." His brusque manner is the defense of the shy. When I heard that Dirk was also a terrific cook, I had emailed him to ask if I could help him make dinner. His terse reply: "There are no recipes. Come at seven."

Following his quick instructions, I start to dice the tomatoes while he debones the fish. "This is the hardest, most complex, and most expressive wine region in the world," he says, eschewing small talk as he dives into his favorite topic. "In the Douro, we have 110,000 acres under vine; 39,000 growers, with vineyards ranging from 250 to 2,500 square feet; and thousands of different exposures to the sun. More than eighty indigenous grape varieties have been grown here for three centuries." This translates to many pockets of nuance that only the old people know about, he continues. "They know their parcels, which grapes to plant. We must keep their small-grower logic. There's power in genetic diversity to craft compelling red wine flavors here."

Dirk cherishes those mixed plantings, and with his Dutch name, German heritage, and Portuguese passport, Dirk is a bit of field blend himself. He's always on the hunt for old, north-facing vineyards, prowling the hills for those hidden crevices that give him the intense dark berry flavors he craves but have a paradoxically fresh brightness in their acidity.

"If we follow the modern logic of ripping up old vineyards and replanting, we will end up in five years where the New World is now—except they know how to do it better. We will be fighting them with uninteresting wines, and it won't matter where we come from."

Still, he doesn't ignore modernity. Dirk has teamed up with five other producers in their thirties and forties, calling themselves the

Douro Boys. ("Some people think we are a boy band," he says, smiling.) The others include Quinta do Crasto, Quinta do Vale Dona Maria, Quinta do Vallado, and Quinta do Vale Meão. "We need to lead with our best here, as Bordeaux does. The five first-growths lift the reputation of the whole region."

He stirs, I chop. We're both relieved that this isn't a face-to-face interview without anything for our hands to do. He's peeling tiny squid now, so I ask what he's making.

"I don't know," he says. "They looked interesting in the market, but I'm not sure what to do with them. If you start with respect for raw products, something good will happen." Then abruptly changing the subject, he asks, "What kind of wine do you like?"

"Your wines!" I almost say, but I know he'll despise sycophancy. Instead, I blurt out, "Old wines!"

Old wines? Why did I say "old wines," I wonder. Why not "mature wines" or "wines from the upper Douro, especially the spectacular 1978 and 1982 vintages"? But no, all I've managed is something that sounds as though I've just graduated from vodka coolers.

"Old wines?" he asks, squinting at me as though I'm dangerously stupid. I nod and decide to shut up.

"Come," he says, leading the way out of the kitchen and downstairs. He opens a door and I follow him into his cellar, with rows and rows of cobwebbed bottles, many so encased you can't see the labels.

"Old wines," he says, pointing. There must be thousands of bottles here, and from the few labels I can see, they date back decades, if not centuries. They're not just Portuguese; there are also some of the finest wines from Burgundy, Bordeaux, Spain, and other regions.

"How about this one?" he asks, pulling out a bottle. The amber liquid shows through streaks of dirt, and the ragged, moldy label barely clings to the glass, but I can just make out the vintage: 1893.

"Yes, please," I whisper.

Back in the kitchen, Dirk pours his tawny port into a decanter, and the amber essence of another century wafts out of the bottle. He gently swirls the decanter to aerate the wine that has been waiting for us for 117 years. He pours us a small glass each, we clink, and, hand shaking, I lift the glass to my lips.

The wine isn't oxidized as I had expected. In fact, it's absolutely fresh. It's not robust or rich, either; it's just a slip of a wine. Still, its aromas swirl around my head, like I'm sitting in a steam room billowing with spice-smoke. Fleeting whiffs of pan-seared tangerines, honey-dipped violets, and plums dusted with cinnamon appear, then vanish. This is a wine to chase all the way to the bottom of the decanter.

Tawny ports start out like ruby ports, but they're aged in wood for much longer. There are four types: fine tawny, tawny, tawny with an indication of age, and colheita. Fine tawny, contrary to what it suggests, is not the best type, just the simplest; it's made by blending ruby and white port, and results in a style even lighter than ruby. It's a quick and inexpensive production method, like mixing red and white wines to make cheap rosé. Tawny from the second category is also fairly simple and usually blended with white port.

Tawnies with an indication of age are labeled by their decade, as ten, twenty, thirty, or forty years old. Each of these is the average age, not the absolute age of the wine. So a ten-year-old tawny may contain some wine that was aged for seven years and some for thirty years. The Port Institute makes the final call when their tasters evaluate a sample to determine if the blend has the character of a ten-, twenty-, thirty-, or forty-year tawny. Colheitas are tawnies that come from a single vintage and are aged for at least seven years in the barrel, but often for decades. These are the rarest of all ports, comprising less than half a percent of total production. On the whole, ruby and tawny port account for 90 percent of sales, but vintage port drives profitability and sales growth.

We continue to sip on the port and chop vegetables until the other dinner guests arrive. The first is Dirk's cellar master, Luís Seabra, who is mesmerizingly charming and, I sense, quite a cad, with those flashing dark eyes and suggestive eyebrow action. He, too, drinks some of the 1893, toasting us with the traditional "Saude!" More guests arrive; few bother ringing the doorbell—most just stroll into the kitchen, deposit a bottle or two on the table, have a drink, and then drift out to the living room to chat. There's an orthopedic surgeon, a landscape photographer, a woman who makes jewelry, and several people from the Port Wine Institute, presumably writing off the evening as media relations work. One of the latter asks me where the 1893 is. I shrug and say that I think it's out in the living room—hoping he doesn't see the decanter behind me on the counter.

Dirk starts frying Galicia pimentos in olive oil, salting them so they lose their toughness and their skins peel off. He looks over at my sun-dried tomatoes and says, "There must be twenty-five pieces all the same size, not twenty-four, not twenty-six."

"I thought you said there are no recipes?" I ask, feeling flustered.

He smiles. "We are guided by intuition, not science—twenty-five feels right."

He turns back to the fish, which he's flipping deftly in the saucepan. "It's easy to overcook fish," he says. "You must understand how high heat affects food. The best cook I ever knew was Joerg Woerther from Austria. I never met anyone so sensitive to heat—he would take the pan on and off the heat constantly, as though he were cooking himself. We try to do the same thing with wine: to feel the outer limits of the wine . . . how far can we take it without ruining it?" He nods as though satisfied with his analogy and with the crispy fish that he teases out of the pan to a large plate. "Yes, to cook and to make wine—to create at the moment of destruction."

The kitchen is now filled with savory cooking aromas and chatty guests. It's so crowded that when I try to move the bowl of chopped tomatoes nearer to Dirk at the stove, I bump into Maria. She glowers at me, turns her back, and starts chopping the celery furiously. I slink back to my corner to console myself with another nip of the 1893 as I angle my body to hide it.

Dirk serves a starter of the steaming grilled squid to anyone in the kitchen not too wrapped up in conversation to notice the food. Then he, Maria, and I carry out the platters of roasted vegetables and fried fish to the dining room. He sits at the head of a long table, and sixteen of us slide into chairs. As the platters are passed around, the conversation continues unabated—Dirk seems to have invited the gastronomic equivalent of a literary salon. Fortunately, I'm seated at his right, because he mostly just chats quietly with the people closest to him. The languages around us weave in and out of French, English, Portuguese, and Spanish. Again, Dirk has an apt analogy: "Making wine is like speaking English: easy to learn but difficult to master."

Dirk pours his 2004 Redoma, an expressive white wine made from a cooler site in the Douro. Its acidity is an electric spine, holding together the flesh of the wine. He explains that a former assistant winemaker with obsessive tendencies had the entire staff, including Dirk, de-stemming the grapes by hand for days.

"Did it make a difference?" I ask.

"To the wine, no. To us, yes, it changed our lives. I'll never do it again, and he's gone," Dirk says, smiling.

As we continue to enjoy the tender fish, Dirk pours his Charme, a blend of tinta roriz and touriga grapes. They come from vines that are seventy to a hundred years old and were trodden by foot in the old lagars. It's a lovely, delicate wine, with great length and polish.

"Fruity wines are a modern disease," Dirk says, clearly moved by his own words. "If I want to drink fruit, I'll have cherry juice. Fruit just sits there on top of wine, facing outward to impress; it's psychopathic. The point of wine is deeper than fruit—it's the essence of the land."

He has a particular passion for Old World pinot noir, which seems to me almost the antithesis of port. However, he seeks to infuse his wines with Burgundian elegance. "We live in a region that gives us rich, ripe wines, but we don't want heavy, fat wines—we want elegance and finesse," he explains. "Most modern wines hurt you; they flatten your senses. We need wines that make us sing."

I ask him what he means by elegance and finesse. His response: "Wines that are of one sensory piece from start to finish."

Turning a question on me, he asks, "So what do you say when you think a wine is complete crap?"

As I search for an answer, my mouth opens and closes, opens and closes, like a fish dying on a dock. Finally, I splutter, "Interesting, very interesting—unlike anything I've ever tasted before."

"*Interesting* answer," he replies, with a sidelong glance and wolfish smile.

He pours his forty-year-old tawny, brimming with aromas of toffee, butterscotch, cedar, and almonds. Dirk explains that this port is drier than younger tawnies and will pair better with the dessert. How can one port be "drier" than another, I ask him—aren't they all sweet? He tells me to think of the difference between a caramel candy and the caramelized but slightly bitter top of crème brûlée. The toffee signature is in both, but there's a wide spectrum of sweetness.

"A great sweet wine finishes dry," Dirk declares. "It starts sweet in your mouth, but the acidity acts like little brushes, sweeping away the sweetness and making your palate feel clean, refreshed, and ready for the next sip. Acidity is the cleanup crew."

Tawny is both lighter and sweeter than vintage port, so it marries well with any egg-based dessert: crème brûlée, sabayon, sponge cake, or custard pudding. The lighter, berry-fresh aromas of ruby ports go better with fruit-based desserts, such as flans, pies, cobblers, and crumbles. These don't go well with the caramel notes in tawnies, which do better with dried, toasted, or spiced fruit, including fruit-cake, toasted almonds, nut-based tarts, pear frangipane, almond cake, tarte tatin, crème caramel, or on their own. Tawny also loves to tango with salty, pungent blue cheeses, such as Stilton, Bleu d'Auvergne, and Gorgonzola. It's the liquid line drawn after the meal.

Port is also autumn in a glass, with its fiery tawny-red tones. It pairs well with many harvest dishes, such as foie gras, pumpkin pie, and pecan tart. However, Dirk even pairs tawny port with game meats and birds, such as smoked duck, quail with black figs, and boar in a red wine reduction sauce, because it brings out their darker, savory flavors. However, it won't obliterate the flavors of the meat itself because it doesn't slink across your mouth the way some sweet wines do. Many people don't understand the concept of sweet. A lot of what they eat is sweet, and not just for dessert. Think of glazed ham, teriyaki sauce, sweet potatoes, creamed corn. Dirk likes vintage port with pepper steak because the pepper reduces the perception of sweetness so that the robust flavors in the dish and glass marry well.

In North America, we don't have much of a history with port, as we don't pair them with our entrées. We drink 75 percent of our wine with dinner, rather than afterward. By the time dinner's over, we're usually too stuffed (or drunk) to have a digestif. When did we lose the pleasant ritual of lingering after dinner for more talk and drink?

So just as you might propose other daring ideas at the end of a meal when your companion is more open to suggestion, try a little port. The ideal way to enjoy it is about a two- to three-ounce serving, only about half the amount of a dry wine; thus, one bottle can easily serve eight to thirteen people. Being a bit greedy, I find the traditional port glasses too small; I prefer drinking my port from the luxurious roundness of a brandy snifter, so I can cradle it in my hands. Although some wine lovers advise serving port slightly chilled, I prefer the aromatic sensuality of a tawny cupped in my hand.

"You can drink tawnies anytime, they're like wearing jeans; but drinking vintage port makes you feel like you should be wearing a tuxedo," Dirk says, as we clink glasses.

He tells me that as tawnies age, they lose about 3 percent of their volume every year through evaporation from the barrel. So they're topped up by younger, fruiter wine to "refresh" them. This builds differing layers of freshness, maturity, flavor, and complexity, much like a modified version of the *solera* system used to make sherry. The oldest barrel is topped up with younger wine. Without careful blending, the wines can taste disjointed: the young fruit doesn't marry the mature character. The longer the wine stays in the barrel, the more its color changes, from the deep violet of youth to the fiery amber and topaz of maturity. This creates a smooth wine of luminescent amber that doesn't need to be decanted because it was filtered before being barreled.

It also doesn't need aging by the buyer, since the winemaker has already matured the port before bottling and selling it. In fact, most tawnies are best consumed within two to three years of bottling. In the liquor store, ten-year-old tawnies are the best value: prices double with every decade, but the hedonistic pleasure doesn't. This was quite a revelation to me—and one that's saved me a lot of money.

Ten-year tawnies have the most vibrant fruit flavors, twenty-year-olds display candied fruits wrapped in toffee, thirty-year tawnies start to taste drier and more honeyed, and by forty, tawnies have darker depths of dried figs and spice-coated clementines. For years I felt less evolved because I loved tawny more than vintage ports.

Now I've just accepted myself as an uncomplicated, unrepentant hedonist: I can't resist tangerine zest, cinnamon, and butterscotch.

Another advantage tawnies have over vintage ports: they retain their taste for one to two months after opening the bottle rather than having to be consumed within a day or two. That's an enormous benefit when you just want to sip an ounce or two a few evenings a week. They've already had to toughen up against oxidation during the aging process, when they're exposed to air as they're transferred (racked) from barrel to barrel several times.

Before I came to Portugal, I didn't even know what made a colheita different from a tawny, but I'm learning quickly now. Dirk has an amazing vertical collection of them: the oldest colheita is from 1906 and spent seventy-two years in cask before being bottled. Some winemakers believe that colheitas confuse the consumer and shouldn't be produced (most tawnies are a blend of years, whereas colheitas are tawnies from a single vintage and are bottle-dated).

Naturally, Dirk disagrees. "Port needs to have different expressions; they make it exciting. Colheitas have always been some of our very best wines."

He pours one for me now but covers the label. Oh joy, we're going to play my favorite game: make the wine writer guess that vintage for a slow and measured disgracing that yields maximum satisfaction to the vintner. This colheita has a surprisingly vibrant freshness that reminds me of the verbal zingers my grandmother used to fling from her corner of the kitchen during dinner.

"I don't like selling these old wines," he surprises me by saying. "I prefer to drink them with my family and friends."

I am so very glad he feels this way. I glance around the room, now saturated with the rich heady haze of honey, spices, and toffee. This wine hasn't been ruined with words—it seems to have been created around a longing.

Dirk prompts me for my answer, and so I guess a few vintages, all too old or too young, of course. Finally, unable to resist, he tells me: he did a little research himself to find what year I was born and has opened a 1966. I'm touched. Families here reserve heirloom wines from various vintages the way we in North America pass down antique watches, cars, and paintings.

This port reminds me of a dessert I created when I was six: tangerine slices rolled in brown sugar. These aromas re-create the entire atmosphere in my mind, and I'm on my grandparents' veranda again. I have such a feeling of beautiful resignation that I sit there smiling at nothing. Stravinsky said that music is the best way to digest time. I think port is better—and certainly tastier. This bottle is a memory palace.

Field Notes from a
Wine Cheapskate

Although port tends to be more expensive per bottle than dry table wines, a little goes a long way, since we usually only indulge in a few ounces at a time. Therefore, a bottle can serve many more people or, in the case of non-vintage ports, be enjoyed over a month or two.

INSIDER TIPS

- Ten-year-old tawnies represent the best value on the liquor store shelf because their prices roughly double with every decade, but their quality doesn't.

- Portugal's native grapes are not well-known to North Americans, but that translates to great values. Varieties like tinta roriz and tinta barroca just don't have the brand awareness and cachet of cabernet sauvignon and merlot. Therefore, producers must compete more aggressively on price.

- The best-known vintages for port will always command the highest prices, just as they do in Bordeaux and Tuscany. So seek out the well-rated vintages close to a star vintage. For example, 2007 is considered one of the best in decades, so try 2006.

WINERIES VISITED

Dow's: www.dows-port.com
Graham's: www.grahams-port.com
Niepoort: www.niepoort-vinhos.com
Sandeman: www.sandeman.eu
Symington Family Estates: www.symington.com
Warre's: www.warre.com

BEST VALUE WINES

Croft Pink Port
Dow's Crusted Port
Dow's Fine White Port
Graham's Late Bottled Vintage
Niepoort 10 Years Old Tawny Port*
Sandeman Ruby Port
Sandeman Tawny Port
Warre's Otima Tawny Port

My first pick for my own Saturday dinner.

TOP VALUE PRODUCERS

Altano (Symington)	Quinta do Bomfim
Cálem	Quinta do Casal
Callabriga (Sogrape)	Da Coelheira
Croft	Quinta do Cerrado
Delaforce	Quinta do Crasto
Duas Quintas	Quinta do Portal
(Ramos Pinto)	Quinta do Vallado
Ferreira	Quinta do Vesuvio
Fonseca	Quinta dos Aciprestes
Kopke	Ramos Pinto
Monte da Cal	Taylor's
Quinta de Cabriz	Vinha Longa

SATURDAY DINNER FOR A WINE CHEAPSKATE

You'll find the recipes for the dishes I enjoyed with Rupert Symington at www.nataliemaclean.com/food.

Bacalhau in Cream Sauce (Fresh Cod Casserole)

Wood-Oven Baked Lamb

Duck Rice

Crème Queimado (Crème Brûlée)

TERRIFIC PAIRINGS

Port is a magnificent, rich, and long-lived dessert wine, with signature aromas of toffee and almonds in the tawnies, and black fruits in the vintage ports. My favorite pairings include:

Almond desserts
Apples: baked, pie, tart
Baked Alaska
Biscotti
Brownies: chocolate
Cheese: cheddar, Stilton,
    Roquefort
Chicken with dates
Chocolate: all types, with
    nuts or caramel

Chocolate-chip cookies
Crème caramel
Donuts: chocolate with sprinkles
Pavlova
Pecan pie
Pizza: blue cheese and
    buffalo chicken
Toffee pudding

RESOURCES

For more information about Portuguese wines and port:

Wine and Food Lover's Guide to Portugal by Charles Metcalfe
The Wines and Vineyards of Portugal by Richard Mayson
Portugal's Wines and Wine Makers: Port Madeira and Regional Wines by Richard Mayson
Wineries of Portugal: www.nataliemaclean.com/wineries
Institute of Port Wines: www.ivdp.pt
Wines of Portugal: www.viniportugal.pt
Body and Soul of Portugal Wine Club Toronto: www.bodyand soulwine.com
For the Love of Port: www.fortheloveofport.com

RELATED READING

The following books, while seemingly unrelated to the main subject matter of this chapter, provided some enjoyable reading before, during, and after my travels:

Heart of Darkness by Joseph Conrad
The Egoist by George Meredith
Notes on a Cellar-Book by George Saintsbury

EIGHT

SUNDAY

La Vie en Rosé en Provence

As I DRIVE down the autoroute du Soleil, the yellow fields of Provence around me are ablaze with the red and blue of poppies and lavender. I can see orchards heavy with apricots and plums, and smell the wild thyme and rosemary that grow around Roman ruins and the villages of cream-colored cottages. Everything is drenched in golden Mediterranean light.

Cypress trees flit by my open car windows: *fwip—fwip—fwip*. Henry IV of France planted those trees along the roads to help buffer the mistral, the infamous wind that sweeps down into Provence from the Rhône Valley. It can reach speeds of fifty-five miles an hour, hard enough to knock people off their feet. The mistral has even been cited as an extenuating circumstance in murder trials: its unceasing howl can drive a person crazy. The wind is most intense during the winter; but even now, on a quiet summer evening, the ivy rippling along a stone wall is a reminder that the mistral is never far away.

Still, the mistral also blows in fresh weather to Provence, keeping the vines dry and preventing disease and rot. That is one reason why winemaking is an ancient tradition here: Phoenicians or Greeks are believed to have planted the first vines sometime in the sixth century BCE, making this France's oldest wine region. After Julius Caesar ousted the Greeks, he considered this region his favorite among the many provinces he owned and affectionately named it "my provence." The name stuck, as did the Romans who continued to cultivate vines there until their eventual decline. Today, there are more than eighty thousand acres of vineyards here and some four hundred producers.

Provence's most famous wine is its deliciously carefree rosé. As a knock-it-back drinker, I love the indiscriminate guzzling of this pink wine—especially over a long Sunday lunch. It combines the fleshy fruit flavors of red wine with the airy lightness of white. Rosé is the world's greatest mindless wine. Every time I taste it, I wonder why I don't drink more of it.

Actually, I *do* know why: for many of us, rosé has never managed to shake that cheap and nasty image from the 1970s. Cast your mind back to the saccharine pink bog-wash we downed in college: Mateus, Lancers, Piat d'Or. Ugh. None of those wines came from Provence, but they still influence how we think of rosé: Kool-Aid with a kick, seemingly a blend of alcohol and fuchsia food coloring—with no fruit flavor and little balancing acidity.

The biggest brand was Mateus, that syrupy concoction in the squat bottle inspired by a World War I water canteen. Although we may shudder at its taste now, it was pure marketing brilliance when first launched back in 1943. Designed by a committee in a Portuguese conglomerate, it paired perfectly with 1950s fare: hotdog wedges on toothpicks and canned fruit trapped in Jell-O. The bonus: when the bottle was empty, you could use it as a candleholder.

By the 1960s, Mateus was the world's biggest selling wine brand; twenty years later, it still accounted for 40 percent of Portugal's wine export. Mateus was the favorite of both royalty and celebrity: Queen Elizabeth, crooner Sir Cliff Richard, and even Saddam Hussein. (In 2002, U.S. inspectors reportedly found several cases of the wine stockpiled in the dictator's palace. There was some debate as to whether these qualified as weapons of mass destruction.)

In the 1970s, North American drinkers moved on from Mateus to even sweeter Californian white zinfandels, which tasted more like the Coca-Cola they had grown up drinking. Bob Trinchero of the Sutter Home winery first popularized the style: he bottled and sold the light pink runoff juice from pressing red zinfandel grapes. The third year he made the wine, the fermentation got stuck, leaving a lot of unfermented sugar in the wine. It sold even better than his dry version—he could barely keep up with demand. Other wineries jumped on his blush bandwagon.

However, most of the buyers of these wines tended to be women, because rosés had cultural associations that gave burly men pause: Mary Kay Cadillacs, Jackie Collins book covers, and heart-shaped resort beds in Niagara Falls. Even today, many people still think of these wines as the vinous equivalent of love beads, lava lamps, and Tom Jones, with his open shirts and gold chains. (After a glass or two of rosé, I've been known to perform a hairdryer-microphone solo in the bathroom of "It's Not Unusual.")

Still viewed as the Rodney Dangerfield of wine, rosé gets little respect. That fact spurred the formation, in 2005, of a group of U.S. wine lovers called Rosé Avengers and Producers (RAP). Every year, they host "Pink Out" tastings across the country to convince consumers, retailers, and sommeliers that rosé can be both versatile and tasty.

What a difference a few decades can make. Rosé is now the new white—a light, approachable wine without oak or heavy flavors. North American sales have jumped 26 percent in the past five years. By comparison, the entire category of table wines increased only

7 percent. Dry rosés are popping up on many restaurant wine lists and liquor store shelves. Younger drinkers are discovering rosé as a bridge between sweet coolers and dry wines. The beautiful bonus is that most of these wines are less than $20, often $15.

However, one challenge remains: few wine regions specialize in the style. Most vintners stake their reputation on "serious" red or white wines: chardonnay, riesling, pinot noir, cabernet sauvignon, or merlot. Not so in Provence, where rosé makes up more than 80 percent of its production. The remaining 20 percent is mostly red wine, with just a little white. That makes Provence the world's largest producer of good rosé, which is why I'm here.

I turn off the autoroute and drive down increasingly narrow back roads. The cicadas make their wheezy summer song. An indigo sky stretches out ahead, with a few corrugated clouds rippling over the hills. It looks like some of them have actually landed on the road itself, but as I get closer, I realize it's a herd of more than a hundred sheep wandering across the lane. I honk, a few of them look at me with their bored gray eyes, and then they go back to grazing. It takes a good fifteen minutes until the woolly scavengers amble on, giving me time to slow down my internal clock.

The vineyards of Provence hug the Mediterranean coast from Marseille to Nice. It's the land of daydream getaways and the playground of the rich: Monte Carlo gambling, the Cannes film festival, Saint-Tropez sunglasses bigger than the bikinis. The shimmering luminous light streaming in my windows has also drawn many artists here: Pablo Picasso, Henri Matisse, Marc Chagall, Paul Cézanne. In fact, it feels like I'm driving through a Van Gogh painting as I pass sun-dappled bales of hay and swaying sunflowers. The artist once wrote how much he loved this countryside for "the limpidity of its atmosphere and gay color effects."

I've always been fascinated by Van Gogh's prodigiously crazed talent, epitomized by his cutting off of his own ear. After that incident, he checked himself into a local asylum, where he could see the swirling stars above the fields. Apparently, when he painted, he no longer saw the bars on his bedroom window. A year later, he checked out, walked into one of those fields, and shot himself. He was thirty-seven years old and left the world with 189 paintings.

I believe that Van Gogh would have painted many more masterpieces had he drunk the local wine rather than absinthe, a spirit distilled from wormwood at 140 proof. (I vaguely recall the one evening I ever drank absinthe. The next morning, I prayed for quick and painless death, but it did not come. I spent the day with my head in the green fairy's vise grip.) Van Gogh wrote to his brother Theo that "to attain the high yellow note, I really had to be pretty well keyed up." Such a hallucinatory drink was hardly the ideal tipple for a bipolar artist, yet perhaps it was this mad mixture that gave us *Starry Night*.

These thoughts bring me back to the present-day genius I'm on my way to see now: vintner Raimond Villeneuve. I became intrigued with him when I read the back label of a bottle of his Château de Roquefort wine, written by Tim Johnson, owner of the renowned Willi's Wine Bar in Paris:

> These wines are the result of the courage of a man who once could easily have been the Court Jester, a man with a touch of madness and a genuine love for what he does best: make wine!
>
> —TIM JOHNSON

When I drank his rosé, I knew I had to meet Raimond, and as I get out of my car in front of Château de Roquefort, I hear his deep, sonorous voice before I see him. As he emerges from the cellar into the sunlight, the picture matches the sound—a tanned, muscular man in his forties, who looks like a war correspondent: multipocketed khaki vest, cargo shorts, hiking boots. He pushes his sunglasses up onto his head as he says hello, revealing electric blue eyes.

"Let me show you the vineyards," he says with a rolling French accent. I follow him up the castle steps and through the one-room apartment where he lives. *"Pas de luxe,"* he acknowledges, smiling. ("No luxury.") The walls are covered with maps, old photos, and rusting farm tools; the kitchen table is stacked with viticultural and history books. Raimond evicted himself from the other twenty-three rooms in his grand château in favor of storing almost two hundred thousand bottles of his precious wine.

"Voilà!" he says, taking me out onto a small balcony and gesturing at the sweeping rows of vines below us that run up to the opposite rock face. We're twelve hundred feet above the turquoise Mediterranean sparkling off in the distance—its breezes keep the fruit cool, allowing the grapes to ripen slowly and to be picked later in the fall, when their flavors have matured. The vineyard is sheltered in a stony, amphitheater-shaped hollow. The soil, mostly clay and limestone, rests on beds of fossilized shells and intrusions of flint.

Outside the vineyard is the wild, harsh countryside, dotted with tough little shrubs where the ground is uncultivated. The Romans built this fortified castle to defend their settlements in Marseilles and Cassis, and named it after the rocky hillside (*rocca fortis*), which became Roquefort in French. Over the centuries, the property has been variously owned by the princes of Baux and the bishops of Marseilles.

Wine has been made in these cellars since the Middle Ages. The place has been in Raimond's family since 1812, when his ancestor, the Earl of Gardanne, bought it. When I admire the château's beautiful bell tower, he tells me that his grandmother built it in 1880. "But the house is much older, 1568."

Raimond takes me through one shadowy ballroom after another, stacked with boxes of wine. The once-stately rooms are uninhabited otherwise: chandeliers darkened, gold-embossed paper peeling from the walls, and dusty velvet curtains shutting out the sunlight. I almost expect to find Miss Havisham here, with her yellowing wedding dress and cobwebbed gray hair. I imagine her sampling Raimond's wine and haughtily dismissing it into the spittoon—great expectorations.

As we wander though the box-filled rooms, Raimond tells me that although he was raised at the family château, where his father made bulk wine for other wineries, his first love was antique wood furniture. He originally trained as an artisanal carpenter and "learned the value of natural materials and craftsmanship." But after several years in that business, Raimond yearned to be back in the wine industry, so he became the export manager for the big Burgundian firm Mommessin. After six years, in 1995, he returned home and took over from his father, making better quality wines under the Château de Roquefort label.

The château has some fifty acres under vine, more than one-third of which are older than forty years. All are farmed biodynamically. Raimond replaced chemicals with manure, and insecticides with wild grasses and beneficial insects. He also uses the natural yeasts on the grape skins to start fermentation, rather than commercially cultivated ones. "I'm not religious about biodynamic farming, but I do see the value in trying to make natural liquids born of experience and observation."

Through an open window, I hear a donkey bray, then again. "Ah, that's Polie—she knows I have a guest, and she gets so jealous." Raimond chuckles. "Would you like to meet her?"

We go down the stone steps of the château and over to a hayfield, where a life-sized Eeyore trots over to greet us. She angles her body to the fence sideways, eyeing me suspiciously, her long gray velvet ears cocked back so as not to miss any of our conversation. Raimond strokes her nose affectionately, and she looks at me as if to say, see, he's still mine.

"Mules are better at tilling vineyard rows than horses or machines," he says. "They're smaller and more careful where they step. But unlike horses, they need lots of companionship. We go for long walks, don't we, Polie? She carries the picnic basket."

Raimond usually allows Polie to wander freely on the estate, and she often follows him on his chores. Laughing, he tells me about one evening when he was hosting an outdoor dinner party. His friends were mingling by the campfire, and he set down a platter of sardines and several open bottles of rosé on a picnic table before going down to the cellar to fetch more wine. When he came back, Polie had already polished off all the sardines and was lifting a bottle of wine in her teeth—drinking what wasn't splashing over her mouth.

"You like your rosé, don't you, Polie?" Raimond asks, as she paws the ground, presumably in agreement.

On our way back to the château, I ask the impertinent question that's been topmost in my mind since I arrived. "Raimond, why is Provence better known for rosé than anywhere else? I know you make a lot of it, but the Rhône Valley produces great rosés, too, and hardly anyone knows about them. What gives?"

"In the Rhône Valley, rosé is the afterthought of red wine," he says, smiling. "But in Provence, rosé is all we think of."

The big difference between the Rhône and Provence is how rosé is made. When red grapes are first crushed, the resulting juice is a light pinkish color. Only after a long soak with the skins does the juice take on a deeper ruby hue, after its acidity breaks down the skins to release their color and flavor. The longer this period of maceration, the more color the juice absorbs. Dark red wines often macerate for several weeks to a month, whereas white wines usually spend no more than twenty-four hours in contact with the skins.

When winemakers want to produce a particularly strong and deep red wine, as they do in the Rhône, they can concentrate the skin-to-juice ratio by removing some of the pink juice early in the process. This "bleeding the vats" is known as *saignée*, which sounds to me like a medieval operation involving leeches. The siphoned-off juice is then fermented like white wine and bottled early in the spring to capture its exuberant fruit flavors. "One advantage of the saignée method," Raimond says, "is that it allows vignerons to create two rivers of wine from one harvest. But it doesn't always make the best rosés—they have high alcohol, like the reds, and too much tannin for my taste."

He has a point. Rhône rosés tend to be beefy vino, often weighing in at 14 percent alcohol, with chewy red fruit flavors. They hint at the big bruiser reds this region can produce. But to me, rosé with that much heft is like a hairy man in a tutu: it just doesn't fly. And if the juice soaks too long on the skins, there's the danger of too much bitter tannin for such a delicate wine, not to mention the lurid lipstick red color of the wine. Conversely, if the grapes don't soak for long enough, the wine looks and tastes pallid. Some vintners try to correct this by adding a little red wine, but that can cause the rosé to lose its ethereal vivacity.

The best-known rosé region in the Rhône is Tavel—a small town just south of Châteauneuf-du-Pape—where all they think of is rosé as well. In fact, it's the only appellation in France that produces nothing but rosé—and has done so for more than five hundred years. At just two thousand acres, the growing area is only 2.5 percent of the size of Provence. Nevertheless, I love the robust style of Tavel rosé, which still manages to be refreshing. Fans throughout history have included Honoré de Balzac, King Louis XIV, and King Philippe le Bel. The latter, traveling through the area in the thirteenth century, reportedly declared, "There is no good wine but for the wine of Tavel!" (Always a politic thing to say about the local wine, wherever you are.)

"We don't use the saignée method here," Raimond says. "We pick the grapes at a ripeness level for a lively rosé, not a big red, then we gently press whole bunches of grapes rather than crushing them individually, so we don't extract too much color and tannin from the skins." Provençal winemakers cold-soak the grapes and skins for just a few hours, or at most, a day, to preserve their delicate flavor and color. The invention of temperature-controlled fermentation has also helped to keep the fruit fresh and lively.

"There is no miracle in my wine," Raimond says. "It's just the quality of the grapes. We use the same grapes here as they do in the Rhône: grenache, mourvèdre, carignan, cinsault. They make great rosé, but they create too tannic red wines here because of the heat." The ideal grapes for red wine in other regions don't necessarily work as well for rosé. Cabernet sauvignon, for example, is too tannic a base—though its parent, cabernet franc, is terrific because it creates a lighter, more aromatic wine.

The best Provençal rosé is perfumed with the lighter spectrum of red wine aromas, such as field raspberries and strawberries, but with the structure and lightness of white wine. Yet those ripe fruit flavors don't mean that the wine is sweet, even though it may taste that way. In fact, all Provençal rosés are bone-dry: they don't even make a sweet style. Wine is sweet only if the vintner stops fermentation before the yeast consumes all the sugar, leaving some sweetness and less alcohol. Usually the higher the alcohol level, the drier the wine; a wine with 12 percent or more is usually dry.

However, in other regions, an insouciant touch of sweetness can be charming in a pert little pink wine, like a coquettish flutter of eyelashes. It tames the tannins and highlights the fresh fruit flavors, like sprinkling sugar over fresh berries and cream.

"Making white wine is more difficult than making red wine, and making rosé is the most difficult," Raimond explains. "If you make the smallest mistake, you throw the acidity out of balance and end up with a wine that's too flabby or too tart. You can't hide your mistakes behind oak, as you can with red wine and some whites, because you want the fresh fruit flavors. It's like cooking: it's easier to ruin a delicate fish than a hearty steak."

The third way to make rosé is the down-market method of mixing red and white wines. It takes only 3 percent of red wine blended into white to make rosé. Even with this small amount, the red wine tannins and bitterness are apparent, so the taste is quite different from the other production methods. This method is illegal in most of Europe. In 2010, when the European Union proposed legalizing this blending method to give producers a way to use up cheap wines, the Provençal wine council lobbied hard against it. They argued that French rosé had finally achieved a reputation as a quality wine, and cheap knockoffs would ruin the whole industry. Fortunately, they were successful, and the legislation was quashed.

That was only the latest salvo in the ongoing battle for the good name of Provence. Back in the 1970s, the government paid vintners to grub up inferior vines and replant with better ones, such as syrah and grenache. Other regions around the world slowly followed suit, and the quality of rosé started improving as more and more wineries planted better vines and improved their techniques. Despite this, wine quality in Provence, like in the rest of France, ranges from the most basic *vin de table* (table wine) to *vin de pays* (country wine) to the highest quality in nine designated growing areas, or *appellation d'origine contrôlée* (AOC). The largest and most important appellation is Côtes de Provence with 115,000 acres, France's sixth largest appellation.

Regardless of how it's made, rosé has traditionally filled a vinous gap in many regions when the locals wanted something to drink while they waited for the red wines to mature. In areas too warm to produce crisp white wines, such as the Rhône Valley, Provence, Portugal, and Spain, rosés are the wines of refreshment. Conversely, cool regions that can make crisp whites, like the Loire Valley, aren't warm enough to produce rich, deep reds. So those places use the thin-skinned, quick-ripening pinot noir and gamay grapes to produce rosés that have a little more weight than their whites.

Fashion has turned to pale rosé, boosting the popularity of Provençal wines. The most ragingly stylish rosé is Domaines Ott, with its distinctive curvy bottle that looks like the glass-blowing machine had a meltdown. The Ott family still runs the winery today, even though Louis Roederer, producer of the prestigious Cristal Champagne, bought a controlling interest in 2004. The wine is a perennial favorite of the jet set, who dubbed it "D.O." Casually drop that moniker into your conversation and everyone will know that you've wintered on the Côte d'Azur or at Cap d'Antibes.

To achieve a color range between translucent onionskin to ballet-slipper pink, the Provençal grape of choice is often grenache, which dominates Raimond's vineyards. Its skin is only lightly pigmented because it has low levels of anthocyanin, the compound that gives red grapes their deep bluish tint. Still, color can be deceiving: it doesn't indicate the wine's quality or body. Pale rosés can be full-bodied, and raspberry-red ones can be lightweights. Some Provençal rosés pack a surprising alcoholic punch, known as "pink pain." Drinking them can give you that same feeling of disbelief after sunbathing on a cloudy day, then discovering that you look like a radioactive lobster.

The challenge with grenache is that it can oxidize quickly because it has low acidity, so it can easily lose its freshness and color after a couple years. This is why most rosé is best drunk young. (The wine, that is, not the drinker.) Ideally, the rosé you drink is from the current vintage or, at most, one to two years old. That said, there are a few exceptions, such as robust rosés from the Rhône, which can age well for five to ten years. But beware if you see that the wine's pink color has acquired an orange-brown tint; that means it's most likely oxidized and will taste tired and faded.

Color is so important to Raimond that he names his wines for their hues. Les Mures, French for "blackberry," is a rich dark red blend of grenache noir, carignan, and syrah; Rubrum Obscrum, the Latin for "obscure red," is mostly old grenache. Corail, or "coral," is a rosé made mostly from grenache, syrah, and cinsault. He pours me a glass as we walk through his cellar, a luminous pink wine with salmon highlights. I inhale its vibrant scents of strawberry and summer-flush raspberries. It's a vivacious wine, made for immediate rejoicing.

Raimond also pours me his other rosé: Sémiramis, a bone-dry, delicate, herb-scented wonder that perfumes my mind. It tastes of the season's first fruit and fresh fields; sipping it, I can feel the juice of ripe grapes running through my fingers.

As we taste, Raimond reflects on his career change. "When I was a carpenter, I was able to see the chair within the tree," he says. "That required observation, creativity, and stillness. Now I have to see the wine within the grape. But either way, craftsmanship is the combination of work and energy—and art as intellect applied to good raw materials," he says, as we emerge back into the sunlight.

"The only escape in this world is through what you produce," he explains. "You cannot escape your fate. When I'm not busy with the vines, I don't feel well."

One of his pockets starts ringing, and he feels in his vest and pulls out a cell phone. It's not the right one, so he pulls out another and answers it. When he's done, he says to me, smiling, "This one is for the cellar—I can drop it on the floor.

"*Alors!* Shall we get some lunch?"

Oui, oui, merci! I am always hungry—tasting wine builds the appetite.

Raimond's battered jeep proves that transportation, like accommodation, is a much lower priority to him than wine. On the glove compartment, scribbled in gold pen, is a note by his friend Tim Johnson, the Paris wine bar owner: "Stick with me and I'll show you the world! TJ, 1995." It's the record of a road trip they took together when Raimond was just starting to sell his first small production of rosé to restaurants in the countryside.

In the heart of bustling Cassis, the town best known for its black currant liqueur, Raimond parks the jeep half up onto a sidewalk, right under a sign with a severe warning that all cars will be towed. He sticks one of his wine labels on the dashboard—the local police enjoy free samples of his wines.

On a vine-covered terrace overlooking the Mediterranean, the day's heat hasn't released its hold, though it's relieved by a breeze from the ocean. Below us, bathers sprawl on the creamy sand, children's voices trail across the water, and heady gusts of thyme, rosemary, and pine from the hillside fill my lungs. Our server pours a cool coral stream of Raimond's rosé into my glass, misting it over. Its raspberry ripeness mixes with the dried salt of sun-baked sweat on my lips. I lick them and gulp some more, feeling it wash away the dust.

Rosé is one of the few wines that satisfies a searing thirst. As I slosh it down, I feel myself reviving, like my dried-out ferns when I remember to water them. Don't get me wrong, I like a good palate-whacking shiraz as much as the next gal—but not when it's so hot that the pavement is curdling.

Rosé should be served almost as cool as most dry white wines: about 60°F. Low temperatures tame those riotous fruit flavors and highlight the wine's acidity, making it more refreshing and less cloying, rather than a mushy mess of hot strawberries. Another bonus is that this wine's soft tannins enable it to chill without losing its fruity flavors. In fact, several rosé producers encourage drinkers to drop in an ice cube. The South African brand Frozé, for instance, is a dark, concentrated, off-dry rosé that's been crafted to be diluted with ice. The producers claim it actually tastes better on the rocks, like an instant sangria.

Despite their delicate reputation, rosés can hold their own against the strong aromas of al fresco dining, like freshly cut grass, barbecue smoke, and suntan lotion. The notes of raspberry, strawberry, cherry, pomegranate, guava, and watermelon are never jammy or candied. Underlying these exuberant fruits is often a mouthwatering layer of herbal, spice, and mineral notes. A brisk finish is like the invigorating "Ah!" of an Alpine hike.

Rosé's association with hot weather is why some wine critics advise us to start drinking it when we get our first sunburn and to stop after Labor Day—when we stop wearing white. Nonsense. We don't drink white wine only in the summer. Rosé is also a year-round pleasure, especially with food. In fact, with their eyes closed, many people can't tell the difference between an aromatic rosé and a light red wine.

"Rosé is a wine of climate, not terroir," Raimond says, lifting his glass to the light. "My wines are free of 'mass terroir-ism,'" he says, referring to the overused wine term that confuses more than illuminates. "This is the wine to drink when you want to be on permanent vacation."

Indeed, Provençal rosé seduces you because you want to live the life here, not just drink the wine. With the sun on my shoulders and a cool river of wine running down my center, I haven't moved in an hour and feel in touch with my inner amoeba. But is drinking rosé back in a North American apartment on a cold, rainy day like looking at the photos you took of Niagara Falls: just not the same thing?

Great wines are often described as tasting of the place from which they come, but I think the best wines are those that take you back to the places that mean the most to you. They unlock those times and places at the edge of memory. This wine will always take me back to this hilltop terrace. In my mind, I will taste again the glistening ivory-satin fish and grilled vegetables, the bowl of sun-warmed cherries topped with a cool dollop of mascarpone, and the rosé that released me from myself for a few hours.

AFTER I SAY good-bye to Raimond and drive off to my next visit, I think about the other regions that produce rosé. Burgundy and Bordeaux, for instance, though best known for their red wines, also make blush wine. Burgundy's finest is Rosé de Marsannay, made from pinot noir grapes; Bordeaux makes it from merlot and cabernet sauvignon. The result is called clairet, to differentiate it from the deep-red wine known as claret.

The Languedoc region of southern France makes deeper-colored rosés, with riper red fruit flavors from mourvèdre and other grapes. However, a lighter, sparkling version from the region's Domaine de Boyer is called TendreBulle Gay Vin. The label shows two stylized heads almost kissing, and on the capsule are the letters *G* and *L*, for *gay* and *lesbian*. In a similar playful vein, New Zealand winery Kim Crawford called their wine Pansy Rosé.

Rosés from the Loire Valley in northern France, where the climate is cooler, tend to be lighter, with more acidity, fresher fruit flavors, and even a little carbon-dioxide fizz. The Lorraine region of the Loire uses the thin-skinned gamay grape to make *vin gris*, or "gray wine"— it doesn't sound appetizing (and it's not actually gray), but it's the term the French use because this rosé is paler than most others. It's produced like white wine, only with red grapes. The grapes are pressed to extract the juice and a tiny amount of color from the skins, but there is no further skin contact. The eastern Loire also uses pinot noir, which gives the wine its copper pink tone. None of these should be confused with inferior rosés made elsewhere from cheap grapes, whose juice is filtered through charcoal to get the pink color.

However, not all Loire rosés have a good reputation. Rosé d'Anjou, for instance, is known for its cheap and nasty sweet blends made from malbec, gamay, and groslot. The latter grape, so aptly named, is remarkable only for its ability to produce oceans of insipid wine. Cabernet d'Anjou, made from cabernet franc, is drier and more palatable, with some pleasant herbal notes. Chinon, farther west in the Loire, makes rich rosés from cabernet franc.

Outside France, many other countries make rosé. In Spain they're called rosados. Navarra, in the northeast, is the traditional heart of production. The wines are usually made from either tempranillo or garnacha (the Spanish name for grenache). Cheaper Spanish rosés are made from the little-known bobal grape—one of the world's most widely planted, even though it's only grown in Spain. Rosado juice gets a teasingly short contact with the skins: less than twenty-four hours. That's why the wine is known as *vino de una noche*, or "one-night wine." (Sounds like a fleeting summer romance.)

The most famous fan of rosados was Ernest Hemingway, who reportedly gulped down two bottles a day during those sultry afternoons spent watching the bullfights in Pamplona, Navarra's capital. He also filled wineskins to take with him when he went off to fight in the mountains during the country's civil war. Who says pink can't be manly? I love the way Hemingway described the taste of rosado in *Dangerous Summer*: "The wine was as good as when you were twenty-one."

Italy also makes some rosé, though most of it is consumed locally. Known as rosato, it's usually made from the sangiovese grape, the base for chianti, which has juicy red fruit flavors and good acidity. Some vintners prefer to use the white grape pinot grigio, which has a natural copper tinge to it. Left on the skins for an extended maceration, the wine emerges a lovely salmon color.

Then there's the New World. In North America, many wineries now produce dry rosé. In Canada, both Ontario and British Columbia make some great wines in the cool-climate style of the Loire, usually from the same grapes: cabernet franc or gamay. Several Canadian producers, such as Malivoire, Flat Rock, and Southbrook Vineyards, specialize in rosé. They believe that it's a natural wine for Canada, where ripening red grapes can be a challenge.

The California winery Bonny Doon makes Vin Gris de Cigare, a delicious blend of grenache, marsanne, cinsault, sangiovese, colombard, syrah, viognier, barbera, and dolcetto. It's impertinently labeled as "Pink Wine." In fact, there must be something about rosé that makes producers cheeky. My favorite description on the Napa winery Renard Rosé's label: "The nose suggests smoky strawberries, raspberry cigars and blah, blah, blah . . . Isn't wine indescribably fun? Just enjoy it!"

Personally, one of my favorite styles of rosés is sparkling, now that I've managed to move past those early awful associations with the saccharine fizz of Baby Duck and the like. I love the naughty color of a rosé sparkler and its sexy raspberry aroma. It conjures up the decadence of a weekday afternoon picnic beside the Seine, eating caviar and quaffing pink bubbles with a seductive Frenchman whom you have to slap occasionally. I read recently that a poll in Switzerland revealed that when those stoic Swiss see a man drinking rosé champagne with a woman, two out of three conclude that she is *not* his wife.

For winemakers, it's especially difficult to get the color of pink bubbly right. In the Champagne region of France, the most common method is to blend chardonnay, pinot meunier, and pinot noir so that the pinot noir dominates. An even more difficult and time-consuming approach allows the juice of all three grapes to sit on the skins for a short time to create the coveted pale-salmon color known as *oeil de perdrix*, or "eye of the partridge." The challenge is to produce the same color, year after year, even though the proportions of the grapes may change. But the reward is a wine with a wonderful delicate flavor. Rosés are considered among Champagne's most prestigious wines and comprise just 5 percent of all champagne production. They're priced accordingly: bottles sell for $80 or more.

JUST OUTSIDE THE village of Saint-Antonin, Domaine du Clos d'Alari is hidden among the trees on the slope of Saint-Antoninus. Inside this fifteenth-century stone winery in the heart of Provence, Nathalie Vautrin-Vancoillie and her family produce wonderfully aromatic rosés. I've heard that Nathalie loves to cook local dishes and pair them with rosé: what better way to spend this evening?

As I get out of my car, Nathalie, an athletic woman in a T-shirt and jeans, comes to meet me. "I'm surprised you found us," she says, smiling.

Nathalie grew up in the old farmhouse, a creamy yellow stone building with blue shutters—a palette typical of the region. Her parents sold their grapes to local winemakers for years but began making their own wine in 1998. A year later, Nathalie joined them to make wine.

"Dad was also in the meat business, and mother loved to cook," she says as we walk into her kitchen—a warm, blue-and-white-tiled cavern filled with wooden tables laden with fresh prosciutto and melon, gorgeously red tomatoes, glistening olives, and bushy heads of romaine lettuce. At the far end, her oven, gas stove, and microwave are winking red-and-orange-eyed creatures, beckoning us to come deeper into the cave. "They transmitted that love of food to me. Then I married Paul."

Her husband, Paul Vautrin, who owns a gourmet deli in Paris, works all week in the city and comes home only on the weekends. Some of his specialty products are on the kitchen shelves: mustard blended with truffle oil, Bloody Mary ketchup, caviar-brined pickles.

Their children's artwork covers the walls throughout the house—colorful pictures on paper as well as crayon drawings on the walls themselves. They feature smiling stick children holding hands, climbing trees, and running through the vineyards. There's also a large photograph of Nathalie and Paul facing each other and laughing, bare shouldered and presumably with no clothes below the frame. It's signed by hundreds of friends. The children have drawn dialogue bubbles for each of them and printed inside "J'taime!" Nathalie's son and daughter are in their early twenties now, both in university.

"I love discovering new flavors, whether it's food or wine," Nathalie says, pushing her thick dark hair behind her ears. "And I love feeling the products in my hands: the small roundness of a grape, the smoothness of a tomato, spices running through my fingers."

Just as I'm feeling those first stirrings of hunger, Nathalie suggests that we "go pick dinner." We walk through the golden September evening, heady scents of sage, rosemary, and lavender wafting up from the warm earth. I finally understand that wine descriptor *garrigue*: the savory blend of wild herbs, cedar, and shrubs.

"Welcome to the field," she says quietly, gesturing to the land beyond the garden. Vintners here refer to their vineyards as "the field." It's a romantic, rolled-up-sleeves notion that evokes the struggle to cultivate one patch of dirt all your life. Of the family's twenty hectares, seven are planted with syrah, grenache, carignan, mourvèdre, merlot, cinsault, and rolle grapes, which the family pick by hand and press lightly using a low-tech method called "the drop": only the weight of the grapes themselves for first-run juice. The result is about thirty thousand bottles a year of wine.

I watch as Nathalie squats down to snip some fennel, her weathered, scarred hands marking her intimate knowledge of this field. "The old people used to call this wild salad," she says, pointing to the tangle of herbs and other plants around us. She offers me a bouquet of wispy yellow fennel. I bury my nose in it and inhale childhood memories of eating licorice on my grandparents' veranda.

We pass a shimmering silvery grove of more than three hundred olive trees, from which Nathalie produces about four hundred litres of olive oil a year. Nearby is a cluster of massive, century-old oak trees. I'm curious about the circle of dead-looking yellow grass around each tree.

"That's from the fungus on the tree roots," Nathalie explains. "That's how you know there are truffles underground."

Ah, truffles: those glorious, exotic cousins of potatoes, with their pungent aromas of wet, musky fall leaves; fresh-turned soil; ripe cheese; and underground caves. Unlike other kinds of fungus, which are parasites on their hosts, truffles are beneficial: they feed minerals to the tree along its roots as they absorb small amounts of sugar from it. The Cadillac of French truffles is the coveted "black diamond" from the Périgord region of Provence. More than 90 percent of French truffles grow in the southwest: Provence, Languedoc, and the Rhône Valley.

To the uninitiated, a truffle can seem almost repellent: a black, lumpy growth that looks like a diseased potato. However, in the right dishes, they're slivers of the netherworld. My most memorable meal was at Alain Ducasse restaurant in New York several years ago, when my husband, Andrew, and I were celebrating a James Beard journalism award. We ordered the eight-course truffle menu. By the time our server was shaving truffle onto our pistachio pastry cream atop a Napoleon of raspberries, I begged for mercyand chocolate sauce.

Nathalie's truffles aren't ready yet, since the season runs from mid-December to March. But even if they were here, nature doesn't give up her treasures easily. "That's the mystery of the truffle," she says, shrugging. "You can't cultivate them; you can only discover them and hope they grow back the next year."

Finding truffles is famously difficult, since they grow about six inches underground—and not necessarily in the same spot as the previous year. The best detection is scent, so most truffle hunters use a dog to sniff them out. Pigs have keen truffle noses, too, but unfortunately, they love them as much as humans do and will gobble down their discoveries if the handler doesn't pay close attention. Nathalie's dog Ubu is a dachshund, more popularly (and aptly in this case) known as a sausage dog. "He's king of the truffles!" she says, smiling. Ubu is enjoying an off-season romp on Nathalie's parents' farm a few miles away. She trained him from a pup, hiding a truffle in a sock and rewarding him every time he found it in ever more difficult and buried locations.

Now when he finds a truffle, he paws the ground and points his nose at the exact spot until Nathalie walks over. She gently digs around the precious tuber with a trowel—breaking it would decrease its value and freshness. The market in truffles is a lucrative one, and often as black as the fungus itself. A good-sized truffle is worth about $2,000 a pound at the local outdoor market, where they're often sold in stealthy cash transactions from a farmer's car (often a Mercedes or BMW). By the time the mushrooms reach fancy restaurants in cities such as Toronto, London, or New York, they've tripled in price. No wonder Nathalie hesitates when I ask her how many truffles she finds in a year—sources and yields are closely guarded secrets. Nobody wants to attract midnight poachers, and dark stories are told of truffle dogs that mysteriously disappear.

Under one of the trees, we see that the ground has been dug up even though truffle season doesn't start for another three months.

"Sanglier!" Nathalie spits out. It sounds like a swear word until she translates. "Wild boar," she explains, kneeling down to fill the dirt back into the holes. Wild pigs have the same penchant for truffles as the tame ones, and will dig them up and eat them whenever they can. They also enjoy the vineyard grapes for dessert. "That's okay," Nathalie says, smiling. "The boars eat the truffles, and then we eat the boars." As we walk to the house, she tells me about her spice-marinated rack of wild boar with pistachio crust.

Back in the kitchen, Nathalie flits from counter to fridge to stove, while I try to anticipate her next move to stay out of her way. As she inserts a laurel bay leaf into the center of each half-boiled potato on a tray, coats them with olive oil, and slips them into the oven, she explains that Provençal cuisine is lighter than most French fare. It relies on olive oil more than butter, on fresh vegetables and seafood more than heavy meats, and it's seasoned with garlic and herbs rather than with salt. Most Provençal recipes seem to begin with the words "Peel one clove of garlic." This is the dream of the Mediterranean diet: eat as much as you want of delicious, flavorful foods and still maintain your weight. And yes, you get to drink wine—especially rosé.

Rosé is brilliant with the herbed dishes of Provençal cooking: basil-infused *pistou* vegetable soup, roasted chicken with rosemary, and succulently stewed tomatoes and vegetables in ratatouille. Many styles of wine work well with herbs because those same aromas are often found in both, especially sauvignon blanc, syrah, and cabernet sauvignon. For example, the tomatoes in a tomato sauce require an acidic red, such as chianti, whereas the basil in a pesto sauce might pair better with a crisp white, such as sauvignon blanc. The beautiful thing about rosé is that it works with both, having the flavor to pair with many foods.

"Rosé doesn't have the interfering elements of heavy oak, alcohol, big fruit, and butter notes," Nathalie says, pouring us each a glass of her wine. After a few sips, I can taste how its ripe berry aromas and natural acidity would allow it to pair with foods that might defeat other wines: ones with sharp, salty, spicy, or smoky flavors, such as green olives, anchovies, pesto, and tapenade. This wine would be perfect on a sultry summer evening; it would flesh out the flavors of mild dishes and lighten the richer fare. Well-made rosés are fragrant with field berries and often sprinkled with pepper notes.

Another challenging ingredient in the game of pairing is garlic, which is so potent that it can make almost any wine taste sour. That's true even of cooked garlic, which is relatively mild. Raw garlic, such as in pesto sauce, is tougher on wine because it numbs the palate the way chili peppers do. But rosé works with both, a crisp counterpoint that cools a seared palate. My mouth waters just thinking of rosé with bouillabaisse, the traditional fish stew of Marseilles. The pairing will mentally transport you to a bistro in the Vieux Port—you may even mistakenly call your husband Jean-Jacques, as I did the other evening while enjoying the dish.

Nathalie is now pouring olive oil into a roasting pan and shredding tiny bits of fennel into it. She also inserts slivers of fennel into some half-slit chicken breasts, turns them over in the oil, and pops them into the oven with the potatoes. Olive oil, one of the delicious staples here in Provence, coats the mouth and makes it hard to taste the wine. Fortunately, it's rarely alone in a dish, like aioli, that masterful blend of just three ingredients: olive oil, garlic, and egg yolk. Rosé cuts through this luxuriously rich mayonnaise.

As the savory aromas of the baking chicken and potatoes waft out from the oven, Nathalie prepares us a simple starter dish of diced fresh tomatoes adorned with salt, pepper, and shredded leaves of fresh thyme. Over this she scoops a dollop of chèvre, meadow-fresh goat cheese. There's nothing I love more than a chin-drippingly juicy tomato, so I'm delighted that they feature in many Provençal dishes, from vegetable soup to ratatouille. While they're terrific at flavoring food, their acidity is hard on wine: like lemon and vinegar, tomatoes can make most wines taste dull. Rosé, however, matches their acidic tang. Rosé dances with acidic citrus sauces, like duck à l'orange. The wine's acidity also cuts through the fat in soft cheeses like Nathalie's chèvre, as well as cream sauces and fried foods. Rosé is revolutionary with a cheeseburger.

My pet theory, though, is that pink wine and pink food go best together. I love a pale, crisp rosé with raw or lightly cooked seafood, such as tuna tartare and cod carpaccio. Think of lobsters cooking over a fire on the beach, glowing roseate as the sun slowly sinks into the ocean. On a picnic table are platters of freshly steamed crabs and barbecued salmon. A row of rosé bottles beside them have the frivolous symmetry of lipstick samples.

While I've been counting the ways that rosé pairs with food, Nathalie has finished cooking. We take our plates outside to an old wooden farm table and sit under an ancient cypress tree, through which sparkles the shattered crystal of a thousand stars around a shard of moon. I'm feeling quite twinkly myself. The September evening is warm, and I'm pleasantly hungry. Nathalie's rosé pairs beautifully with the tomato and goat cheese as well as the fennel-infused chicken and potatoes. This gossamer wine is a midnight run through a field of raspberries in a sheer nightdress shot through with moonlight.

"I hate big, body-builder wines," Nathalie says, as we sip contemplatively on the rosé. "These wines are slender, like the body of a woman. Wine is seduction—women are better at that, yes?" she asks with a sly smile. Certainly, the steroid of the wine world, oak, is absent from this transparent, limpid wine. Notions of lingering over another glass, or four, come to mind.

As we talk in the darkness, I love listening to Nathalie's voice; her laugh is free and uneven, the kind loosed among friends. I believe that as the evening progressed, toasts were made, backs were slapped, promises were not kept. I do recall informing Nathalie that she was *très sympa* and that we were both marvelous citizens of a marvelous world.

Eventually, Nathalie's steaming apricot tart magically appears on the table. (Perhaps Nathalie nipped into the kitchen to bring it out, but I don't recall pausing from sharing my brilliant observations with her.) For all its versatility, Provençal rosé does have a limitation: desserts make the bone-dry wine taste bitter. So we drink a dessert wine from the Languedoc instead.

By this time it's nearly midnight, I'm feeling contentedly wine-heavy, and realize I'm emitting a low, sybaritic purr. Nathalie and I bid each other a drowsy good evening, and I trudge upstairs to bed. I immediately plunge into a deep sleep. But at 2:47 a.m., I'm jerked awake by a thousand bullfrogs that had organized themselves below my window during the night and are now croaking in unison. "Those damn frogs!" I shout. Then I hope no one has heard me. Eventually, I fall back to sleep and spend the rest of the night dreaming of *cuisses de grenouille*—tender frogs' legs sautéed in finely chopped onions and garlic, garnished with a sprig of revenge parsley.

Early the next morning, I throw open the bedroom shutters to watch the sun brush over the dark violet hills, slowly painting them into lavender and pink. Mercifully, the frogs have dispersed. I had thought I'd skip breakfast so I wouldn't be charged for extra luggage on the flight home. However, I can't resist sharing warm homemade bread, local cheeses, and peach preserves with Nathalie before leaving. As she says, "It's a good way to live."

MY FINAL VISIT in Provence isn't with a winery but rather with the man who put this region and its wines in my daydreams. Certain writers are associated with certain places: Émile Zola with Paris, E. M. Forster with India, Woody Allen with New York. And for this heavenly place, it's an author whose book *A Year in Provence* has sold more than six million copies in forty languages. In fact, the man who's been called the Pied Piper of Provence created a whole new genre of travel memoir: leave a dreary job, move to a warm climate, renovate a derelict farmhouse. Think of the books that have followed: *A Piano in the Pyrenees* by Tony Hawks, *Driving Over Lemons* by Chris Stewart, *Under the Tuscan Sun* by Frances Mayes, and even a parody, published in France, called *An Eternity in Provence.*

Peter's book celebrates life here: the abundant fresh food and wine, the long, lazy walks in the herb-scented countryside, the sunny afternoons in the hammock, the quaint and odd village folk and local customs. Since that first bestseller, he's written more than twenty books, most about his beloved Provence. I love them all, so I'm more than a little nervous about meeting him for drinks this afternoon. My heart thuds heavily, like dough flipped over and over as it's kneaded.

"Are you Peter Mayle?" I pose the ridiculous question in a bat-squeak to the only man in the lobby of the inn where we're to meet.

He smiles warmly at me as we shake hands, his bronzed face radiant under silver hair.

"Nice to meet you, Natalie," he says in a soft British accent. He wears an untucked Ralph Lauren shirt, blue trousers, leather loafers without socks, and no watch. At seventy-one, he's Mediterranean cool.

As we walk down into the postcard village of Lourmarin (a thousand inhabitants and eleven restaurants), Peter tells me he decided to become a writer because he was "useless at mathematics and anything technical. I was not drawn to politics or big business, or to any endeavor where I had to report to committees and bosses. English was my favorite subject at school, and the only one at which I was any good. I wanted independence and thought that writing would give me that." Journalism didn't appeal to him, but "advertising seemed like much more fun, and it was better paid."

Peter found breaking into the field difficult. Despite the aristocratic Oxbridge accent, he doesn't have a university degree. "The Brits are sticklers for that sort of thing, so I couldn't get an advertising job in London." So in the early 1960s, he moved to New York and worked for advertising giants David Ogilvy and George Lois, first as a copywriter and eventually as a creative director. He was one of the real-life *Mad Men* on Madison Avenue. He looks back on that time now as good training for his future career as a novelist. "You have to stick to the plot—to be concise, informative, and if possible entertaining. If one idea didn't work, you tried something else. No one was going to wait for your muse to inspire you."

Even though he was successful in the field, he decided to leave Madison Avenue in 1975 and become a full-time writer. Was it hard, I ask him, to leave the security of an advertising-executive income to become a writer? He laughs and tells me that advertising was always a precarious occupation. "But I was able to leave the business because my first books were starting to make money, and I was able to get freelance advertising work."

The stories about Provence were far from his first foray into print; by the time *A Year in Provence* was published in 1989, he had already been an author for sixteen years. His first book, a children's sex-education primer called *Where Did I Come From?* was published in 1973. This was followed by several more as part of a series, then by the hilarious *Wicked Willie* series of cartoon books. They're still in print today, having sold more than three million copies.

"Here we are," Peter says, as we walk up to the patio of a small bistro. Ever the gentleman, he pulls out a seat for me at a table. We sit in the bright sunshine sipping on icy rosé, watching villagers walk by. He tells me that after readers found out that this café was his favorite spot for drinks, they started sending letters and gifts here.

"I've had some addressed simply to 'Peter Mayle, France,'" he says, shaking his head. "I've also received many, many jars of marmalade, because I mentioned in an interview that's what I missed most about Britain."

We talk about England, America, and France. What's the key difference among them? Peter pauses for a moment, then responds, "Lunch. Sunday lunch, in particular. Until you've watched a Frenchman enjoying his Sunday lunch, you can't possibly imagine how religious an experience eating can be in France," he says, smiling. "It's not just rich people at fancy restaurants, either; it goes all the way through society. Farmers and plumbers have their favorite restaurants and their own special recipes, and they like to talk about them. This fascination with the stomach is a very pleasant addition to life."

So why don't those outside France enjoy their food and wine the same way, I ask. "The North American business ethic says that if you're having a two-hour lunch, you're being unproductive, wasting time," Peter responds. "The French are not ashamed to admit to liking pleasure, whether it's two hours for lunch or a month's holiday in August. They like to have a good time, and they're not guilty about it. Let me put it this way: When an American looks at a duck, he says, 'Oh, how cute.' When a Frenchman looks at a duck, he wonders, 'How shall I cook him?'"

In 1986, Peter and his wife, Jean, were on vacation on the Côte d'Azur when they stumbled upon the Lubéron valley, in the heart of Provence. They loved the area so much that a year later, they bought an old farmhouse, figuring they had just enough money to last them while Peter wrote his first novel.

"We started to renovate our home, but I became completely distracted—and much more taken with the curiosities of life in Provence than with getting down to work on the novel," he explains. "The daily dose of education I was getting from the stonemason, the mushroom hunter, the lady with the stubborn donkey, the electrician, the farmer next door, and so on, was infinitely more interesting than anything I could invent. Months went by without my committing a word to paper. Eventually, I felt so guilty that I sent my agent a long letter explaining why I hadn't even started the novel and describing some of the distractions. To my enormous surprise and relief, he wrote back saying that if I could do another two hundred and fifty pages like the letter, he might be able to find a publisher."

The agent was right, but the publisher evidently didn't expect much: he printed only three thousand copies, and told Peter that there'd be plenty of unsold ones that he could give as Christmas presents. But six weeks after the book went on sale, his agent called to say that every copy had been bought. The reprints started, and by the end of the year, it had become a runaway bestseller. Its popularity was such that over the next few years, Peter followed up with *Encore Provence*, *Toujours Provence*, and *A Good Year*, another escapist novel with a London stockbroker who inherits his uncle's Lubéron château and vineyard. The book was later made into a film by Peter's vacation-home neighbor, the film director Ridley Scott, and starred Russell Crowe.

Such was the success of his books that some people accused Peter of spoiling Provence by fueling an invasion of tourists: more than ten million tourists now visit the region every year. "I've been accused of causing everything from the village baker running out of bread to a surfeit of Germans in the café," he says, smiling. "But the tourist in Provence is an unfairly maligned creature—the good they bring far outweighs the bad." Peter argues that without tourism, there wouldn't be money to maintain the churches, châteaux, and other historic buildings. Most Provençaux recognize this fact, and their reaction has generally been positive. "They know tourism is an important part of the local economy, and they're happy that a foreigner has fallen so publicly in love with their region."

I love that Peter proudly declares himself a "permanent tourist" rather than the more fashionable and intellectual descriptor of traveler. Like rosé itself, he shrugs off snobbery and admits to simple pleasures.

Peter didn't change the names of the people in his book or disguise the village. He thought that would make the story less authentic. "Besides, I never expected many people to actually read it," he confesses, chuckling. The result is that many of the characters, unintended beneficiaries of Peter's success, have become minor local celebrities—like the builder Didier Andreis, described in *A Year in Provence* as "half man, half forklift truck." Since then, he and his wife have opened a flourishing guesthouse. Visitors often bring a well-thumbed copy of the book with them to help them savor Peter's eye for the cultural peculiarities of France.

As we're sitting there, for instance, a small man with a mustache roars up in his open-top convertible, stops in the middle of the cobblestone street, hops out over the door, and goes into a bar. "The

French have such imaginative ways of parking," Peter says with affectionate humor.

Peter had his first notion of the book's success when strangers started showing up on his doorstep. "I remember the first fan well—a man in a BMW," he says. "I invited him in, plied him with wine, and signed his book at least twice. At first it was exciting. People came from Australia, Germany, England, Sweden, America. Then it increased until we had four, five, six visits a day."

One February day, Peter discovered a photographer from a British tabloid newspaper hiding in his bushes. The cameraman explained, "Well, you never know . . . someone might be outdoors naked." Another day, a bus pulled up in front of his home and let out twenty Japanese tourists; their Tokyo travel agent had told them that their tour of Provence included a visit to Peter Mayle's house. Several local bars started selling maps to his house. The final straw came one Sunday. As Peter and Jean were sitting down to lunch, they heard splashing water in the backyard. Peter walked around to find a group of Italians videotaping themselves swimming in his pool.

To escape their unwanted celebrity, Peter and Jean sold their home and fled to America. They settled in Long Island, New York, and Peter entered himself into the self-devised Author Protection Program. "That's the great thing about America: you can be anonymous if you want," he says. They were content there for four years, especially since four of his five adult children lived in the United States. But eventually, the lure of Provence proved too strong. In 1997, after Peter and Jean watched a video of friends enjoying Sunday lunch there, they knew they had to return. "You can live outside eight months a year there, and the rhythm of daily life is slower. In America, I missed the moments that make up the daily texture of life. In America, I felt deprived of oxygen."

So they moved back and found another farmhouse just outside the village of Lourmarin—Peter's cagey now about the address. He writes in the mornings, but keeps afternoons and evenings free for friends, family, food, and appreciating the life he chronicles. As one of his characters says, "Nowhere else in the world can you keep busy doing so little, and enjoying it so much." Indeed, that's the reason not much has changed in his life since publishing his books. "I drink better wine," he says, noting that he drinks about a liter a day. "It sounds like a lot, but you have two or three glasses at lunch and two or three at dinner, and that's a bottle gone."

His latest book, *The Vintage Caper*, is a lighthearted mystery novel about the theft of a $3 million wine cellar. The plot takes a private investigator to Marseilles, Bordeaux, Paris, and Hollywood in a wonderful romp that displays Peter's deep knowledge of wine. When I tell him so, he responds, "I'm light entertainment; I'm not Proust. Writing, like wine, doesn't have to be complicated to be good. I can tell a good story because I enjoy what I write about."

That's probably why I—and millions of other readers—love Peter's books so much. Like a chilly glass of rosé, they wash away thoughts of finishing chores, making plans, returning from vacation, getting old. Rosé is a great wine because it's fleeting, reminding us that all things end, so seize the day.

"I've got this scene worked out for my death," Peter says, as he smiles and pours us more wine from the carafe. "I've just had the most extraordinary three-hour lunch. As I raise my hand for another glass of wine, I have a mammoth heart attack—just before the bill arrives."

And until then?

"Learning about food and wine is a series of edible adventures and surprises—you never finish."

Field Notes from a
Wine Cheapskate

INSIDER TIPS

- Forget those notions of pink wine being sweet: today's rosés are bone-dry and refreshing. With Provence, you're guaranteed to get a dry rosé.

- Look for wines that have never been taken seriously by connoisseurs, always considered lightweights. You'll find pleasure at a pittance there.

- Rosé is best served chilled, as it's more refreshing. So here's a tip that will give wine snobs a coronary: if your wine's too warm, drop an ice cube in it for ten seconds, then scoop it out. It has an immediate chilling effect and doesn't dilute the flavors—and after all, we're not trying to ice Châteaux Margaux, just an everyday good value wine. Consider this your license to chill.

WINERIES VISITED

Château de Roquefort: www.deroquefort.com
Domaine du Clos d'Alari: www.leclosdalari.fr

BEST VALUE WINES

Château de Roquefort Corail*
Château de Roquefort Les Mures

Château de Roquefort Sémiramis
Domaine du Clos d'Alari Côtes de Provence Rosé
Domaine du Clos d'Alari Grand Clos Rosé

My first pick for my own Sunday lunch.

TOP VALUE PRODUCERS

Bieler Père et Fils
Carte Noire
Château Barbeyrolles
Château Calissanne
Château Constantin-
   Chevalier
Château de
   Fonscolombe
Château la Tour
   de l'Évêque
Château Routas
   Rouvière
Château Simone
Clos Mireille
Domaine de la Petite
   Cassagne

Domaine de la Sauveuse
Domaine de l'Olivette
Domaine de Suriane
Domaine de Trévallon
Domaine des Peirecèdes
Domaine Houchart
Domaine Sorin
Domaine Tempier
Domaines Ott
La Bastide Blanche
Les Vignerons de la
   Cadierenne
Sables d'Azur

SUNDAY LUNCH FOR A WINE CHEAPSKATE

You'll find Nathalie Vautrin-Vancoillie's recipes for the dinner we made together and shared at her home at www.nataliemaclean.com/food.

Tomato with Goat Cheese

Chicken with Fennel

Baked Potatoes with Bay Laurel Leaf

Apricot Tart

TERRIFIC PAIRINGS

Asian, Indian, and
    Thai dishes

Charcuterie

Cheese: Brie,
    Camembert,
    Parmesan

Chicken club sandwich

Curries: mild and spicy

Pasta with tomato and
    seafood sauces

Pâté

Pizza: cheese, pepperoni

Pork roast

Quiche

Salmon with herbs

Tuna: grilled

Turkey: roast

Veal piccata

Vegetables and salads

RESOURCES

For more information about Provence and rosés:

Adventures on the Wine Route by Kermit Lynch
Extremely Pale Rosé: A Very Pale Adventure by Jamie Ivey
Touring in Wine Country: Provence by Hubrecht Duijker
Wines of Provence: www.vinsdeprovence.com
Provence Wines USA: www.provencewineusa.com
Rosé Avengers and Producers: www.rapwine.com
Wines of Provence: www.nataliemaclean.com/wineries

RELATED READING

A Year in Provence by Peter Mayle

Toujours Provence by Peter Mayle

The Vintage Caper by Peter Mayle

Encore Provence: New Adventures in the South of France by Peter Mayle

Provence A–Z: A Francophile's Essential Handbook by Peter Mayle

DRINKING MY WORDS

Closing-Time Comments

CANDY-COLORED BOTTLES OF spirits glow against the mirrors behind the bar of the Algonquin Hotel. I've perched myself on a bar stool on this brisk May evening after having found the collected essays of my favorite New York City writer with the acid pen, Dorothy Parker, at a nearby bookstore. I've mentioned more than twenty books throughout the chapters. I'm often reading the work of one of the country's beloved authors while I'm traveling in a region to sharpen my observations, whether it's *The Leopard* by Sicily's Giuseppe di Lampedusa, the short stories of Argentina's Jorge Luis Borges, or Peter Mayle's books about Provence. This gets me thinking about my journey and the connection between writing and drinking as a way of understanding a place and its people.

Now that my own book of adventures is coming to an end, I can contemplate all that I've seen through a wine-soaked looking glass. Frankly, I just want a drink (or four) without making even one tasting note, so perhaps I'll go with cocktails tonight. And what better place than the Algonquin Hotel? Rich aromas of leather, oak, and booze fill the air. A man sitting in one corner of the bar seems as remote as a lighthouse, looking down on the afterwork tipplers at the tables throughout the room. The buttery tones of Ella Fitzgerald fill the spaces between their scattered conversations.

The Algonquin is famous as the gathering spot of the city's leading wits in the 1920s: humorist Robert Benchley, theater critic Alexander Woollcott, playwrights Edna Ferber and George Kaufman, *New Yorker* founder Harold Ross, and Dorothy Parker.

Almost a century later, their boozy lives still speak to us almost as eloquently as their literary legacy. Their writing back then had a prominence impossible in today's multimedia clutter, though they'd all be brilliantly pithy on Twitter. Still, they remain memorable. My favorite Parker lines come from her comments at the wake of a fellow writer. A friend by the open coffin remarked, "Doesn't he look wonderful?"

"Why shouldn't he?" Parker replied. "He hasn't had a drink in three days."

Perhaps these writers fascinate me, as this book surely attests, because I've always freely admitted to loving the hedonistic joys of wine (okay, the buzz). Alcohol makes me happy and stops me from being a tightly wound control freak, as some people (*quite* unjustly) characterize me. After a few glasses, I magnanimously forgive those people . . . for now.

James Joyce said that drinking is the revenge of shy people, but I'd say it's the passport of the socially awkward. Wine is a universal language of pleasure that has helped me connect with hundreds of people around the world for this book. It has allowed me to slip into social situations and feel an immediate connection. Many of the vintners I met along the way were scary smart or famous or forbidding. But exchanging a few oenophile-geeky references made the initial bond that allowed our conversation to flow with the wine.

Establishing a trust that says "you share my passion; you're like me" enabled my questions and their answers to become less protected and get downright indiscreet in some cases. As a fully immersive writer, much of this book was written while I was abuzz with my subject. (Fortunately, a very sober editor went through it before it arrived in your hands.) But why do most wine writers never mention the buzz they get from drinking? Are they afraid of not being taken seriously if they're having fun? This reminds me of the critic who observed that the splendid Irish novelist, Edna O'Brien, was one of the "first writers to have sex in her novels; all the other writers just had children."

The title of my first book—*Red, White, and Drunk All Over*— made people smile, but it also drew some criticism. I claimed, rather weakly, that "drunk all over" simply referred to savoring wines in many places around the world. That said, I'm an equal-opportunity drinker: cocktails, cognac, vodka, whisky, saké, wine, you name it. I got called to the bar years ago for the affirmative action in my glass.

Unwinding at the Algonquin, cocktail in hand, is a welcome respite from my professional focus on wine, and a liquid punctuation for the end of a long journey in this book. Earlier in the day, I was one of twenty journalists at a tasting of more than a hundred Californian cabernets, hosted by their agents. This type of event, when you compare one type of wine made during the same year from many producers, is called a horizontal tasting. (Not to be confused with your likely position by the time you finish.) A vertical tasting, by contrast, would mean tasting many different vintages of one producer's cabernets.

I remember all the times I've tried to convince friends that tasting wine and traveling to far-flung, exotic locales is hard work. The usual response is an amused smile or outright laughter. Ah, the glamorous life of a wine writer, they think: tasting delicious wines in gorgeous settings, being wined and dined by witty people in fine restaurants, getting effusive emails from admiring readers. But tasting wine as a professional is like being a driver in a foreign city—unlike the passenger who's just along for the sensory ride, you have to pay attention and use your wits.

I wish those friends could see me now, after 8 countries, 312 wineries, and 15,267 wines: a crimson flower blooms inside my mouth, its fiery tendrils licking at the back of my throat. I think my lips are starting to peel off. I've definitely lost a layer of enamel from my teeth; bathing them in acidity for three hours will do that. My mouth is a fire-blackened building; my cheeks glow like red-hot metal.

Many of the wines I tasted for this book were high in alcohol, especially port, Australian shiraz, and Argentine malbec. But that was the style they needed to be. Wines such as Niagara pinot noir, German riesling, and Provençal rosé are all creatures of lightness. Tasting this incredible stylistic range made me respect that each wine needs to be true to its own character, and that as drinkers, we need to be true to our own taste rather than follow what's fashionable or expensive.

Wine fascinates us, so it's easy to get caught up in its aroma, flavor, body, and structure. What matters, though, when we lift a glass to our lips are the experiences that become woven into that wine, including where we are and who we're with. Time after time, when I breathe in the aromas of a wine I've had before, those memories are summoned instantly: I see and smell the first time I had the wine, rather than a fruit salad of descriptors. That's what we overlook when we dismiss inexpensive wine as uninteresting; it's we, as drinkers, who make a wine interesting with what we bring to the wine. You won't find this complete experience of wine in tasting notes. It's a lot like this book: your experience of it will depend on who you are.

Many of the winemakers I met understood this because they bring generations of family struggle to every glass. Their legacy is in the blend, and they know what sacrifices have been made to create it. When they taste their wine, they're back in the harvest, dealing with the issues farmers face, wondering how to pay for the new grape press, or remembering the celebratory dinner after the picking was done.

As I flip through my Parker anthology, the old Chinese bartender, whose name tag reads Mr. Hoy, hands me a cocktail list. I order the Parker: vodka, cassis, and fresh lemon juice. The vodka sluices through the crimson liqueur like rain tearing the sky open. The stem of the glass, cool and smooth in my hand, feels as familiar as my own skin. Like Parker's wit, the drink tastes sweet up front but finishes with a nasty bite.

It makes me wonder about the connection between alcohol and the creative process. Does booze loosen writers' inhibitions and heighten their feelings? Are they more susceptible to drink than other artists? Perhaps Tolstoy grasped it better when he observed, "Writing requires two people: the writer and the critic. Alcohol silences the critic until the writer is done." My subject matter relaxes me about my subject. That helps not just because I'm a puddle of neuroses but also because I'm drawn to fully immersive experiences in foreign places, rather than to sitting at a table and interviewing someone who visits my hometown. I've always searched for flesh knowledge—an understanding of life skinned of its social protocols. But all that flitting from experience to experience, emotion to emotion, is draining.

For my first book, I tried the day-in-the-life approach of working as a sommelier, a liquor store staffer, a winemaker, and a grape picker. For this book, and strangely for someone who usually avoids animals, I threw myself into odd situations where I encountered them in almost every chapter: sharks, snakes, sheep, goats, horses, donkeys, dogs, baboons, kangaroos, kookaburras, magpies, ladybugs, and hawks. Perhaps I knew at a gut level that being uncomfortable is the starting point for a good story. You use more of your senses and synapses when you're on strange terrain. Perhaps the animals were also part of my desire to stay connected with nature, especially in a world that's increasingly mediated by social media and technology. I never want to lose my awe of the land, yet I don't want to be overwhelmed by it. It is grand and I am small, but I rise and respond to it. That narrative pattern emerges only when you're finished.

A few more people have seated themselves at the bar. Their cocktails glow like tiny campfires along the dark wood surface. The chatter in the room is cheerful and loud, and their pink faces radiate goodwill. A flowering tenderness floods me with love for all these *beautiful* people.

I ask Mr. Hoy for a cocktail called the New Yorker. As he mixes the tequila, fruit nectar, and a squeeze of fresh lime, I listen drowsily to the clicking ice and chatter from the other end of the room, where a group of women are celebrating someone's birthday. A couple at a nearby table lean into each other, foreheads touching. All these details seem magnified and precious to me, worth recording for posterity. In fact, I think I'll start making a few notes for the brilliant novel that now seems entirely possible to write this week.

The woman at the other end of the bar slowly sips a martini in which three olives float like commas. Her pale skin rests on her face like sheets draped over furniture in an empty summer home. Maybe it's the preponderance here of women drinkers, but it occurs to me that most of the celebrated writer-drinkers were men. Hemingway-style boozing gave a man an attractive aura of both manliness and vulnerability, but a drinking woman was viewed as unladylike and promiscuous.

Drink like a man, write like man. Parker once prayed, "Dear God, please make me stop writing like a woman." So where does that leave me, a woman who writes about wine and comes from a long line of alcoholics? Does my interest in alcoholic writers bode ill for my own sobriety, or is it an encouraging portent for a spectacular boozy memoir that starts with how well-maintained the tennis courts are at the Betty Ford Clinic? There's no doubt that wine tasting is not a profession for lily livers, even though you're supposed to spit out the sample after tasting it. Wine professionals also like to drink for pleasure.

After I started writing about wine, it bothered me that I wasn't a doctor helping to heal people or a teacher guiding children to enlightenment. What ideal had I given my life to? Facilitating bourgeois hedonism? Consumerism? Sloth? I needed a drink to sort it all out. The more I thought about it, the more I realized that there is honor in helping people find pleasure and relaxation. We all work hard, and there are many stresses in our lives. We need the simple joys in life, like a good glass of inexpensive wine, to regain a sense of ourselves. No worrying about how much it cost or what it scored; simply, do I like it, and do I like who I'm with?

I'm on my own, but tonight, the answer is yes. I finish with a small snifter of brandy. My fingers wrap around the bowl of the glass the way two lovers cradle each other lying side by side. It's past midnight now, and most people have left; the remaining drinkers look like party debris.

After communing with spirits all evening—both the bottled and the writerly kind—I feel as though I'm now putting away a family album of faded photographs. As I bid good night to Mr. Hoy and walk out of the Algonquin, an inky drizzle almost hisses as it hits my warm skin. Behind me, I believe I can hear those writers stumbling out, calling cheery, drunken good-byes as they head home to a bed or a desk. I think we all agree with the Irish poet and *New Yorker* writer Brendan Behan's self-assessment: I'm a drinker with a writing problem.

ACKNOWLEDGMENTS

Most of those who make wine are hospitable by nature, but the winemakers I met for this book were congenitally kind, inviting me into their homes and lives. Without their help, this would just be a transcript of dull interviews rather than a tapestry of human stories: Nicolas Audebert, Thomas Bachelder, Charles Back, Giuseppe Benanti, Wolf Blass, Norbret Breit, Nicolás and Laura Catena, Marco de Grazia, Tom Drieseberg, Louise Engel, Andrea Franchetti, Peter Gago, Michael Halstrick, Anthony and Olive Hamilton Russell, Stephen and Prue Henschke, Bevan Johnson, David Johnson, Ernie Loosen, Martin Malivoire, Rusty Myers, Dirk Niepoort, Diego Planeta, Katharina Prüm, George Sandeman, Carmen Stevens, Rupert Symington, Nathalie Vautrin-Vancoillie, Raimond Villeneuve, Nik Weis, and José Alberto Zuccardi.

A special thank-you to Peter Mayle, who helped me wrap up these edible adventures in the last chapter. Peter's irrepressible zest for food, drink, and life is my model. The next bottle is on me, Peter.

In a book about wine, there are thousands of facts that you can screw up. That became clear to me when I sent my manuscript to several wine wizards, whose depth of knowledge and incisive comments made me realize just how much I had yet to learn. They could have been brutal, even mocking, but they were all gentlemen: Steve Beckta, Kent Benson, Ken Goosens, Craig Hosbach, Kevin Keith, Bob McConnell, Grayson McDiarmid, and

Scott Richards. Any remaining errors are entirely my own—they could only do so much given what they had to work with.

Did I mention I can't cook? I just pull corks and twist caps. My deepest thanks to those who tested hundreds of recipes for this book that are now on my website: Pat Anderson, Stephanie Arsenault, Terra Baltosiewich, Kim Beavers, Vicki Bensinger, Tracey Black, Susan Blomeley, Maxine Borcherding, Betty Brown, Tim Brown, Leanna Bullock, Mark Busse, Don Chow, Beryl Cohen, Andrew Coppolino, David Crowley, Kari Cunningham, Veronique Deblois, Kathy Dimson, Lynnmarie Donner, Philippe Dupuy, Steff Ehm, Michelle Gibeau, Winona Godwin, Jacqueline Gomes, Peggy Grace, Deanna Hostler, Nadine Hughes, Heather Jones, Jennifer Kingsley, Honna Kozik, Tracy Lawson, Jennifer Lim, Richard Mahoney, Susie Majesky, Meghan Malloy, Alona Martinez, Jennifer Massolo, Ian McKichan, Craig McKnight, Lisa McKnight, Javier Merino, Liz Milender, Stéphanie Montreuil, Jessica Vilani Nanna, Debbie Patterson, Shari Reed, Ryan Reichert, Anna and Dave Russell, Sylvia Sicuso, Rebecca Stanisic, Lesley Stowe, Coleen Thompson, Lori Tinella, Sandy Trojansek, Maia Welbourne, Kathy Weldy, Robin White, Deborah Wickins, Dianne Willis, Lisa Wood, and Kristin Zangrilli.

For their assistance with the daunting task of planning the logistics of my trips abroad, I would like to acknowledge the help of Ulrike Bahm, Denis Boucher, Maria Cabral, Liz Clement, Ron Fiorelli, Louisa Fry, Magdalena Kaiser-Smit, Laurel Keenan, Valérie Lelong, Giuseppe Longo, Ariel Menniti, François Millo, Andre Morgenthal, and Rebel Neary.

I'd like to thank Antonia Morton, whom I affectionately call my personal word trainer. Antonia has read everything I have ever written professionally—buffing and polishing it before the world saw it.

This book would have remained a Microsoft Word document without the support of my Canadian publishers, Kristin Cochrane and Brad Martin, and my U.S. publisher and editor, John Duff. Working with my editors, Amy Black and John, felt like an intriguing conversation over a long, satisfying dinner. They gently prodded and posed questions that made me believe I had come up with their skillful insights on my own. And when

I stubbornly ignored them, they delivered the necessary unvarnished direction.

I am grateful to my agent, Jackie Kaiser, who provided critical guidance in conceiving the idea for this book and its organization. Jackie is, and always has been, steadfast and gracious.

I considered changing the last name of my superstar assistant, Helena Cody, in these acknowledgments so that you can't find her or hire her. (Note to self: send flowers.)

Most profoundly, I'd like to thank my life editor and dreams agent, Ann MacLean. You're on every page of this book, Mom.

The burden of putting up with my obsession for wine rests most heavily on my husband, Andrew, and my son, Rian. Andrew, universally curious and brilliant, has adopted my field as a subject of interest to him, too. His efforts to make this a shared passion have brought us closer together. Rian, now twelve, kept me afloat with his wry humor and optimism for the book's success, asking earnest questions about how royalties are transferred to relatives when an author dies. Let's hope this book sends your grandkids to college, Rian!

INDEX

Aan De Doorns, 159–60
Abbot (Prince of Fulda), 66
ABSA Cape Epic competition, 148
absinthe, 283
Aconcagua, 227
Adelaide, Australia, 1, 11, 24
Adenauer, Konrad, 73
Adventures on the Wine Route (Lynch), 314
Africa, 125
    See also South Africa
African National Congress (ANC), 139
Africa Uncorked (Platter), 164
agrodolce (desserts), 187
Alain Ducasse restaurant, New York, 300
alberello method, 181
Albert, Prince, 47
alcohol content
    high-alcohol, 237, 238, 240, 253, 320
    low-alcohol, 42, 53, 60, 62, 77
alcoholism in South Africa, 151
Algonquin Hotel, New York, 317, 319, 323
Alice's Adventures in Wonderland (Carroll),
    21, 39, 178
Allen, Woody, 305
Altano, 262, 275
altitude impact, 208, 209, 212, 217–18, 261
Amadeo, Vittorio, II (King), 177, 178
Amadeus (Harris hawk), 103, 104–5
Amani Vineyards, 141–42, 149–50, 151,
    158, 161, 162
American oak, 9, 12–13, 14, 15–16, 18
American Revolution, 86
ancient regions as "new," 197
Andes Mountains, 203, 204, 205, 212, 219,
    223, 227

Andreis, Didier, 309
"angel's share," 13
Antarctica, 124, 202
anthocyanins, 209
Antiques Roadshow (TV show), 20
AOC *(appellation d'origine contrôlée)*, 87,
    289–90
apartheid, 127–28, 138, 139–40, 140, 151
Appellation (restaurant), Australia, 29, 37
Arabs, 174, 187
Argentina
    climate and soils of, 203, 207, 214, 218,
        219–20, 223
    traveling in, 202, 213
    wine, 33, 201–33
Aristotle, 185
asado (cookout), 225, 226, 228, 232
Ashbourne, Lord, 156
Asia, 10, 88
Asrael (opera), 191
Atlantic Ocean, 124, 128, 136, 155, 157, 236
Audebert, Nicolas (Cheval des Andes), 202
auslese riesling, 49, 58, 65, 66–67, 80
Ausonius, 47
Austen, Jane, 127
Australia
    climate and soils of, 1, 2, 3, 17, 23–24,
        28, 29, 219
    traveling in, 11, 20–21, 25
    wine, 1–39, 138, 204, 320
Autobahn, 53, 68
Avola, Sicily, 172

BA (beerenauslese) riesling, 65, 67, 74, 80
baboons, 136, 321

Baby Duck, 87, 296
bacalhua, 260
Bacchus, 168
Bachelder, Mary, 109
Bachelder, Thomas (Le Clos Jordanne),
    109–11, 112, 113, 114, 115–16
Back, Charles (Fairview Wine, Spice Route,
    Fairvalley), 128–32, 134–38, 139
Back, Cyril, 130
Back, Michael (Backsberg Winery), 137
"backwards," 46
"badge wine," 181
Bain & Company, London, 153
Balzac, Honoré de, 288
barbera grapes, 211, 296
bargain wines, xi–xx, 317–23
    Argentine wine, 33, 201–33
    Australian wine, 1–39, 138, 204, 320
    changing world of, xviii
    "experts," xiv, 14
    French wine, 11, 12, 17, 84, 169, 215,
        279–315
    German wine, 32, 41–81, 320
    Niagara (Canadian) wine, 83–121, 320
    Portuguese wine and port, 34, 43, 235–77
    price vs. quality, demystifying, xii, xiii
    Sicilian wine, 167–200
    South African wine, 123–65
    unquenchable journey, xv–xvi
    virtual glass of wine, sharing, xiv, xx
    websites, xiv, xviii–xix, xx
    women and wine, 9, 258–59, 281, 322–23
    See also best value wines; blending;
        climate and soils; dinner picks;
        dinners; insider tips; marketing and
        labels; pairings (food and wine);
        resources and related reading; top value
        producers; traveling
Barossa, Australia, 1, 2, 3–4, 16, 17, 28–29,
    30, 35
Baudelaire, Charles, 127
Bauer, Florian, 146
Beaujolais, 55
beerenauslese (BA) riesling, 65, 67, 74, 80
Behan, Brendan, 323
Belle Époque, 191, 202
Benanti, Antonio, 177, 178
Benanti, Giuseppe (Vinicola Benanti),
    177–80, 181–83, 193
Benchley, Peter, 165
Benchley, Robert, 318
beneficial insects, 24, 94–96, 105, 285

beneficio classification system, 260
Benigni, Roberto, 172
Bernkasteler Doctor, 72, 73, 76
Berry, Halle, 140
best value wines, xvii–xviii
    Argentine wine, 231
    Australian wine, 36
    French wine, 312–13
    German wine, 78
    Niagara (Canadian) wine, 118
    Portuguese wine and port, 274
    Sicilian wine, 198
    South African wine, 162
Bianchi (Seagram, Canada), 214
biodynamical farming, 285
bird bangers, 83–84, 102, 103–4
black currant liqueur, 292
Black Economic Empowerment, 129
Black Hawk Down (film), 84
blackstrap, 253
Black Tower, 55–56
black vintners, 129, 136–37, 138,
    139, 140–41, 141–42, 143–44,
    148–51, 158
black vultures, 235
"black wine," 208
Blass, Wolfgang Franz Otto (Wolf Blass),
    4–11, 15
"blaster's mistakes," 89
"bleeding the vats" *(saignée)*, 287, 288
blending
    Argentine wine, 209–10
    Australian wine, 7, 9–10, 16, 26
    California wine, 48
    French wine, 289, 297
    German wine, not blending, 47–48
    Niagara (Canadian) wine, 115
    Portuguese wine and port, 239,
        240–42, 271
    Sicilian wine, 173, 175, 179, 180,
        193, 194
    South African wine, 130, 144, 147, 156
"blessed mother's milk" *(liebfraumilch)*,
    54–55
blind tasting, 45
"block and tackle" wines, 87
Blue Nun, 55–56, 56
blush wine, 294
Bodega Norton, 205, 207, 213, 214–16,
    216–17, 218–19, 221, 230, 231
Bohemund II (Prince of Trier), 72
Boisset, Jean-Charles (Le Clos Jordanne), 110

Bolero (Ravel), 19
Bond, James (fictional character), 246
Bonny Doon, 131, 296
Bordeaux, France, xi, 13, 14, 43, 55, 58,
    169, 179, 193, 194, 203, 294
bordeaux (claret), 10, 47, 67, 147, 185
Bored Doe, 130
Borges, Jorge Luis, 202, 233, 317
Borges Collected Fictions (Borges), 233
Born Free (film), 106
Bosman, Herman Charles, 149–50, 165
Botrytis cinerea, 67, 69
bottle-aged ports, 240, 255–56
Bottle Shock (film), 107
Bouchard Aîné et Fils, 110
boutique wineries, 11, 12, 33, 175
Bramble, Linda, 120
brand awareness, 70–71, 230, 274
brandy ingredient in port, 238, 240
breakfast wines, 62
Breit, Norbret (Wegeler), 73, 74, 75,
    76, 77
Brettanomyces, 90
Bright, Thomas, 87
Brightman, Sarah, 64
Bright's Disease, 87
Brindisi, 191
British connection to port, 246–47
British Masters of Wine, 145
Broadbent, Michael, 145
Brook, Stephen, 80
Brown, George Massiot, 243
Brown Brothers, 11, 12, 33
Bruno Prats, 262
Bryant, Chris (Fairview Wine), 133, 134
Buenos Aires, Argentina, 201, 202, 214,
    216, 226
bulldozers, 236
bungs, 13
Burgundian site-specific, 109, 111, 115
burgundy, 70, 91
Burgundy, France, 58, 65, 84, 109, 110,
    185, 294
Busby, James, 2
butter on food, drink chardonnay, 61

cabernet, 17, 33, 90, 130, 147
Cabernet d'Anjou, 295
cabernet franc, 101, 106, 149, 196
cabernet franc grapes, 53, 193, 288, 295, 296
"cabernetization" of wine industry, 175
cabernet sauvignon, 7, 48, 161, 212, 282, 302

cabernet sauvignon grapes, 193, 207, 211,
    288, 294
Cabo Tormentoso (Cape of Storms), 126
Ca' d'Oro, Venice, 190–91
Caesar, Julius, 280
California
    climate and soils of, 47
    wine, 48, 55, 64–65, 107, 114, 131, 147,
        174, 215, 281
    winemaking in, xi, 2, 11, 18, 50, 61, 110,
        138, 143, 203, 206, 207
Camuto, Robert, 199
Canada
    climate and soils of, 84, 85, 86, 88, 90,
        111, 112
    Niagara (Canadian) wine, 83–121, 320
    traveling in, 83, 84–86, 89
Canada-U.S. Free Trade Agreement, 87
Canadian Oak Chardonnay, 101
Cape of Good Hope, 124, 126
Cape Town, South Africa, 128, 132
Cape wine region, South Africa, 124–27
Captain Morgan, 243
Carey, Peter, 39
carignan grapes, 288, 299
Carroll, Lewis, 21, 39, 178
Casella Wines, 8, 9
Casino Royale (film), 246
Cassis, France, 284, 292
Cat Amongst the Pigeons, 8
Catania, Sicily, 176, 177
Catena, Domingo (Catena Zapata),
    206, 207
Catena, Elaina (Catena Zapata),
    206, 207
Catena, Laura (Catena Zapata), 210, 233
Catena, Nicola (Catena Zapata),
    206, 207
Catena, Nicolás (Catena Zapata), 204,
    205–10, 211–12, 213, 214, 230, 231
CBS, 138
cellaring port, 255
cellar palate, 147
cenosilicaphobia (fear of empty glass), 182
Cézanne, Paul, 282
chablis, 65
Chagall, Marc, 282
Chambolle, 115
Champagne, 5, 14, 61, 116–17, 254, 297
Chapleau, Marc, 113
Chapoutier, Michel, 261
chaptalization, 17, 63–64

chardonnay, 9, 29, 36, 55, 59, 61, 64–65, 106, 107, 110, 111, 112, 113, 116, 117, 130, 139, 149, 153, 156, 157, 174–75, 212, 282
chardonnay grapes, 53, 111, 112, 153, 207, 297
"Chardonnay Shocker," 107
Chassagne, 115
Château Cheval Blanc, 202, 214
Château Cos d'Estournel, 262
Château de Haute House Hooch, xi
Château de Roquefort, 283–85, 286–87, 288, 289, 290, 291–92, 293, 312
Château de Roquefort Corail (pick for Sunday lunch), 291, 312
Château des Charmes, 119
Château d'Yquem, 63, 67, 69, 127
Château Génot-Boulanger, 110
Château-Grillet, 221
Château Lafite-Rothschild, 205, 214, 258
Château Margaux, 57, 114, 143
Chateau Montelena Chardonnay, 107
Château Mouton-Rothschild, 57, 113
Châteauneuf-du-Pape, 287
cheap-and-sweet image, 55–56, 70, 87
cheap wine, 131–32
    See also bargain wines
cheese and wine, 130, 134–35, 229
"chemist's wine," 17
chenin blanc (Steen), 135, 161
Cheval des Andes, 201–2, 204, 230
chianti, 296
Child, Julia, 256
Chile
    climate and soils of, 47, 203, 218
    wine, 33, 55, 131, 138, 140, 169, 203, 211, 212, 215, 255
chilling wine, 312
Christie's wine auction house, 145
Christoffel, 71
Chryseia, 262
Churchill, 246
cinsault grapes, 127, 144–45, 288, 296, 299
clairet, 294
claret (Bordeaux), 10, 47, 58, 67, 147, 179, 185
Claystone Terrace Vineyard (Le Clos Jordanne), 111, 113, 116
cliffs and vineyards, 59, 72, 76
climate and soils, xii, xvii
    Argentina, 203, 207, 214, 218, 219–20, 223
    Australia, 1, 2, 3, 17, 23–24, 28, 29, 219

California, 47
Canada, 84, 85, 86, 88, 90, 111, 112
Chile, 47, 203, 218
France, 219, 279–80, 284, 290, 294
Germany, 42–43, 53, 54, 57, 59, 67–68
Portugal, 236, 245, 254, 260, 268
Sicily, 167, 171, 172–73, 173, 176–77, 179, 180, 181, 185, 186, 192–93, 193, 194, 196
South Africa, 124, 125, 128, 135, 152, 153, 158, 161
clones, 174, 208
Clooney, George, 152
Clos de Vougeot, 110
Clos Jordanne Single Vineyard (Le Clos Jordanne), 111
clubs (milongas), 216
CNN, 132
Cockburn (Symington Family Estates), 246
cocktails mixed with port, 245–46
cold-climate vs. warm-climate regions, 35
Cold War, 131
cold weather, drinking wine, 32, 35
colheitas, 266, 272
Collins, Jackie, 281
color-coding labels, 8
Como, Perry, 155
competitions, 6–7, 14, 148
Conrad, Joseph, 235, 277
Conservationist (Gordimer), 165
Contarini family, 191
"controlled neglect" of plants, 27
corks vs. screwcaps, 30–31, 35, 48
"correcting" finished wine, 17
Corto Maltese (comic books), 191
Cosa Nostra, 176
Côte d'Azur, France, 290, 308
Côte d'Or, 130
Côte Rôtie, 1, 129
Côtes-du-Rhône, 129
country wine (vin de pays), 175, 289
Courtney Gamay, 97
cover crops, 24, 105, 112
Coyote's Run, 87
Cristal Champagne, 290
Cristoforo Colombo (opera), 191
"critter craze" wine labels, 8–9, 129, 130–31
Crocodile Rock, 8
Croft, 246, 258, 274, 275
Crotta, Jorge (Catena Zapata), 205
Crow, Russell, 309
cru bourgeois wines, 55

Crushed by Women: Women and Wine (Port), 38
crusted port, 257
currency advantage, 230
"custodian," 11, 20
cut *(corte)*, 250
Cuvaison winery, 263
Cyclops, 168

Damon, Matt, 136
Dangerfield, Rodney, 281
Dangerous Summer (Hemingway), 296
Darwin, Charles, 226
De Bortoli, 171
decanting port, 243–45, 255–56
Declaration of Independence, 62
"deep calling to deep," 29
de Grazia, Marco (Tenuta delle Terre Nere), 184–89, 193, 198–99
de Grazia, Sebastian, 184, 200
de Klerk, Frederick Willem, 139
Depardieu, Gérard, 178
Deserioux, Cindy, 100
dessert wines, 65, 67, 69
de Villiers, Marq, 121
Diageo, 249
diamond mines, South Africa, 153
Dickens, Charles, 127
di Lampedusa, Giuseppe Tomasi, 171, 183, 200, 317
dinner picks (asterisk), xviii
    Château de Roquefort Corail (Sunday lunch), 291, 312
    Dr. Loosen's Dr. L Riesling (Monday), 57, 78
    Fairview Shiraz (Wednesday), 162
    Le Clos Jordanne Village Reserve Pinot Noir (Tuesday), 111, 115, 118
    Niepoort 10 Year Tawny Port (Saturday), 274
    Santa Julia Malbec (Zuccardi) (Friday), 222, 227
    Tenuta delle Terre Nere Etna Rosso (Thursday), 186, 198
    Wolf Blass Red Label Shiraz Cabernet Sauvignon (Sunday), 9, 36
dinners for a wine cheapskate
    Friday dinner, 203, 222, 227, 232
    Monday dinner, 42, 57, 78, 79
    Saturday dinner, 238, 274, 275
    Sunday lunch, 291, 312, 313–14
    Sunday dinner, 3, 9, 36, 37–38

Thursday dinner, 172, 186, 198–99
Tuesday dinner, 111, 115, 118, 119
Wednesday dinner, 128, 162, 163
Dion, Céline, 114
Disney World, 125
Ditter, Don (Penfolds), 18
"D.O.," 290
DOC *(Denominazione di Origine Controllata)*, 87, 175
dogs, 154, 155, 300, 321
Domaine de Boyer, 294
Domaine de la Romanée-Conti, 84
Domaine du Clos d'Alari, 297–99, 302–4, 312
Domaines Ott, 290, 313
"Don, The" (Brown), 243
donkeys, 285–86, 321
Donnafugata, 171, 198
dop system, 151
"Douro Boys, The," 264–65
Douro Valley, Portugal, 235–36, 237, 246, 247, 248, 249–50, 251, 254, 261, 262, 264, 268
Dow's (Symington Family Estates), 246, 247, 253, 254, 257, 258, 259–60, 274
Dr. Bürklin-Wolf, 71
Dr. Loosen, 49–54, 55, 56–57, 58–59, 64, 71, 77
Dr. Loosen's Dr. L Riesling (pick for Monday dinner), 57, 78
Dr. Pauly-Bergweiler, 71, 78
Drieseberg, Tom, Anja (Wegeler), 73–77
Drinks Matcher tool, xviii, xix
Driving Over Lemons (Stewart), 305
"drop" method, 299
dry-farming vs. irrigation, 23
dry riesling, 53, 60, 64, 65, 69, 71, 79–80, 174
dry rosé, 55
dry table wine, 13, 14, 22, 260–61, 262, 268–69, 273
Duijker, Hubrecht, 314
Dutch East India Company, 126
Duval, John (Penfolds), 18

Egoist, The (Meredith), 237–38, 277
Egon Müller, 71
Eisenhower, Dwight (U.S. president), 73
eiswein (icewine), 9, 65, 69, 80, 87–89, 102, 114, 118
Ejbich, Konrad, 121
Eleanor of Aquitaine (Queen of England), 246

Elixir of the Gods from Toronto, 88
Elizabeth (Queen of England), 281
Empedocles, 176
Encore Provence: New Adventures in the South of France (Mayle), 308, 315
endothelin-1, 209
Engel, Louise (Featherstone Estate Winery), 98–99, 100, 101–2, 102–5, 106
Erdener Prälat Riesling Auslese Long Gold Capsule, 58, 59
et alaria wind, 188
Etna, Mount, 167, 176–77, 179, 180, 184, 185, 186, 187, 190, 192, 193, 194, 196
Europe and phylloxera, 2, 26, 51, 176, 208
European Union, 289
Evita: The Real Life of Eva Perón (Fraser and Navarro), 233
experience (your) and wine drinking, 320
"experts," xiv, 14
"export" (port-style wine), 239
Extremely Pale Rosé: A Very Pale Adventure (Ivey), 314
"eye of the partridge" (*oeil de perdrix*), 297

Facebook, xiv, xix
Fair Trade wines, 151
Fairvalley, 129, 137–38, 140, 162
Fairview Shiraz (pick for Wednesday dinner), 162
Fairview Wine, 128–37, 162
Falcone Borsellino Airport, 176
Falklands War with Britain, 202, 211
"fallen bright," 245
family and Sicily, 175–76, 181, 197
Faust Part One (Goethe), 66, 81
Featherstone Estate Winery, 87, 98–102, 102–6, 118
Ferber, Edna, 318
Fernando, Carlos (Cheval des Andes), 201–2
Feudo, 185, 198
"field, the" (vineyards), 299
Fielden, Christopher, 233
filtering sediment, 256
Finca, 214, 231
"fine bush" (*fynbos*), 125
fine tawny ports, 266
Fish Hoek, 128
Fitzgerald, Ella, 318
Flat Rock, 87, 114, 119, 296
flavonoids, 209
Florio, 171

Fly Away Home (film), 90
"flying winemakers," 214
food and wine. *See* pairings
Fool and Forty Acres: Conjuring a Vineyard Three Thousand Miles from Burgundy (Heinricks), 121
Forster, E. M., 305
fortified wines, 13, 238–39, 240, 258
Fosters, 10, 12
Foti, Salvo (Vinicola Benanti), 178
fractional blending, 170–71
France
    climate and soils of, 219, 279–80, 284, 290, 294
    traveling in, 279, 282
    wine, 11, 12, 17, 84, 169, 215, 279–315
Franchetti, Alberto, 191
Franchetti, Andrea (Passopisciaro), 190–96
Franchetti, Giorgio, 190–91
Franchetti, Giuditta, 190
Franchetti, Luisa, 191
Franchetti, Nanuk, 191
Franchetti, Raimondo, 191
Fraser, Nicholas, 233
Frederick the Great, 127
freedom (*liberdade*), 250
Freedom Road, 137, 140
Freeman, Morgan, 136
French oak, 9, 13, 16, 18, 157, 207
French Rabbit, 8
French wine, 11, 12, 17, 84, 169, 215, 279–315
Friday dinner, 203, 222, 227, 232
Fritz Haag, 71
frogs, 304
Frozé, 293
Fuddle Duck, 87
Fuzion Malbec Shiraz (Zuccardi), 222, 227, 231

Gago, Peter (Penfolds), 11, 15, 16–17, 17–18, 18–19, 19–20
Gaja, Angelo, 50
Gallo, Gina, 110
gamay, 97, 290, 295, 296
Gamay Noir, 101
Gardanne, Earl of, 284
Gardel, Carlos ("King of Tango"), 216
Garden of Gethsemane, 159
garrigue, 298
gauchos, 225–26
geeks, xv

Gehry, Frank, 108
Geisenheim Grape Breeding Institute, 22
Geisenheim Wine Institute, 22
Germania (opera), 191
German Wine Law of 1971, 54
Germany
  climate and soils of, 42–43, 53, 54, 57,
    59, 67–68
  German wine, 32, 41–81, 320
  growing up in, 4–5
  traveling in, 41, 53, 55, 60, 61, 71
Gimli Goose, 87
Goat Door, 130
Goat-Father, 130
Goat-Rotie, 129
goats, 321
Goats do Roam, 162
Goatshed (restaurant), South Africa, 134
Goat wines, 129, 130–31, 132–33, 162
Godfather, The (Puzo), 174, 200
Goethe, Johann Wolfgang Von, 66, 81
Goodall, Jane, 125
Good Year, A (Mayle), 308–9
Gordimer, Nadine, 165
grafting, 30
Graham's (Symington Family Estates), 246,
  254, 256–57, 274, 275
Grahm, Randall, 50, 131
"grandfathers, the," 26
Grand Prix d'Honneur, 87
granita, 187
Grant Burge, 4, 37
granulometry, 223
Grass, Günter, 81
gravity-flow vs. mechanized system, 46, 89
gray wine *(vin gris)*, 295
Grazia, Elena, 189
Grazia, Sebastian de, 200
Greeks, 167–68, 174, 280
"green revolution," 91
grenache grapes, 130, 288, 290, 291,
  296, 299
"grip," 253
Groot Constantia, South Africa, 126–27
Grosser Ring Auction in Trier, Germany, 52
"GSM" (grenache, shiraz, mourvèdre)
  blends, 7
Guevara, Che, 184
Guyot training, 223

Hairspray (film), 90
Halliday, James, 38

Halstrick, Michael (Bodega Norton), 213,
  214–16, 216–17, 218–19, 221
Hamilton Russell Vineyards, 151–54,
  155–60, 161, 162
hands-on approach, 51, 63, 74
Harris, Thomas, 121
Hatcher, Chris, 7
hawks, 98, 103, 104–5, 106, 321
Hawks, Tony, 305
*Heart and Soul: Australia's First Families of
  Wine* (Lofts and Halliday), 38
*Heartbreak Grape: A Journey in Search of the
  Perfect Pinot Noir* (de Villiers), 121
"heartbreak grapes." *See* pinot noir
heart disease and red wine, 209
Heart of Darkness (Conrad), 277
Heinricks, Geoff, 121
Hemingway, Ernest, 191, 295–96, 322
Hendrix, Jimi, 155
Henry II (King of France), 246
Henry IV (King of France), 279
Henschke, 21–34, 29, 35, 36, 219
Henschke, Cyril, 22, 27–28
Henschke, Johann, 34
Henschke, Johann Christian, 22
Henschke, Justine, 34
Henschke, Stephen, 21–22, 23, 24, 25–30,
  31, 32–34
Hepburn, Katharine, 246
Hephaestus, 244
hermitage, 1, 13, 14, 237
Hidden Bench, 114
high-alcohol wines, 237, 238, 240, 253, 320
Highland dancing, xiv–xv, 244
Hill of Grace (Henschke), 33
History of the Peloponnesian Wars
  (Thucydides), 168
Hobbs, Paul (Catena Zapata, Simi), 143, 207
homemade wine, xi–xii
Homer, 168, 244
Homo erectus, 159
horizontal tastings, 319
horses, 201, 204, 321
hot weather, drinking wine, 32
Hoy, Mr. (bartender), 321, 322, 323
Hubert Lamy Clos du Meix, 113
Hucknall, Mick (Il Cantante), 178
Humbrecht, Olivier, 50
hundred-mile diet, 93
Hungarian wine, 67, 131
Hussein, Saddam, 281
Hutton Vale, 32

Ice Age, 85
Icewine: The Complete Story (Schreiner), 120
icewine (eiswein), 9, 65, 69, 80, 87–89, 102, 114, 118
Idle, Eric (Monty Python character), 2–3
IGT *(Indicazione Geografica Tipica)*, 175
Il Cantante, 178
Iliad, The (Homer), 244
India, 126, 305
Inniskillin, 87, 88–89, 107, 108, 114, 117, 119
INSEAD, 247
insider tips, xvii
    ancient regions as "new," 197
    brand awareness, 230, 274
    butter on food, drink chardonnay, 61
    chilling wine, 312
    cold weather, drinking wine, 32, 35
    currency advantage, 230
    family-run operations, 197
    hot weather, drinking wine, 32
    labels, 77
    late-bloomer wineries, 230
    lemon juice on food, drink riesling, 61
    lesser-knowns, 197, 230
    lightweight wines, 312
    low-alcohol wines, 77
    organically grown grapes, 92, 118
    perceptions, checking your, 161
    regional food and wine pairings, 197
    reputation and repositioning, 55–56, 77
    rosés, 312
    screwcaps vs. corks, 30–31, 35, 48
    supporting-actor wines, 118
    tawny ports, 273
    trade bans and competition, 138–39, 161
    value, relativity of, 117–18
    warm-climate vs. cold-climate regions, 35
    well-rated vs. best-known vintages, 274
insolia grapes, 174, 180
"interesting" wine, 269
"in the air" *(lada all'aria)* vineyard, 188
Invictus (film), 136
Iraq War, 131
Italy, 3, 34, 50, 59, 169, 215, 296
    See also Sicily
Ithemba, 140
"It's Not Unusual," 281
Ivey, Jamie, 314

J. Walter Thompson, 152
Jackson-Triggs, 108, 110, 119
Jacob's Creek, 33

Jaffelin, 110
James Halliday Australian Wine Companion (Halliday), 38
Jaws (Benchley), 165
Jefferson, Thomas, 62, 127
Jiko (restaurant), Disneyworld, 125
Jimmy Watson Trophy, 6–7
Johnny Walker, 243
John Platter South African Wine Guide (Platter), 164
Johnson, Bevan (Newton Johnson Winery), 124, 128
Johnson, David (Featherstone Estate Winery), 98, 99, 100, 105, 106
Johnson, Hugh, 50, 56
Johnson, Samuel, 238
Johnson, Tim, 283, 292
Jones, Tom, 281
Joseph Drouhin Clos des Mouches, 107
Journey Among the Great Wines of Sicily (Zanfi), 199
Joyce, James, 318
Judgment of Montreal, 107, 113–14

kabinett riesling, 62, 63, 65, 73, 78, 79–80
kangaroos, 20–21, 321
Kaufman, George, 318
Keller, Helen, 12
Kim Crawford, 294
Kistler chardonnay, 174
kookaburras, 28, 321
KWV *(Kooperatiewe Wijnbouwers Vereeniging)*, 139, 145

labels, 77
    See also marketing and labels
"ladder brands," 14–15
ladybugs, 24, 94–96, 105, 321
lagars, 250, 251, 252, 268
Lailey Vineyard, 87, 114
"lambmowers," 99
Lancers, 260, 280
"land of midday sun" *(mezzogiorno)*, 183
Langes-Swarovski, Gernot (Bodega Norton), 214
Languedoc, France, 132, 299, 304
La Petite Vineyard (Le Clos Jordanne), 111, 112, 115
large wine-growing states *(grosslagen)*, 54–56
late-bloomer wineries, 230
Late Bottled Vintage (LBV) port, 257
Late Harvest Cabernet Franc, 101

late-harvested grapes, 51, 59, 66–67
Lawrence, D. H., 196
leaf-roll virus, 146–47
Le Cigare Volant, 131
Le Clos Jordanne, 87, 107–9, 110–13, 114, 115–16, 118
Le Clos Jordanne Village Reserve Pinot Noir (pick for Tuesday dinner), 111, 115, 118
"leg opener" wine, 9
Leiwener Laurentiuslay Riesling Beerenauslese, 67
Lemelson Vineyards, 110
lemon juice on food, drink riesling, 61
Leopard, The (Lampedusa), 171, 183, 200, 317
Leopard tortoises, 154
L'Espresso, 192
lesser-knowns, 197, 230
Life Is Beautiful (film), 172
light effect on grapes, 208–9, 210, 217
lightweight wines, 312
"limeys," 126
Lion in Winter, The (film), 246
Lion King, The (film), 125
Liszt, Franz, 191
Little Penguin, 8
Lofts, Graeme, 38
loggia, 155
logo, first wine, 243
Loire Valley, France, 135, 137, 290, 294–95, 296
Lois, George, 306
Lombardo, 171
London Times, 146
longboats *(barcos rabelos)*, 236
Longfellow, Henry Wadsworth, 127
Long Walk to Freedom: The Autobiography of Nelson Mandela (Mandela), 137, 165
loons, 28
Loosen, Ernst "Ernie" (Dr. Loosen), 49–54, 55, 56–57, 58–59
Loosen's Dr. L Riesling, 71
Louise (resort), Australia, 29, 37
Louis Philippe (King of France), 127
Louis VII (King of France), 246
Louis XIV (King of France), 217, 288
low-alcohol wines, 42, 53, 60, 62, 77
Lurton, Jacques, 208
Lutherans, 2, 22, 25, 27
Lynch, Kermit, 314

Machiavelli in Hell (de Grazia), 184, 200
MacLean, Natalie, xi–xx, 3, 21, 84, 125–26, 142–43, 317–23, 318–19
MacQuitty, Jane, 146
madeira, 258
Mad Men (TV show), 306
Madonna, 177, 178
Mafeking Road and Other Stories (Bosman), 165
Magic Mountain, The (Mann), 70, 81
magpies, 28, 321
Malamado, 229
malbec, 32, 205, 212, 213, 217, 219, 227, 228–29, 230, 232, 233, 320
malbec-cabernet sauvignon blends, 202
malbec grapes, 207–8, 209, 210, 211, 220, 295
Malivoire, Martin (Malivoire Winery), 84, 85, 89–90, 91, 92, 93, 94, 95–98, 105, 118, 296
Mandela, Nelson, 125, 137, 139, 140, 142, 158, 165
Mann, Thomas, 70, 81
Mansilha, Maria José da Fonseca, 263, 268
Maradona, Diego, 202
Marchand, Pascal (Le Clos Jordanne), 109–10
Maria Carolina (Queen of Naples), 171
marketing and labels
    Argentine wine, 212, 215–16
    Australian wine, 3, 5–6, 6–7, 8–9, 14–15, 33
    French wine, 57, 280–81
    German wine, 49, 54–55, 56–57, 63, 70, 71, 77
    Niagara (Canadian) wine, 88, 94, 116
    Portuguese wine and port, 239, 242–43, 257–59
    Sicilian wine, 175, 181
    South African wine, 129, 130–31, 132, 140
Marqués de Riscal, 108
Márquez, Gabriel García, 173
Marsa el Allah ("port of God"), 170
marsala, 170–71
Marseilles, France, 282, 284, 302
Martinez, 171
Marx, Karl, 52
"mass terroir-ism," 293
Master of Wine (MW) program, 148–49
Mateus, 55, 260, 280–81
Matisse, Henri, 282
Mayes, Frances, 305
Mayle, Jean, 308, 310, 311

Mayle, Peter, 305–11, 315, 317
Mayson, Richard, 276
McNamara, Mark, 37
Mediterranean, 124, 160, 168, 173, 181, 185, 186, 196, 206, 279, 282, 284, 292, 301, 306
Mendoza, Argentina, 201, 214, 218, 219, 221, 222
Meredith, Carole, 221
Meredith, George, 237–38, 277
merlot, 48, 90, 149, 172, 173, 282
merlot grapes, 56, 193, 294, 299
Metcalfe, Charles, 276
Methuen Treaty, 247
M'hudi, 140
Michelin-starred restaurants, 61
microoxygenation, 225
microwinemakers, 30
Middle Ages, 47
milking a goat, 133–34
minerality, 67–68, 193
mistral wind, 279–80
mobile apps, xix
modernists vs. traditionalists, 193
Moira's Vineyard Pinot Noir, 97
Mommessin, 110, 285
Mona Lisa, 26
Mondavi people, Argentina, 207
Monday dinner, 42, 57, 78, 79
Monty Python (comedy), 2–3
"Mosella" (Ausonius), 47
Mosel Valley, Germany, 41–42, 43, 47, 49, 50, 51, 52, 53, 71, 76–77
mountain climbing, 227–28
"mountain has broken" ("scassau a muntagne"), 176
Mount Edelstone Shiraz (Henschke), 31
mourning doves, 104
mourvèdre grapes, 130, 135, 220, 288, 294, 299
Mouton, Donald (Fairview Wine), 133, 134
Mouton Cadet, 57
Mövenpick, 263
Mulderbosch, 125, 162
muscat, 127, 221
Museo Franchetti alla Ca' d'Oro, 191
mushroom compost, 105
My Big Fat Greek Wedding (film), 90
Myers, Jim, 141
Myers, Rusty and Lynde (Amani Vineyards), 141

Napa Valley, California, xi, 11, 203, 206
Napoleon, 47, 127, 171
nataliemaclean.com, xiv, xviii, xix, xx, 36, 37, 79, 119, 163, 198, 232, 275
"natural" farming. See organic farming
Navarro, Marysa, 233
Navarro Correas, 214, 231
Nederburg, 128, 162
Nelson, Horatio, 170
nerello grapes, 179, 180, 186
nero d'avola, 172–73, 174, 179, 199
nets to protect vineyards, 102, 112
New Beginnings, 140
Newton Johnson Winery, 124, 162
"new viognier," 220–21
New vs. Old World wines, 107, 114
New York, 85, 305
New Yorker, 318, 323
New Yorker cocktail, 322
New York Times, 108
New Zealand wine, 8, 29, 99, 114, 137, 294
Nguni of South Africa, 140
Niagara (Canadian) wine, 83–121, 320
    See also Canada
Niagara Escarpment, 85–86, 91, 98
Niagara Falls, 85, 86, 117, 281, 294
Niagara-on-the-Lake, 86, 117
Niagara Peninsula, 85, 86
Niagara's Wine Visionaries (Bramble), 120
Niehaus, Charles, 145
Niepoort, Dirk (Niepoort), 262, 263–66, 267–69, 270, 271, 272–73, 274
Niepoort 10 Years Old Tawny Port (pick for Saturday dinner), 274
nitrogen, 91
Nobel prizes, 206
noble rot (edelfäule), 67
North American Free Trade Agreement, 87
Norton. See Bodega Norton
nose of human, xiii
Notes on a Cellar-Book (Saintsbury), 238, 277
Notte di Leggenda (opera), 191
Nuits-Saint-Georges, 115

oak for aging, 9, 12–13, 14, 15–16, 18, 106, 157, 207
Obikwa, 128, 162
O'Brien, Edna, 319
Ockfener Bockstein, 63, 66
Odysseus, 168
oenology, 12
"Oenotria" (Land of Vines), 168

Ogilvy, David, 306
Olde English Babydoll Southdowns, 100
"old people's faces" *(oumensgesiggies)*, 127
Olympus, Mount, 168
one-night wine *(vino de una noche)*, 295
Ongniaahra ("point of land cut in two"), 85
Ontario, Lake, 84, 85, 86, 89, 112, 113
Ontario Wine Content Act, 87
Onyx Cabernet Franc Merlot, 101
opening port, 255–56
Oporto, Portugal, 235, 237
organically grown grapes, 92, 118
organic farming, 85, 91–92, 93, 105,
    112–13, 118, 218
organic wine, 92–94, 118
Oscar and Lucinda (Carey), 39
O'Toole, Peter, 246
Ott family, 290, 313
"overnight sensation," 2
Oxford Companion to Wine (Robinson), 21
Oxford University, U.K., 22, 152, 153,
    205, 247
oxidization, 13

Pacific Ocean, 126, 203
pairings (food and wine), xviii
    Argentine wine, 221, 226, 227, 228, 229,
        232–33
    Australian wine, 29, 30, 32, 33, 34,
        37–38
    French wine, 294, 299, 301–3, 313–14
    German wine, 60–61, 62, 63, 66, 67, 69,
        70, 79–80
    Niagara (Canadian) wine, 96–98,
        100–101, 105, 106, 119–20
    Portuguese wine and port, 257, 260, 264,
        267, 268, 269, 270, 275–76
    regional food and wine pairings, 197
    Sicilian wine, 173–74, 184–89, 193, 197,
        198–99
    South African wine, 136, 156, 157–58,
        159–60, 163–64
Palermo, Sicily, 168–69, 176, 177
"palliative vines," 126
Palmento: A Sicilian Wine Odyssey
    (Camuto), 199
Pamplona, Spain, 295
Pansy Rosé, 294
Parker, Dorothy, 317, 318, 321, 322
Parker, Robert, 59
parral-trellising, 223
parrots, 224

Passopisciaro, 189–90, 192–96, 197
Patagonia, 202
Pendock, Neil, 164
Penfolds, 4, 5, 11–20, 24, 35, 36, 114
perceptions, checking your, 161
Périgord region of Provence, France, 299
Pernod Ricard/Allied Domecq, 249
Perold, Abraham, 144–45
Perón, Evita, 202, 211
Perón, Juan, 211
Pessoa, Fernando, 263
Peter Lehmann Wines, 4, 36–37
petit verdot, 193, 195
petrol, 68
Pétrus, 73
phenolics in grapes, 209
Philippe le Bel (King of France), 288
phosphorous, 91
photosynthesis, 209, 217
phylloxera, 2, 26, 51, 127, 176, 189, 220
Piano in the Pyrenees, A (Hawks), 305
Piat d'Or, 280
Picasso, Pablo, 282
Piesporter Goldtröpfchen Riesling Spätlese,
    63, 66
"Pink Out" tastings, 281
"pink pain," 290
"Pink Wine," 296
pinotage, 144–48, 157, 158, 161
pinot noir, 65, 70, 84, 89, 91, 95, 97–98,
    106, 110, 113, 114, 115–16, 117–18,
    120, 152, 153, 158, 282, 295, 297, 320
pinot noir ("heartbreak") grapes, 56, 84,
    90–91, 95, 97, 111, 112, 144–45, 153,
    290, 294, 297
pizza *(spinchone)*, 186
Planeta, Alessio (Planeta), 175, 176
Planeta, Diego (Planeta), 174–75, 175–76,
    178, 198
Planeta, Diego (Settesoli), 172
Planeta, Francesca (Planeta), 175
Plantagenet, Henry (Duke of
    Normans), 246
Plato, 185
Platter, John, 164
*Pocket Guide to Ontario Wines, Wineries,
    Vineyards, and Vines, A* (Ejbich), 121
polyphenols, 209
Pontallier, Paul (Tukulu), 143–44
Ponzi, Dick, 110
Ponzi, Luisa, 110
Ponzi Vineyards, 110

port, 47, 236–49, 250–62, 266–67,
    269–73, 276, 320
Port, Jeni, 38
Portugal
    climate and soils of, 236, 245, 254,
        260, 268
    traveling in, 235, 247, 249–50
    wine and port, 34, 43, 235–77
*Portugal's Wines and Wine Makers: Port
    Madeira and Regional Wines*
    (Mayson), 276
Prälat, 58, 59
"predicated" *(prädikat)* wines, 65, 70
prehistoric artifacts, South Africa, 158–59
Price, Freddie, 80
Price, Janet, 80
price vs. quality, demystifying, xii, xiii
Prohibition, 2, 87
Provence, France, 279–80, 282, 286, 288,
    289, 290, 293–94, 297, 299, 301, 305,
    308, 309, 310, 314, 317
*Provence A–Z: A Francophile's Essential
    Handbook* (Mayle), 315
Prüm, Johann Josef, 43–47, 48–49, 57, 64, 77
Prüm, Katharina (Johann Josef Prüm),
    44–46, 48–49, 58, 64
Prüm, Manfred (Johann Josef Prüm),
    43–44, 49
Pulitzer Prize, 184
Pussycat, 87
Puzo, Mario, 200
pyrazine, 95

QbA *(Qualitätswein bestimmter
    Anbaugebiete)*, 65
QmP *(Qualitätswein mit Prädikat)*, 65
Quest for Fire (film), 90
Quinta da Senhora da Ribeira, Portugal,
    247, 250, 253
Quinta de Roriz, 262
Quinta do Bomfim, 247, 254, 275
Quinta do Noval National, 254
Quinta do Vale Dona Maria, 265
Quinta do Vale Meão, 265
Quinta do Vallado, 265, 275
Quinta do Vesuvio, 254, 259, 260, 262, 275

rabelos (boats), 249
"rack-and-return," 18
racking, 13
"rainbow nation," 140
Ravel, Maurice, 19

recipes, xix
recorking clinics, 19–20
Red, White, and Drunk All Over (MacLean),
    319, 321
red wines, 71, 131, 135, 139, 180, 209, 289,
    290, 294
Reeves, Keanu, 251
regional food and wine pairings, 197
Renard Rosé, 296
reputation and repositioning, 55–56, 77
resources and related reading, xviii
    Argentine wine, 233
    Australian wine, 38–39
    French wine, 314–15
    German wine, 80–81
    Niagara (Canadian) wine, 120–21
    Portuguese wine and port, 276–77
    Sicilian wine, 199–200
    South African wine, 164–65
Rhodes, Cecil John, 153
Rhône Valley, France, 1, 13, 131, 221, 279,
    286, 287–88, 290, 291, 299
Richard, Sir Cliff, 281
Rickman, Alan, 107
riding trousers *(bombachos)*, 201
riesling, 282
    Australian, 29
    German, 32, 41–42, 43, 47–48, 50, 53,
        55, 56, 58, 59, 61, 62, 64–65, 71, 75,
        80, 127, 320
    Niagara (Canadian), 32, 84, 105, 118
    port vs., 237–38
    South African, 134
riesling grapes, 88, 112
Riesling Renaissance (Price and Price), 80
Riesling Rendezvous, 54, 80
Riesling Taste Scale, 71
Rilke, Rainer Maria, 29, 39
Rizzuto, 198
Robert Mondavi winery, 206
Robert Oatley, 37
Robert Weil, 71
robins, 104
Robinson, Jancis, 21, 68
robotic treaders, 251–52
rock stars (winemaker), 50
rocky hillside *(rocca fortis)*, 284
"Rocky Horror Riesling Show, The," 54
Roederer, Louis, 290
Rolland, Michel (Val de Flores, Clos de los
    Siete), 214
Romans, 47, 52, 63, 168, 176, 280, 284

rosado (rosé), 290, 295–96
rosato (rosé), 296
rosé
    California wine, 296
    French, 280–82, 283, 286–91, 292–94, 296–97, 301–2, 303–4, 311, 312, 314, 320
    Italian, 296
    Portuguese, 280–81, 290
    South African, 293
    Spanish, 290, 295–96
Rosé Avengers and Producers (RAP), 281, 314
Rosé d'Anjou, 295
Rosemount, 14, 37
rosé-style port, 258–59
Roseworthy College of Agriculture, Australia, 12, 18, 22
Ross, Harold, 318
roto-fermenters, 225
ruby ports, 266–67
Rüssel, Ruth and Harald, 61–62, 79
Russell, Anthony Hamilton (Hamilton Russell Vineyards), 151–52, 153, 154–60
Russell, Olive (Hamilton Russell Vineyards), 155, 156, 157–58, 159–60, 163
Russell, Tim Hamilton (Hamilton Russell Vineyards), 152–53, 159
Rüssels Landhaus St. Urban (restaurant), Germany, 61–62, 79

Saganski, Moira (Malivoire Winery), 90
Saintsbury, George, 238, 277
Sambuca di Sicilia, 174
Sandeman, George Thomas David (Sandeman), 239–46, 274
Sandeman, Walter (Sandeman), 242–43
sangiovese, 172, 211, 296
Santa Julia Malbec (Zuccardi) (pick for Friday dinner), 222, 227
Santenay, 115
Sapienza, Lisa (Vinicola Benanti), 177–78, 179–80, 181, 183
Sassicaia, 114, 170, 172
Saturday dinner, 238, 274, 275
sauvignon blanc, 29, 125, 137, 152, 156, 157, 161, 163, 164, 302
Schloss Vollrads, 71
Schreiner, John, 120
Schubert, Max (Penfolds), 12–14, 17, 18, 22

Schug, Bernard "Bernie" (Dr. Loosen), 51
scirocco wind, 173
Scott, Ridley, 309
Scott Henry trellising, 30
Scotus, Duns, 26
"screamers," 102
screwcaps vs. corks, 30–31, 35, 48
scyra. See shiraz
Seabra, Luís (Niepoort), 267
Seagram's, 214, 249
Sebeka, 128, 163
Selbach-Oster, 71
Selected Poetry of Rainer Maria Rilke, The (Rilke), 29, 39
Settesoli, 172
Seven Sisters, 140
Seymour, Jane, 44
"shablie," xi
Shadow, The (radio drama), 243
Shakespeare, William, 101
sharks, 123, 321
Shaw, George Bernard, 86
sheep, 32, 99–101, 106, 321
"sheep's foot," 99–100
sherry, 12–13, 238, 258, 259, 271
shiraz, 1, 7–8, 9, 14, 15, 16, 17, 18, 21, 31–32, 32–33, 128, 136, 163, 172, 204, 302, 320
shiraz grapes, 1–2, 13, 38, 130, 135–36, 161, 172–73, 296, 299
Sicily
    climate and soils of, 167, 171, 172–73, 176–77, 179, 180, 181, 185, 186, 192–93, 194, 196
    traveling in, 177, 183
    wine, 167–200
Silence of the Lambs (Harris), 121
silver nitrate, seeding clouds with, 224
Simi Winery, 143
Simonsig, 128, 163
Simply Red, 178
Singh, Rajinder, 227
single-malt whisky, 258
Singleton, Kate, 199
single-variety wines, rarity of, 262
site-specific method, 109, 111, 115
60 Minutes (TV show), 139
Skor, 257
Slate, 74
smartphone apps, xix
Smith Woodhouse (Symington Family Estates), 246

snakes, 1, 4, 321
Snow White, 88
soils. *See* climate and soils
solera method of aging, 170–71, 271
Solo Tango (cable channel), 216
"somewhereness," 26, 156, 225
Sopranos, The (TV show), 174
Sour Grapes (Pendock), 164
South Africa
  climate and soils of, 124, 125, 128, 135,
    152, 153, 158, 161
  traveling in, 124
  wine, 123–65
Southbrook Vineyards, 119, 296
Southern Right Sauvignon Blanc (Hamilton
  Russell), 157, 162
Spanish conquistadors, 210–11
Spanish wine, 34, 108, 215, 236, 290,
  295–96
sparkling rosés, 296–97
spätlese riesling, 48–49, 63, 65, 66, 72–73,
  74, 76, 79–80
Spice Route, 129, 136, 162
spittoons, 130
Springboks (rugby team), 136
squawk boxes, 102, 103
St. Catherine's, 100
St. Helena, 127
St. Urbans-Hof, 61–63, 64, 65, 66, 67, 68,
  69, 70, 71, 78
Stag's Leap Cabernet Sauvignon, 107
stainless-steel tanks, 47, 207
"starboard" (port-style wine), 239
starlings, 83–84, 101–2, 104, 106
Starry Night (van Gogh), 283
steak houses *(parrillas)*, 226
Steen (chenin blanc), 135, 161
Stellenbosch, South Africa, 126, 127, 141, 152
Stellenbosch Farmers Winery (Distell), 143
Stellenbosch University, South Africa, 138,
  142, 144, 146
Stevens, Carmen (Amani Vineyards),
  140–41, 141–42, 143–44, 148–51, 158
Stewart, Chris, 305
stomping grapes *(pigeages)*, 250–51, 268
Stravecchio marsala, 171
Stravinsky, Igor, 273
Sumac Ridge, 108
Sunday lunch, 291, 312, 313–14
Sunday dinner, 3, 9, 36, 37–38
"sundial" *(sonnenuhr)*, 44
Super Tuscans, 170, 172

supporting-actor wines, 118
sustainable agriculture, 93
Switzerland, 263, 296–97
Sydney Wine Show, 14
Symington, Charles (Symington Family
  Estates), 248
Symington, Clare (Symington Family
  Estates), 248
Symington, Dominic (Symington Family
  Estates), 248
Symington, Johnny (Symington Family
  Estates), 248
Symington, Paul (Symington Family
  Estates), 248
Symington, Rupert (Symington Family
  Estates), 246, 247–48, 249, 251–52, 253,
  256–58, 259–60, 261, 262, 263, 275
syrah. *See* shiraz

table wine *(vin de table)*, 289
Tachis, Giacomo, 172
Talon Ridge Vineyard (Le Clos Jordanne),
  111–12, 115
tango, 202, 216
tawny ports, 248, 256, 257, 266–67,
  269–70, 271–72, 273
Tawse, 87, 114, 119
Taylor's, 246, 258, 275
TBA (trockenbeerenauslese) riesling, 65,
  69–70, 80
"Tempest in a Wine Glass," 107
tempranillo grapes, 135, 211, 295
TendreBulle Gay Vin, 294
Tenuta delle Terre Nere (Black Earth
  Estate), 184–89, 193, 197, 198–99
Tenuta delle Terre Nere Etna Rosso (pick for
  Thursday dinner), 186, 198
"termite specials," 16
Terrazas de los Andes, 202, 214, 231
Thandi, 140
Theron, Charlize, 125
"thisness" *(haecceitas)*, 26
Thackeray, William Makepeace, 154
Thucydides, 168
Thursday dinner, 172, 186, 198–99
Tignanello, 169, 170
Tin Drum, The (Grass), 81
tinta grapes, 261, 262, 268, 274
Tolstoy, Leo, 321
top value producers, xviii
  Argentine wine, 231
  Australian wine, 36–37

French wine, 313
German wine, 78
Niagara (Canadian) wine, 119
Portuguese wine and port, 275
Sicilian wine, 198
South African wine, 162–63
torrontés, 211, 220–21
Toujours Provence (Mayle), 308, 315
touriga grapes, 261, 262, 268
Touring in Wine Country: Provence
(Duijker), 314
trade bans and competition, 138–39, 161
trademark name of port, 239
traditionalists vs. modernists, 193
"Transatlantic Upset," 107
Trapped in Paradise (film), 90
traveling in
Argentina, 202, 213
Australia, 11, 20–21, 25
Canada, 83, 84–86, 89
Germany, 41, 53, 55, 60, 61, 71
Niagara (Canada), 83, 84–86, 89
Portugal, 235, 247, 249–50
Sicily, 177, 183
South Africa, 124
treading grapes *(pigeages)*, 250–51, 268
Treadwell Restaurant, 100–101
Treasury Wine Estates, 10
trellising, 30, 63, 174, 223
Trinchero, Bob (Sutter Home
winery), 281
trockenbeerenauslese (TBA) riesling, 65,
69–70, 80
"trop" (port-style wine), 239
"True Love Chardonnay," xi
truffles, 299–301
Tuesday dinner, 111, 115, 118, 119
Tukulu, 140, 143–44, 148
Tuscany, Italy, xi, 43, 172, 197, 203, 255
Tutu, Desmond, 125
Twain, Shania, 114
Twitter, xiv, xix, 318
Two Oceans, 128, 163

U-boats, 64
U.K., 138
Under the Tuscan Sun (Mayes), 305
ungrafted *(pied frau)* vines, 176
United States, 86, 138, 215
"universally declared" vintage, 254
University of Adelaide, Australia, 12, 18,
22, 34

unquenchable journey, xv–xvi
See also bargain wines
Urban, Saint (Pope Urban I), 61
Ürziger Würzgarten Riesling Spätlese, 57

Valckenberg family, 54
Valeira dam, Portugal, 249–50
value, relativity of, 117–18
van der Stel, Simon, 126–27
Van Gogh, Theo, 283
Van Gogh, Vincent, 282–83
Vanity Fair (Thackeray), 154
van Riebeeck, Jan, 126
Vautrin, Paul, 298
Vautrin-Vancoillie, Nathalie (Domaine du
Clos d'Alari), 297–99, 300, 301,
302–4, 305, 313
Vergine marsala, 171
vertical tastings, 319
Vesuvius, 176
Victoria (Queen of England), 47
Vila Nova de Gaia, Portugal, 236–37, 249
Villeneuve, Raimond (Château de
Roquefort), 283–87, 288, 289, 290,
291–92, 293, 294
Vina Patagonia (Concha y Toro, Chile), 214
Vincor, 108, 110
Vin Gris de Cigare, 296
Vinicola Benanti, 177–80, 181–83, 193,
197, 198
*Vino Argentino: An Insider's Guide to the
Wines and Wine Country of Argentina*
(Catena), 233
Vino-Lok glass stoppers, 31
Vintage Caper, The (Mayle), 311, 315
vintage port, 254–56, 257, 271, 272
vintages, xvii–xviii, 258
Vintners Quality Alliance (VQA), 87, 116
viognier, 211, 220–21, 296
virtual glass of wine, sharing, xiv, xx
volcanic viticulture, 167, 176–77, 179, 181,
186, 192–93, 194, 196
Volgyesi, Andrew, 96
Volnay, 115
von Bismarck, Otto, 127
von Söetern, Christoph (Bernkasteler
Doctor), 72
Vulcan, 176, 192

Walk in the Clouds, A (film), 251
warm-climate vs. cold-climate regions, 35
War of 1812, 86

Warre, George (Warre's), 247
Warre's (Symington Family Estates), 246, 247, 258, 274
wasabi, 74–75
Waugh, Auberon, 128
Wednesday dinner, 128, 162, 163
Wegeler, 72–77, 78
Wegeler, Anja (Wegeler), 73
Wegeler, Carl and Julius (Wegeler), 72–73
Wegeler, Rolf (Wegeler), 73
Wehlener Sonnenuhr, 44, 49, 58
Weir, Prue (Henschke winery), 22, 23, 24, 26, 27, 29–30, 31, 33, 34
Weis, Nikolaus (St. Urbans-Hof), 61–63, 64, 65, 66, 67, 68, 69, 70, 71, 79
well-rated vs. best-known vintages, 274
Welmoed Winery, 148
Wharton School of Business, 153
Where Did I Come From? (Mayle), 307
white port, 259–60
"whites for eternity," 68–69
white wines, 180–81, 220–21, 268, 281, 289, 290
whole-cluster pressing, 50
Wicked Willie series (Mayle), 307
Wiest, Rudi, 74–75
wild boar, 301
Wild Kingdom (TV show), 125
William of Orange, 247
Willi Schaefer, 71
Willi's Wine Bar in Paris, 283
Winds of Change, 140
Wine and Food Lover's Guide to Portugal (Metcalfe), 276
"wine cure," 12
Wine Industry Transformation Charter, 129
wineries visited, xvii
Wine Routes of Argentina (Young), 233
Wines and Vineyards of Portugal, The (Mayson), 276
Wines of Argentina, Chile, and Latin America, The (Fielden), 233
Wines of Germany, The (Brook), 80
Wines of Sicily (Singleton), 199

"winning formula," 6, 7
Woerther, Joerg, 267
Wolf Blass, 4–11, 15, 24, 35, 36
Wolf Blass Red Label Shiraz Cabernet Sauvignon (pick for Sunday dinner), 9, 36
Wolfe, David, 145
women and wine, 9, 258–59, 281, 322–23
wood-aged port, 240, 256, 266, 356
Woodhouse, John, 170
Woollcott, Alexander, 318
World Cup (soccer), 202
World War I, 280
World War II, 91
Worldwide Winery Directory, xix, 36
writing and drinking, 321–23

Yalumba, 4, 11, 12, 33, 37
Yealands, Peter, 99
Year in Provence, A (Mayle), 305, 307, 308, 309, 310, 315
Yellow Tail Shiraz (Casella Wines), 8, 9
Young, Alan, 233

Zakaria, Fareed, 74
Zanfi, Andrea, 199
Zapata, Angelica (Bodega Catena Zapata), 206
Zeus, 168
Zilliken, 71, 78
zinfandel, 55, 147, 281
Zola, Émile, 305
Zonda wind, 218
Zuccardi, Don Alberto (Zuccardi Family Wines), 222
Zuccardi, José (Zuccardi Family Wines), 222–28, 229, 232
Zuccardi, Julia, 222
Zuccardi, Miguel (Zuccardi Family Wines), 222
Zuccardi, Sebastian (Zuccardi Family Wines), 222, 227–28
Zuccardi Family Wines, 213, 222–28, 229, 230, 231, 232

ABOUT THE AUTHOR

Funny, brainy, and unapologetically tipsy, **Natalie MacLean** is an accredited sommelier who operates one of the largest wine websites at www.nataliemaclean.com. She was named World's Best Drink Writer at the World Food Media Awards, and is the only person to have won both the M.F.K. Fisher Distinguished Writing Award from the James Beard Foundation and the M.F.K. Fisher Award for Excellence in Culinary Writing from Les Dames d'Escoffier International. Her first book, *Red, White, and Drunk All Over*, was chosen Best Wine Literature Book at the Gourmand World Cookbook Awards. Her work has appeared in *Bon Appétit*, *Food & Wine*, *Wine Enthusiast*, *Condé Nast Traveler*, and *Bloomberg BusinessWeek*, among others. A Rhodes Scholarship finalist and champion Scottish Highland dancer, Natalie lives with her husband and son in Ottawa.